This book provides a much overdue contribution to our understanding of the developmental dynamics of some of Asia's most celebrated city states: Singapore and Hong Kong. By revisiting the developmental state thesis and analysing the policy challenges posed by the rise of the knowledge economy and the increasing impact of digitization, the author is able to demonstrate how the adoption of smart city strategies is increasingly supplanting traditional approaches to developmental policy, planning and economic management. A timely, thoughtful and innovative book that speaks to students of international political economy, development and policymakers alike.

Darryl S.L. Jarvis, Professor and Head of Department of Asian and Policy Studies, Education University of Hong Kong

The Evolution of the Asian Developmental State

Many East Asian states have undergone profound economic transformations over the last two decades. Singapore and Hong Kong especially have adapted to shifting economic and technological conditions by transforming themselves into 'smart developmental states'. In these cities, the proliferation of digital technologies has given rise to new growth sectors and opened up new areas of political contestation within these early proponents of the developmental state model.

Providing a theoretical and empirical discussion of the Asian developmental state model, the book assesses the evolution of the developmental state model, considers recent developments in the field and evaluates the development state's continued relevance as a conceptual framework for understanding the politics of economic development. Focusing on digital and technology-enabled economic activities in Hong Kong and Singapore, the author explores the various policies that allow developmental states to stimulate economic growth, ensure organizational coherence, and engage businesses and other stakeholders.

This book will be of interest to scholars and researchers of political economy and economic development in Asia as well as business professionals and other practitioners.

J.J. Woo is Assistant Professor of Singapore and Southeast Asian Politics in the Public Policy and Global Affairs Programme of Nanyang Technological University, Singapore. From 2016 to 2017, he was Rajawali Fellow at the John F. Kennedy School of Government at Harvard University, where he worked on policy co-creation in Singapore. Dr Woo received his PhD from the Lee Kuan Yew School of Public Policy, National University of Singapore and holds an MSc (International Political Economy) from the S. Rajaratnam School of International Studies, Nanyang Technological University.

Rethinking Asia and International Relations

Series Editor: Emilian Kavalski, Li Dak Sum Chair Professor in China–Eurasia Relations and International Studies, University of Nottingham, Ningbo, China

This series seeks to provide thoughtful consideration both of the growing prominence of Asian actors on the global stage and the changes in the study and practice of world affairs that they provoke. It intends to offer a comprehensive parallel assessment of the full spectrum of Asian states, organisations, and regions and their impact on the dynamics of global politics.

The series seeks to encourage conversation on:

- what rules, norms, and strategic cultures are likely to dominate international life in the 'Asian Century';
- how will global problems be reframed and addressed by a 'rising Asia';
- which institutions, actors, and states are likely to provide leadership during such 'shifts to the East';
- whether there is something distinctly 'Asian' about the emerging patterns of global politics.

Such comprehensive engagement not only aims to offer a critical assessment of the actual and prospective roles of Asian actors, but also seeks to rethink the concepts, practices, and frameworks of analysis of world politics.

This series invites proposals for interdisciplinary research monographs undertaking comparative studies of Asian actors and their impact on the current patterns and likely future trajectories of international relations. Furthermore, it offers a platform for pioneering explorations of the ongoing transformations in global politics as a result of Asia's increasing centrality to the patterns and practices of world affairs.

China's Relations with the Gulf Monarchies
Jonathan Fulton

The Evolution of the Asian Developmental State
Hong Kong and Singapore
J.J. Woo

For more information about this series, please visit:
https://www.routledge.com/Rethinking-Asia-and-International-Relations/book-series/ASHSER1384

The Evolution of the Asian Developmental State

Hong Kong and Singapore

J.J. Woo

Routledge
Taylor & Francis Group
LONDON AND NEW YORK

First published 2019
by Routledge
2 Park Square, Milton Park, Abingdon, Oxon OX14 4RN

and by Routledge
605 Third Avenue, New York, NY 10017

First issued in paperback 2021

Routledge is an imprint of the Taylor & Francis Group, an informa business

British Library Cataloguing-in-Publication Data
A catalogue record for this book is available from the British Library

Library of Congress Cataloging-in-Publication Data
Names: Woo, J. J. (Jun Jie), author.
Title: The evolution of the Asian developmental state:
Hong Kong and Singapore / J.J. Woo.
Description: Abingdon, Oxon; New York, NY: Routledge, 2018. |
Series: Rethinking Asia and international relations |
Includes bibliographical references and index.
Identifiers: LCCN 2018006044 | ISBN 9781138070264 (hardback) |
ISBN 9781315115139 (e-book)
Subjects: LCSH: Economic development—Government policy—China—Hong Kong. | Economic development—Government policy—Singapore. | Technology—Economic aspects—China—Hong Kong. | Technology—Economic aspects—Singapore. | Technology and state—China—Hong Kong. | Technology and state—Singapore. | Hong Kong (China)—Economic policy. | Singapore—Economic policy.
Classification: LCC HC470.3.Z9 E448 2018 | DDC 338.95125—dc23
LC record available at https://lccn.loc.gov/2018006044

Typeset in Times New Roman
by codeMantra

ISBN 13: 978-1-03-209496-0 (pbk)
ISBN 13: 978-1-138-07026-4 (hbk)

To my wife Debbie and my son Harvey, for being my raison d’être.

And above all, Ad Majorem Dei Gloriam.

Contents

Figures

Tables

Acknowledgements

This book would not have been possible without the love and support of my wife Debbie, who has always been the sounding board for my ideas. This book, like all my other books, therefore bears the imprint of her thoughts and ideas. Unlike my previous books, however, this book also bears the imprint of my son Harvey, who was born shortly before this book was completed. I am grateful for his constant (though not necessarily quiet) company during the final stages of writing this book.

I am also grateful for the support of Nanyang Technological University, which has, as both my employer and alma mater, furnished me with the financial and intellectual resources necessary for putting this book together. During the course of writing this book, I was also a Rajawali Fellow at the John F. Kennedy School of Government, Harvard University. I will always be indebted to the Harvard Kennedy School, and the city of Boston, for providing me with inspiration and intellectual ballast.

If it takes a village to raise a child, it certainly takes one to write a book as well. I am grateful to colleagues and friends who have provided me with much support and company, among them: Jamie Chung and Ong Shun Wei, Alfred Pang, Jerome Leon, Nandhakumar, Simon Pang, Daniel Ouyang, Leong Ching, M. Ramesh, Michael Howlett and Giliberto Capano.

Lastly, I owe a debt of gratitude to my students, who have brought me much joy, inspiration and friendship in my vocation as a teacher. In particular, I am especially grateful to Benjamin Low, Reesa Desker, Wong Jun Jie, Jeremy Ng, and Tan Yutong for their thoughts and well wishes.

J.J. Woo
January 2018
Singapore

Preface

From the 'East Asian Miracle' to the 'Asian Century' (Mahbubani 2008, 2009, Kohli *et al.* 2011, Mahbubani 2014), there has been no shortage of superlatives for describing the economic rise of Asia, particularly East Asia. Similarly, there has been a deluge of scholarly research on the bases and drivers of economic growth and expansion in Asia (Deyo 1987, Johnson 1987, Wade 1990, Henderson 1993, Goh 1996, Kojima 2000, Kasahara 2013, Yeung 2017), with most of these studies aimed at uncovering the role of Asian governments and policymakers in driving such growth.

At the heart of this scholarly interest in the role of government is the developmental state model, which aims to provide a systematic understanding of the political and economic foundations of East Asian economic governance (Douglass 1994, Grabowski 1994, Leftwich 1995, Woo-Cumings 1999, Jomo 2000, Kasahara 2013, Chu 2016, Jessop 2016). Yet at the same time, it is increasingly clear that cracks have appeared in the hitherto flawless facade of the developmental state model, giving rise to questions over its conceptual, normative and empirical relevance (Kim 1993, 1999, Fine 1999, Minns 2001, Carroll and Jarvis 2017).

This book is situated at the intersection of such developmental state studies and their criticisms. While I agree that the developmental state model is facing challenges to its conceptual relevance (whether from globalization, economic liberalization and deregulation, or the emergence of a digital and knowledge-based economy), I also argue that developmental states such as Singapore and Hong Kong have successfully adapted and modified their developmental state models in response to these challenges, specifically by transforming themselves into smart cities.

This book therefore seeks to address these adaptations and modifications to the developmental states of Singapore and Hong Kong. In the process, it aims to provide a sketch of the 'smart developmental state' that has emerged from these adaptations. Singapore and Hong Kong are not the only developmental states seeking to transform themselves into smart cities. Other developmental states, such as China, South Korea and India, are rapidly developing smart cities, with the goal of finding new sources of economic growth and expanding the state's influence in the economic and social spheres.

Aside from an empirical discussion of this shift from developmental state to smart developmental state, this book also provides potential avenues for future research and further theorizing. Specifically, I argue that studies on the developmental state model need to move beyond a narrow political economy focus to take on a more policy-oriented approach. As states continue to adapt and respond to changing global political and economic conditions, it is crucial that the theoretical constructs and analytical frameworks that are used to understand these states adapt as well. This will ensure a closer fit between theory and reality.

1 Introduction

Beginning in the 1980s, rapid economic development in Asia has given rise to the speculation that the twenty-first century will be an 'Asian Century', with economic and political power gradually shifting eastwards (Kohli et al. 2011, Mahbubani 2008, 2009, 2014, 2014). Much of this was fuelled by the 'East Asian Miracle' of the 1990s, which was characterized by rapid economic growth in Japan, China, and the four 'newly industrialized economies' of Hong Kong, Singapore, South Korea and Taiwan (Stiglitz and Uy 1996, Stiglitz and Yusuf 2001).

Not only did the East Asian Miracle result in extensive poverty reduction and more equitable distribution of income among these East Asian economies (Page et al. 1993, Asian Development Bank 2002), it also raised fundamental ideological questions over the extent and nature of state intervention in economic policymaking (Wade 1990, Henderson 1993). In contrast to the neoliberal approaches to economic governance that had held sway in many Western developed economies, economic development in East Asia has from the start featured centralized state planning and extensive government interventions in markets.

At the heart of this centralized model of economic governance and development is what is known as the 'East Asian Developmental State model', or 'Developmental State model' in short.[1] This book will provide a theoretical and empirical discussion of the developmental state model, with a focus on the two cities of Hong Kong and Singapore. It aims to address recent developments in the field and assess the continued relevance of the developmental state as a framework for understanding the politics of development in East and Southeast Asia.

The core argument of this book is that there is a need to update and adapt the developmental state model to reflect an increasingly complex and technologically driven knowledge economy. Indeed, this book is driven by the following research questions:

- Is the developmental state still relevant in today's globalized knowledge economy?
- How have developmental states such as Hong Kong and Singapore adapted in response to the global shift towards a digital and knowledge-based economy?

- How do the two cities' smart city strategies contribute to developmental goals?
- What does this twenty-first-century 'smart' developmental state look like?
- What are the conceptual adaptations and modifications required in order to ensure the continued relevance of the developmental state model?

However, and with many East Asian economies undergoing profound transformations from manufacturing-based and export-led economies to a services and knowledge-based economy, the developmental state model, with its traditional focus on industrial planning, is receiving less attention in scholarly research and discourse on Asian economic development. There has therefore been a decline in scholarly studies and theorizing on the Asian developmental state, especially in light of evolving political-economic realities.

As political scientist Richard Stubbs has articulated in the title of his 2009 article 'What ever happened to the East Asian Developmental State?' this is by no means a rhetorical question. Rather, there is a need to take stock of the developmental state in the twenty-first century, both as theoretical construct and empirical reality. This book will seek to achieve this, by examining the developmental state and its evolution in the context of Hong Kong and Singapore, both of which are city-states that are known to be strong proponents of the developmental state model, albeit with variations in their interpretation and implementation of the model (Huff 1995, Low 2001a, Painter 2005).

Before discussing the two cases, however, it is important to establish a clear understanding of the developmental state that will guide the discussions that follow in the rest of this book. In the following section, I will provide an overview of the existing literature on the Asian developmental state. In this instance, a geographical focus on Asia is necessary, as the aim is to understand the developmental state as it pertains to Asian cities such as Hong Kong and Singapore. This is followed by a brief discussion of the two cases, a section on the research and methodology that underpins this book, and a chapter-by-chapter outline of the rest of this book.

The Asian developmental state: a concept

The origins of the developmental state can be traced to Chalmers Johnson's 1982 work on Japan's Ministry of International Trade and Industry (MITI), in which he argued that economic development in Japan was driven by extensive state intervention, through the role of an elite and insulated state bureaucracy and the coordination of pilot organizations such as MITI (Johnson 1982). The developmental state model would prove highly applicable to other East Asian states, given their similar trajectories of economic development, in what was known as the 'flying geese' pattern of development (Korhonen 1994, Kojima 2000, Kasahara 2013).

This would spark off a flurry of scholarly research on the developmental state model in East Asian countries such as South Korea, Taiwan, Hong Kong and Singapore through the 1980s and 1990s (Lim 1983, White 1984, Evans 1989, Haggard 1990, Wade 1990, Kim 1993, Douglass 1994, Kohli 1994, Moon and Prasad 1994, Perry 1997). While these case studies sought to identify and adapt the various aspects of the developmental state that Johnson had identified to other East Asian economies, efforts at further theorizing on the developmental state were in no way lacking.

Much of this theoretical work was, and continues to be, focused on understanding the sources and exercise of state capacity by Asian developmental states (Evans 1985, 1989, Woo-Cumings 1999, Cheung 2008, Lee 2009, Evans 2014). This is particularly the case with regard to understanding a developmental state's capacity to mobilize and direct economic and socio-political resources (White 1984). Also of particular interest to many of these scholars is the ability of developmental states to control, influence or 'discipline' firms into cooperating with the state's industrialization efforts and policies (Grabowski 1994).

Much of this focus on state strength or capacity has to do with an association of the developmental state model with political authoritarianism (White 1984, Douglass 1994). It should, however be noted that the developmental state model is much more than simply a justification of authoritarianism, since in most cases state interventions tend to conform to market principles, rather than contradict or subvert them (Johnson 1982, Wade 1990). Understood through the lens of the developmental state model, government interventions in economic development tend to be exercised through market-based tools such as capital re-allocation or implicit subsidies.

This again places the focus on economic bureaucracies such as MITI, since these tend to be staffed with economists who are well attuned to the various market-based tools for spurring economic development. A more significant implication of this focus on state capacity is an associated desire to understand the various organizations, channels and mechanisms through which state authority and interventions are exercised and transmitted to industry and societal actors. This has meant a need to develop a more systematic and comprehensive understanding of the various components of a typical developmental state.

This is provided by Leftwich (1995), whose oft-cited article identifies the six major components of a typical developmental state:

- A developmental elite
- Relative autonomy of the state
- A powerful, competent and insulated economic bureaucracy
- A weak and subordinated civil society
- Effective management of non-state economic interests
- Repression, legitimacy and performance

Much of the discussion that will follow in the rest of this book draws extensively from Leftwich's formulation of the developmental state, especially regarding the six components that he has identified, although the other studies discussed above are important in guiding the discussion as well. While theoretical development and research on the developmental state model tailed off in the 2000s, with the 1990s typically seen as the peak of theoretical and empirical studies on the subject, there has recently been a revival of sorts, especially with the onset of the 2008 Global Financial Crisis and a consequent refocusing of attention on the role of the state in policymaking (Wade 2010, Howlett and Lejano 2013, Capano et al. 2015).

Indeed, and despite expectations to the contrary, particularly those arising from neoliberal sources, the developmental state has proven exceptionally resilient, even in the face of seismic shifts in the global political economy, such as globalization, financialization, economic liberalization, and even the institutional and ideological challenge of neoliberal politics, particularly in terms of the 'Washington Consensus' (Beeson and Islam 2005, Hayashi 2010, Wade 2010, Jessop 2016). Furthermore, structural shifts in the global economy, such as the emergence of the knowledge economy, have resulted in the reconfiguration, rather than the decline, of the developmental state (O Riain 2000, Low 2003a, Chu 2009).

In light of these ongoing 'reconfigurations' in the modern, or 'postmodern', developmental state, there is a need to devote closer attention to the theoretical implications of these reconfigurations, even as the exact nature and extent of these reconfigurations require deeper empirical examination. This book aims to achieve both these aims through a theoretical and empirical study of the twenty-first-century developmental state, as exemplified by Hong Kong and Singapore. In doing so, I seek to provide an updated conceptual understanding of the developmental state model, as it pertains to the digital and knowledge-based economy of today.

Methodology and design

The findings of this book are derived from field research in the two cities, conducted over the past four years. This research began as an inquiry into the financial services sector of the two cities, seeking to understand the various policy drivers of the two cities' rise to prominence as leading Asian financial centres (Woo 2015a, 2016a). However, my research revealed a deep socio-political component to economic and financial sector development in the two cities, particularly in terms of their approaches to economic governance (Woo 2015b, 2015a, Woo and Howlett 2015).

In particular, it became increasingly clear that state capacity remains an important determinant of successful economic development in the two cities (Woo 2014, 2016b, 2016a, Woo et al. 2016). In light of these, there was a need to devote closer attention to the governance systems that drive policymaking and economic development in the two cities. As I discuss below and in Chapters 2 and 3, both Hong Kong and Singapore have been associated with the Asian developmental dtate model of economic governance and development. It is therefore within this context that this book is situated.

Derived from the work of political scientists and developmental studies experts, the developmental state model is strongly geared towards understanding the political systemic aspects of economic governance and development. As discussed above, this includes elements such as embedded autonomy, performance legitimacy and elite governance. Paradoxically, the bureaucratic insulation that lies at the heart of the developmental state model requires the state to possess a significant extent of political clout and authority.

As a consequence of this focus on politics and governance, along with my training as a political scientist, this book takes a qualitative case study approach in understanding the developmental state model in Hong Kong and Singapore. This involves the collection and analysis of qualitative data, both primary and secondary, that includes in-depth interviews with senior policymakers and industry professionals, official reports and publications from governments, firms and research institutions, as well as the existing body of research and writing on the subject.

Taking such a qualitative approach is crucial for studies on political and economic development in Asia, where interpersonal connections or *guanxi* play a crucial role in determining or influencing policy decisions (Leung et al. 1996, Wilkinson 1996, Ewing et al. 2000, Hamilton-Hart 2002, Woo 2015b). The analysis of qualitative data allows for the formulation of 'thick' descriptions that are particularly useful for understanding such relations, which often border on the informal (Cheng and Womack 1996), and the derivation of 'causal inferences' on how such variables impact policy outcomes (King et al. 1994, Maguire and Ball 1994, Creswell and Miller 2000, Bennett and Elman 2006).

Certainly, there are limitations to taking a qualitative approach, such as issues pertaining to generalizability and, in some instances, validity (Maxwell 1992, Bernard 2000, Creswell and Miller 2000, Neuman 2011). Considerable attention was placed on ensuring the validity of this research, whether in terms of enhancing validity through triangulation, ensuring interviewee candour by providing the option of anonymity, and where possible equitable distribution of data points, especially in terms of selecting as broad an array of interviewees as possible, representing differing viewpoints and interests.

Hong Kong and Singapore: Asian developmental city-states

As cases, Hong Kong and Singapore exhibit an astounding level of comparability. Indeed, the two cities have often been juxtaposed against each other as either complementary 'sister' cities with a common history and destiny, opposite ends of a liberal–conservative political spectrum, differing models of policymaking or public administration, or simply direct competitors for the crown of Asia's top financial centre (Young 1992, Ng 1998, Lim 1999, Lam 2000, Cheung and Sidhu 2003, Lee and Haque 2006, Painter and Wong 2007, Tan and Lim 2007, Woo 2016a).

In all instances, Hong Kong and Singapore are often seen as highly comparable and hence amenable to comparative case studies. There are several reasons for this. First, the two cities share a common British colonial history, with Singapore achieving independence in 1965 and Hong Kong coming under Chinese rule with the 1997 handover. In both cities, the British established the common law system and put in place an efficient public service. These continue to form the bedrock of the two cities' governance and public administration.

Furthermore, both Hong Kong and Singapore were important trade hubs for the British Empire and served as respective gateways to East and Southeast Asia. This port city identity would result in striking similarities in the economic structure and composition of the two cities. For instance, both cities placed an important emphasis on manufacturing (although this is much less the case in Hong Kong today), while their current position of pre-eminence as leading Asian financial centres can be traced back to their early success as port cities and their strategic position along major trade routes (Woo 2016a).

More broadly speaking, both cities boast a highly skilled workforce with a strong command of English as their working language. These, too, arguably, are legacies of their British colonial history. Yet and in part due to their majority Chinese populations, both Hong Kong and Singapore are characterized by a significant level of conservatism and the prevalence of Confucian values such as obedience to authority and family-centrism (Kuah 1990, Chua 1997, Lam et al. 1999, Lin and Ho 2009, Kaplan 2015).

From a more practical perspective, Hong Kong and Singapore are highly comparable in terms of their size. Hong Kong's current population is 7.24 million, while that of Singapore is 5.6 million. In terms of demographics, both cities are made up of a majority Chinese population, most if not all of whom are descendants of migrants from Mainland China. Perhaps most importantly, Hong Kong and Singapore are among the few functioning city-states of the world. While Hong Kong operates under the jurisdiction of China, it enjoys significant autonomy in its economic policies as a 'Special Administrative Region' (SAR).

Yet despite all these similarities in size, demographics and historical development, Hong Kong and Singapore differ in one important way: their political systems. First, Hong Kong does not enjoy universal suffrage. Rather, its leaders are elected by a select group of business and societal elites, with the Chief Executive chosen from a panel of approved candidates. In contrast, Singapore's political leaders are popularly elected through general elections that take place once every five years, under a majoritarian parliamentary system. However, these institutional differences are not necessarily reflected in the political culture of both cities.

For instance, Hong Kong is known for its liberal political culture that favours freedom of speech and expression, with strong levels of political activism and an active civil society (Lam 2004, Ma 2007, Lee and Chan 2008). This is in contrast to the depoliticization and state dominance of Singapore's political culture, with civil society relatively weak and media outlets operating under strict government controls (Lee 2002, 2005, George 2007, 2012, Tan 2012). These contrasts have also resulted in differences in how the developmental state model is interpreted and applied in Hong Kong and Singapore.

Singapore Inc.

There is very little doubt that Singapore is generally known as the exemplary model of the Asian development state, even more so than many other East Asian cities, including Hong Kong (Painter and Wong 2007, p. 180). Much of this is driven by the existential turmoil that had accompanied its ejection from the Federation of Malaysia and subsequent independence in 1965, with its founding leaders deeply preoccupied with seeking out new sources of economic growth in the absence of a natural hinterland (Huff 1995).

Naturally, this focus on economic development necessitated as well as spurred the establishment of the various institutions that are associated with the typical developmental state, such as an economic bureaucracy or pilot agency (the Economic Development Board), the embedded autonomy of a civil service that is at once insulated from socio-political pressures but deeply embedded within Singapore's socio-cultural milieu, a weak civil society, and perhaps most importantly, political legitimacy derived from economic performance (Huff 1995, Hamilton-Hart 2000, Low 2001a, Olds and Yeung 2004).

This overarching focus on economic growth and development has led to the characterization of Singapore's approach to economic governance as 'Singapore Inc.' (Haley et al. 1996, Low 2001b, 2003b, 2006, 2006). This corporate metaphor for policymaking in Singapore is further emphasized by the government's efforts at incorporating private sector management practices into its policy processes (Haque 2002, 2004, Lee and Haque 2006, Aoki 2015, Aoki and Tay 2015).

Hong Kong's administrative state

An important consequence of the lack of universal suffrage and political elections in Hong Kong is the high level of insulation that its government, particularly the civil service, enjoys from political and societal forces (Painter 2005). This lack of socio-political pressure has resulted in a high level of continuity and stability in Hong Kong's bureaucracy that is buttressed by the extensive political clout of civil servants, whether through their membership and participation in legislative bodies or their possession of technical domain knowledge (Cooper and Lui 1990), although the flipside of this is its 'seclusion' from the rest of society (Lau and Liu 1984).

Owing to such bureaucratic stability, insularity and influence, Hong Kong's approach to governance and policy has often been depicted as that of an 'administrative state' (Harris 1988, Painter 2005, Cheung 2008, Painter and Yee 2012). More importantly for the purposes of our discussion, the Hong Kong administrative state features several important elements of the developmental state, such as performance-based legitimacy, the central role of civil service elites and the embedded autonomy of its bureaucracy (Cheung 2008).

More fundamentally and despite relatively liberal socio-political context, economic development involves a significant extent of centralized state intervention and action, albeit framed more subtly as 'positive non-intervention' (Glassburner and Riedel 1972, Lui and Chiu 1993, Schenk 2001, 2002, Li 2012). Like Singapore, the Hong Kong government has also often sought to incorporate private sector management practices to enhance efficiency in policy delivery (Lee and Haque 2006).

Varieties of developmental states

As the discussion above shows, there are variations in the interpretation and implementation of the developmental state model in Hong Kong and Singapore, with the former characterized by an 'administrative state' and the latter by 'Singapore Inc.' Hence while the existing literature appears to point towards a relatively consolidated understanding of the developmental state, there are in reality 'varieties of developmental states' (Joshi 2012) that differ in terms of not only their policy choices, but the state's relations with labour, capital and the external economy as well (Douglass 1994).

There is therefore a need to take a nuanced and contextual approach when studying developmental states. As is evident from the brief discussion above and the more detailed expositions in Chapters 2 and 3, even Hong Kong and Singapore, which are typically seen as paragons of the Asian developmental state, exhibit differences in the ways in which the various elements and components of the developmental state are represented or developed in the governing and policy processes.

Such variations in the developmental state are further complicated by ongoing shifts in the political-economic contexts of both cities, the most significant of which is a shift towards a knowledge-based and digital economy that is driven by the proliferation of data and 'smart' technologies. Indeed, the growing complexity that is often associated with such shifts in the domestic economy has gradually led to the view that the state can no longer manage such complex and diverse economies on their own (Stubbs 2009, p. 12, Morley et al. 2015).

Yet at the same time, others have noted that the developmental state remains alive and well in the knowledge economy, albeit with modifications, adaptations and reconfigurations (O Riain 2000, Low 2003a, Chu 2009). These variations and reconfigurations of the developmental state form the crux of this book. Drawing on recent theoretical developments such as 'policy capacity' and 'policy co-creation' (Painter and Pierre 2005, Needham 2008, Gleeson et al. 2011, Peters 2015, Woo *et al.* 2015, Wu *et al.* 2015, Woo 2016a), this book will seek to provide an updated account of the Asian developmental state, focusing on the various means through which the developmental state remains able to direct and influence economic development, albeit with the involvement of business actors.

Outline of the book

Having provided an introduction to the existing developmental state literature, articulated the rationale and arguments of this book, and discussed its research methodology and design, the remainder of this book will serve to elaborate and flesh out the arguments presented in this introductory chapter.

Chapter 2 begins with a discussion of Singapore's historical development and current existence as a developmental state, locating and examining within Singapore's socio-economic and political context the various components of the developmental state that have been identified by Leftwich. This approach is replicated for Hong Kong in Chapter 3. In doing so, these two chapters provide an overview of Singapore's and Hong Kong's unique interpretations and conceptions of the developmental state.

This is followed by Chapter 4, which discusses a recent shift in the two cities towards a digital and knowledge-based economy that is marked by the emergence of disruptive technologies that have given rise to both new developmental opportunities and new spaces of political contestation and negotiations. This chapter will also discuss relevant policy initiatives such as Singapore's Smart Nation initiative and Hong Kong's recent drive to become a smart city.

Having discussed these economic shifts and transformations, in Chapter 5 we discuss their implications for the developmental state as a concept and theoretical construct. This chapter will also propose several conceptual modifications to the developmental state model that aim to update and enhance the model's relevance as an analytical framework. Chapter 6 will then summarize the findings of this book, sketching out the broad elements of the modified developmental state model required for understanding the politics of economic development in twenty-first-century Asia. Potential limitations and caveats will also be discussed, along with potential avenues for future research.

Note

1 For the rest of this book and the discussions that follow, I will use the shorter and more inclusive term 'developmental state model'. Not only does this provide brevity, it also allows for a broader conception of the developmental state model. Such conceptual inclusivity is important, given that other non-Asian states have since adopted the developmental state model (Hochstetler and Ricardo Tranjan 2016, Mann and Berry 2016).

References

Aoki, N., 2015. Institutionalization of New Public Management: The case of Singapore's education system. *Public Management Review*, 17 (2), 165–186.

Aoki, N. and Tay, M., 2015. Managerialism Meets Regime: A Distinctively Singaporean Marriage? *Asian Journal of Political Science*, 23 (3), 346–365.

Asian Development Bank, 2002. *Growth and Poverty: Lessons from the East Asian Miracle Revisited*. Tokyo: Asian Development Bank.

Beeson, M. and Islam, I., 2005. Neo-liberalism and East Asia: Resisting the Washington Consensus. *The Journal of Development Studies*, 41 (2), 197–219.

Bennett, A. and Elman, C., 2006. Qualitative Research: Recent Developments in Case Study Methods. *Annual Review of Political Science*, 9 (1), 455–476.

Bernard, H.R., 2000. *Social Research Methods: Qualitative and Quantitative Approaches*. London: Sage.

Capano, G., Howlett, M., and Ramesh, M., 2015. Bringing Governments Back in: Governance and Governing in Comparative Policy Analysis. *Journal of Comparative Policy Analysis: Research and Practice*, 17 (4), 311–321.

Cheng, T. and Womack, B., 1996. General Reflections on Informal Politics in East Asia. *Asian Survey*, 36 (3), 320–337.

Cheung, A.B.L., 2008. The story of two administrative states: state capacity in Hong Kong and Singapore. *The Pacific Review*, 21 (2), 121–145.

Cheung, W.-L. and Sidhu, R., 2003. A Tale of Two Cities: Education Responds to Globalisation in Hong Kong and Singapore in the Aftermath of the Asian Economic Crisis. *Asia Pacific Journal of Education*, 23 (1), 43–68.

Chu, Y., 2009. Eclipse or reconfigured? South Korea's developmental state and challenges of the global knowledge economy. *Economy and Society*, 38 (2), 278–303.

Chua, B.-H., 1997. *Communitarian Ideology and Democracy in Singapore*. London, U.K.: Routledge.

Cooper, T.L. and Lui, T.L., 1990. Democracy and the Administrative State: The Case of Hong Kong. *Public Administration Review*, 50 (3), 332–344.

Creswell, J.W. and Miller, D.L., 2000. Determining Validity in Qualitative Inquiry. *Theory Into Practice*, 39 (3), 124–130.

Douglass, M., 1994. The 'developmental state' and the newly industrialised economies of Asia. *Environment and Planning A*, 26 (4), 543–566.

Evans, P.B., 1985. Transnational Linkages and the Economic Role of the State: An Analysis of Developing and Industrialized Nations in the Post-World War II Period. In: P.B. Evans, D. Rueschemeyer, and T. Skocpol, eds. *Bringing the State Back In*. Cambridge: Cambridge University Press, 192–226.

Evans, P.B., 1989. Predatory, developmental, and other apparatuses: A comparative political economy perspective on the Third World state. *Sociological Forum*, 4 (4), 561–587.

Evans, P.B., 2014. The Capability Enhancing Developmental State: Concepts and National Trajectories. In: E.M. Kim and P.H. Kim, eds. *The South Korean Development Experience*. London, U.K.: Palgrave Macmillan UK, 83–110.

Ewing, M., Caruana, A., and Wong, H., 2000. Some Consequences of Guanxi. *Journal of International Consumer Marketing*, 12 (4), 75–89.

George, C., 2007. Consolidating authoritarian rule: calibrated coercion in Singapore. *The Pacific Review*, 20 (2), 127–145.

George, C., 2012. *Freedom from the press: journalism and state power in Singapore*. Singapore: NUS Press.

Glassburner, B. and Riedel, J., 1972. Government in the Economy of Hong Kong. *Economic Record*, 48 (1), 58–75.

Gleeson, D., Legge, D., O'Neill, D., and Pfeffer, M., 2011. Negotiating Tensions in Developing Organizational Policy Capacity: Comparative Lessons to be Drawn. *Journal of Comparative Policy Analysis: Research and Practice*, 13 (3), 237–263.

Grabowski, R., 1994. The successful developmental state: Where does it come from? *World Development*, 22 (3), 413–422.
Haggard, S., 1990. *Pathways from the Periphery: The Politics of Growth in the Newly Industrializing Countries*. 1st ed. Ithaca, N.Y: Cornell University Press.
Haley, U.C.V., Linda Low, and Toh, M., 1996. Singapore Incorporated: reinterpreting Singapore's business environments through a corporate metaphor. *Management Decision*, 34 (9), 17–28.
Hamilton-Hart, N., 2000. The Singapore state revisited. *The Pacific Review*, 13 (2), 195–216.
Hamilton-Hart, N., 2002. *Asian States, Asian Bankers: Central Banking in Southeast Asia*. New York: Cornell University Press.
Haque, M.S., 2002. Structures of New Public Management in Malaysia and Singapore: Alternative Views. *The Journal of Comparative Asian Development*, 1 (1), 71–86.
Haque, M.S., 2004. Governance and Bureaucracy in Singapore: Contemporary Reforms and Implications. *International Political Science Review*, 25 (2), 227–240.
Harris, P.B., 1988. *Hong Kong: A Study in Bureaucratic Politics*. Hong Kong: Macmillan.
Hayashi, S., 2010. The developmental state in the era of globalization: beyond the Northeast Asian model of political economy. *The Pacific Review*, 23 (1), 45–69.
Henderson, J., 1993. Against the economic orthodoxy: on the making of the East Asian miracle. *Economy and Society*, 22 (2), 200–217.
Hochstetler, K. and Ricardo Tranjan, J., 2016. Environment and Consultation in the Brazilian Democratic Developmental State. *Comparative Politics*, 48 (4), 497–516.
Howlett, M. and Lejano, R.P., 2013. Tales From the Crypt The Rise and Fall (and Rebirth?) of Policy Design. *Administration & Society*, 45 (3), 357–381.
Huff, W.G., 1995. The developmental state, government, and Singapore's economic development since 1960. *World Development*, 23 (8), 1421–1438.
Jessop, B., 2016. The Developmental State in an Era of Finance-Dominated Accumulation. *In*: Y. Chu, ed. *The Asian Developmental State*. Palgrave Macmillan US, 27–55.
Johnson, C.A., 1982. *MITI and the Japanese Miracle: The Growth of Industrial Policy, 1925–1975*. 1st ed. Stanford, California: Stanford University Press.
Joshi, D.K., 2012. Varieties of Developmental States Three Non-Western Pathways to the Millennium Development Goals. *Journal of Developing Societies*, 28 (3), 355–378.
Kaplan, R.D., 2015. Asia's Rise Is Rooted in Confucian Values. *Wall Street Journal*, 6 Feb.
Kasahara, S., 2013. *The Asian Developmental State and the Flying Geese Paradigm*. Washington, D.C.: United Nations, UNCTAD Discussion Paper No. 213.
Kim, E.M., 1993. Contradictions and Limits of a Developmental State: With Illustrations from the South Korean Case. *Social Problems*, 40 (2), 228–249.
King, G., Keohane, R.O., and Verba, S., 1994. *Designing Social Inquiry: Scientific Inference in Qualitative Research*. New Jersey: Princeton University Press.
Kohli, A., 1994. Where do high growth political economies come from? The Japanese lineage of Korea's 'developmental state'. *World Development*, 22 (9), 1269–1293.
Kohli, H.S., Sharma, A., and Sood, A., 2011. *Asia 2050: Realizing the Asian Century*. New Delhi: SAGE Publications India.
Kojima, K., 2000. The 'flying geese' model of Asian economic development: origin, theoretical extensions, and regional policy implications. *Journal of Asian Economics*, 11 (4), 375–401.

Korhonen, P., 1994. The Theory of the Flying Geese Pattern of Development and Its Interpretations. *Journal of Peace Research*, 31 (1), 93–108.

Kuah, K.-E., 1990. Confucian ideology and social engineering in Singapore. *Journal of Contemporary Asia*, 20 (3), 371–383.

Lam, N.M.K., 2000. Government intervention in the economy: a comparative analysis of Singapore and Hong Kong. *Public Administration and Development*, 20 (5), 397–421.

Lam, S., Lau, I.Y., Chiu, C., Hong, Y., and Peng, S., 1999. Differential emphases on modernity and Confucian values in social categorization: the case of Hong Kong adolescents in political transition. *International Journal of Intercultural Relations*, 23 (2), 237–256.

Lam, W., 2004. *Understanding the Political Culture of Hong Kong: The Paradox of Activism and Depoliticization*. New York: M.E. Sharpe.

Lau, S. and Liu, Z., 1984. *Society and Politics in Hong Kong*. Chinese University Press.

Lee, E.W.Y. and Haque, M.S., 2006. The New Public Management Reform and Governance in Asian NICs: A Comparison of Hong Kong and Singapore. *Governance*, 19 (4), 605–626.

Lee, F.L.F. and Chan, J.M., 2008. Making Sense of Participation: The Political Culture of Pro-democracy Demonstrators in Hong Kong. *The China Quarterly*, 193, 84–101.

Lee, J., 2009. Developmentalism, social welfare and state capacity in East Asia: integrating housing and social security in Singapore. *Journal of Asian Public Policy*, 2 (2), 157–170.

Lee, T., 2002. The Politics of Civil Society in Singapore. *Asian Studies Review*, 26 (1), 97–117.

Lee, T., 2005. Internet Control and Auto-regulation in Singapore. *Surveillance & Society*, 3 (1), 74–95.

Leftwich, A., 1995. Bringing politics back in: Towards a model of the developmental state. *Journal of Development Studies*, 31 (3), 400–427.

Leung, T.K.P., Wong, Y.H., and Wong, S., 1996. A study of Hong Kong Businessmen's perceptions of the role 'Guanxi' in the People's Republic of China. *Journal of Business Ethics*, 15 (7), 749–758.

Li, K.W., 2012. *Economic Freedom: Lessons of Hong Kong*. 1st ed. Singapore: World Scientific Publishing Company.

Lim, L., 1983. Singapore's Success: The Myth of the Free Market Economy. *Asian Survey*, 23 (6), 752–764.

Lim, L.Y.C., 1999. Free Market Fancies: Hong Kong, Singapore, and the Asian Financial Crisis. In: T.J. Pempel, ed. *The Politics of the Asian Economic Crisis*. Ithaca and London: Cornell University Press, 101–115.

Lin, L.-H. and Ho, Y.-L., 2009. Confucian dynamism, culture and ethical changes in Chinese societies – a comparative study of China, Taiwan, and Hong Kong. *The International Journal of Human Resource Management*, 20 (11), 2402–2417.

Low, L., 2001a. The Singapore developmental state in the new economy and polity. *The Pacific Review*, 14 (3), 411–441.

Low, L., 2001b. *The Political Economy of a City-State: Government-Made Singapore*. Oxford: Oxford University Press.

Low, L., 2003a. Sustaining the competitiveness of Singapore Inc in the knowledge-based global economy. *In*: R.S. Rajan, ed. *Sustaining Competitiveness in the New*

Global Economy: The Experience of Singapore. Cheltenham, UK: Edward Elgar Publishing, 135.

Low, L., 2003b. Singapore Inc: A success story. *South African Journal of International Affairs*, 10 (1), 49–63.

Low, L., 2006. *The Political Economy of a City-State Revised*. Singapore: Marshall Cavendish.

Lui, T.-L. and Chiu, S., 1993. Industrial Restructuring and Labour-Market Adjustment under Positive Noninterventionism: The Case of Hong Kong. *Environment and Planning A*, 25 (1), 63–79.

Ma, N., 2007. *Political Development in Hong Kong: State, Political Society, and Civil Society*. Hong Kong: Hong Kong University Press.

Maguire, M. and Ball, S.J., 1994. Researching politics and the politics of research: recent qualitative studies in the UK. *International Journal of Qualitative Studies in Education*, 7 (3), 269–285.

Mahbubani, K., 2008. The Case against the West: America and Europe in the Asian Century. *Foreign Affairs*, 87 (3), 111–124.

Mahbubani, K., 2009. *The New Asian Hemisphere: The Irresistible Shift of Global Power to the East*. New York: PublicAffairs.

Mahbubani, K., 2014. *The Great Convergence: Asia, the West, and the Logic of One World*. New York: PublicAffairs.

Mann, L. and Berry, M., 2016. Understanding the Political Motivations That Shape Rwanda's Emergent Developmental State. *New Political Economy*, 21 (1), 119–144.

Maxwell, J., 1992. Understanding and Validity in Qualitative Research. *Harvard Educational Review*, 62 (3), 279–301.

Moon, C.-I. and Prasad, R., 1994. Beyond the Developmental State: Networks, Politics, and Institutions. *Governance*, 7 (4), 360–386.

Morley, J.W., Cheng, T., and Lin, C., eds., 2015. Taiwan: a long decade of democratic transition. In: *Driven by Growth: Political Change in the Asia-Pacific Region*. Armonk, N.Y.: M.E. Sharpe, 224–254.

Needham, C., 2008. Realising the Potential of Co-production: Negotiating Improvements in Public Services. *Social Policy and Society*, 7 (2), 221–231.

Neuman, W.L., 2011. *Social research methods: qualitative and quantitative approaches*. Boston: Allyn & Bacon.

Ng, B.K., 1998. *Hong Kong and Singapore as International Financial Centres: A Comparative Functional Perspective*. Singapore: Nanyang Technological University, SABRE Working Paper No. 6–98.

Olds, K. and Yeung, H., 2004. Pathways to global city formation: a view from the developmental city-state of Singapore. *Review of International Political Economy*, 11 (3), 489–521.

O Riain, P.S., 2000. The flexible developmental state: globalization, information technology and the 'Celtic Tiger'. *Politics and Society*, 28 (2), 157–193.

Page, J., Kim, C.-S., Stiglitz, J.E., Sabor, R., Campos, J.E.L., Birdsall, N.M., Corden, W.M., MacDonald, L. [editor, and Pack, H., 1993. *The East Asian miracle: economic growth and public policy*. Washington, D.C.: The World Bank, No. 12351.

Painter, M., 2005. Transforming the Administrative State: Reform in Hong Kong and the Future of the Developmental State. *Public Administration Review*, 65 (3), 335–346.

Painter, M. and Pierre, J., 2005. Unpacking policy capacity: issues and themes. *In*: M. Painter and J. Pierre, eds. *Challenges to State Policy Capacity: Global Trends and Comparative Perspectives*. Basingstoke: Palgrave Macmillan, 1–18.

Painter, M. and Wong, S., 2007. The telecommunications regulatory regimes in Hong Kong and Singapore: when direct state intervention meets indirect policy instruments. *The Pacific Review*, 20 (2), 173–195.

Painter, M. and Yee, W.-H., 2012. Agencies and policy in an administrative state: The case of Hong Kong. *Policy and Society*, 31 (3), 223–235.

Perry, M., 1997. *Singapore: a developmental city state.* Chichester: Wiley.

Peters, B.G., 2015. Policy capacity in public administration. *Policy and Society*, 34 (3–4), 219–228.

Schenk, C.R., 2001. *Hong Kong as an International Financial Centre: emergence and development 1945–1960.* New York: Routledge.

Schenk, C.R., 2002. Banks and the emergence of Hong Kong as an international financial center. *Journal of International Financial Markets, Institutions and Money*, 12 (4–5), 321–340.

Stiglitz, J.E. and Uy, M., 1996. Financial Markets, Public Policy, and the East Asian Miracle. *The World Bank Research Observer*, 11 (2), 249–276.

Stiglitz, J.E. and Yusuf, S., 2001. *Rethinking the East Asian Miracle.* World Bank Publications.

Stubbs, R., 2009. What ever happened to the East Asian Developmental State? The unfolding debate. *The Pacific Review*, 22 (1), 1–22.

Tan, C.H. and Lim, J.Y.S., 2007. *Singapore and Hong Kong as Competing Financial Centres.* Singapore: Saw Centre Financial Studies.

Tan, K.P., 2012. The Ideology of Pragmatism: Neo-liberal Globalisation and Political Authoritarianism in Singapore. *Journal of Contemporary Asia*, 42 (1), 67–92.

Wade, R., 1990. *Governing the Market: Economic Theory and the Role of Government in East Asian Industrialization.* New Jersey: Princeton University Press.

Wade, R., 2010. After the Crisis: Industrial Policy and the Developmental State in Low-Income Countries. *Global Policy*, 1 (2), 150–161.

White, G., 1984. Developmental states and socialist industrialisation in the third world. *The Journal of Development Studies*, 21 (1), 97–120.

Wilkinson, B., 1996. Culture, Institutions and Business in East Asia. *Organization Studies*, 17 (3), 421–447.

Woo, J.J., 2014. Singapore's policy style: statutory boards as policymaking units. *Journal of Asian Public Policy*, 8 (2), 120–133.

Woo, J.J., 2015a. Beyond the Neoliberal orthodoxy: Alternative financial policy regimes in Asia's financial centres. *Critical Policy Studies*, 9 (3), 297–316.

Woo, J.J., 2015b. Policy Relations and Policy Subsystems: Financial policy in Hong Kong and Singapore. *International Journal of Public Administration*, 38 (8), 553–561.

Woo, J.J., 2016a. *Business and Politics in Asia's Key Financial Centres – Hong Kong, Singapore and Shanghai.* 1st ed. Singapore: Springer.

Woo, J.J., 2016b. *Singapore as an International Financial Centre: History, Politics and Policy.* London: Palgrave Macmillan.

Woo, J.J. and Howlett, M., 2015. Explaining dynamics without change: a critical subsector approach to financial policy making. *Journal of Asian Public Policy*, 8 (3), 312–328.

Woo, J.J., Ramesh, M., and Howlett, M., 2015. Legitimation Capacity: System-Level Resources and Political Skills in Public Policy. *Policy & Society*, 34 (3–4), 271–283.

Woo, J.J., Ramesh, M., Howlett, M., and Coban, M.K., 2016. Dynamics of global financial governance: Constraints, opportunities, and capacities in Asia. *Policy and Society*, Forthcoming.

Woo-Cumings, M., 1999. *The Developmental State*. Ithaca, N.Y: Cornell University Press.

Wu, X., Ramesh, M., and Howlett, M., 2015. Blending Skill and Resources Across Multiple Levels of Activity: Competences, Capabilities and the Policy Capacities of Government. *Policy & Society*, 34 (3–4), 165–171.

Young, A., 1992. A Tale of Two Cities: Factor Accumulation and Technical Change in Hong Kong and Singapore. *In*: O.J. Blanchard and S. Fischer, eds. *NBER Macroeconomics Annual 1992*. Massachusetts: MIT Press, 13–64.

2 Developmental states

A conceptual overview

The conceptual origins of the Asian developmental state are very much connected to the empirical reality of rapidly industrializing economies in the global south, particularly those situated within the East Asian region, during the 1970s. Indeed, the origins of the Asian developmental state model can be traced to the pioneering work of Chalmers Johnson (1982, 1995) on economic development in Japan, which was instrumental in identifying the developmental state as 'one that gives priority to economic growth, productivity, and technological competitiveness' (Chu 2016, p. 1).

This work, along with those of other subsequent studies on the Asian developmental state, can therefore be seen as an attempt to understand the rapid economic growth that was occurring in East Asia, among states that organized their political systems and bureaucracies very differently from the Western liberal democracies that many of these early scholars belonged to. Theory therefore followed phenomenon, as early scholars of the developmental state model sought to make sense of the political and institutional foundations upon which the rapid economic transformation of East Asian states was founded.

This epistemological priority of empirical phenomenon over theory would recede, as the developmental state model gradually became a major area of study, especially among political scientists, political economists, and area studies experts. Drawing from this relatively large body of work, this chapter will provide a broad overview of the conceptual development of the developmental state model. Specifically, I will discuss the context within which the developmental state model was conceived and developed, sketch out the components and characteristics of an idealized developmental state, and review its ongoing evolution as both theoretical concept and empirical study.

Conceptual development and evolution

The notion of a development-focused state is neither new nor exclusive to the East Asian context. As Leftwich (1995, pp. 401–402) has noted, the notion of using state resources to pursue developmental or capitalist aims had existed in the work of nineteenth-century thinkers such as Friedrich List and Karl

Marx as well as more contemporary thinkers such as Samuel P. Huntington. White and Wade (1988, p. 1) argue that all successful instances of 'late development' among both capitalist and socialist nations can be characterized by the state's 'strategic role in taming domestic and international market forces and harnessing them to a national interest'.

This definition of the developmental state model that has been provided by White and Wade encompasses, at a broad level of conception at least, three major elements or activities that are present in all developmental states: the (i) *harnessing* or directing of market forces and economic resources in a (ii) *strategic* manner that is geared towards the fulfilment of a (iii) *national interest* or objective. Furthermore, developmental states tend to be motivated by a need or desire to 'catch up' with more developed economies (Tan 2005, Block and Negoita 2016, Jessop 2016), although, and as I will discuss below, the focus has since shifted from 'catching up' to 'continues upgrading' (Block and Negoita 2016). Studies of the developmental state model therefore tend to focus on how states employ their political and bureaucratic resources to the pursuit of national economic goals.

While this broad understanding of the developmental state, as White and Wade have argued, apply equally to capitalist and socialist states as well as East Asian and European states alike, there are in reality variances in the ways in which governments of developing economies intervene in their markets (Tan 2005). For instance, Tan (2005) has noted that the Soviet states tended to completely dominate their domestic markets, whereas East Asian developmental states such as Japan allowed for private property ownership, with policies tending to promote the private sector, rather than the public sector (Chu 2016, p. 4).

This exercise of state power in tandem, or even in complicity, with free markets suggests a significant extent of complexity and nuance in the ways that state power is exercised by East Asian developmental states, as well as no small amount of conceptual confusion. For instance, the spate of economic liberalization that had occurred in East Asian states, such as Korea, had led to the mistaken belief that it was the free markets that had driven economic growth when in reality, such 'liberal market' policies were driven by formal and informal state direction (Luedde-Neurath 1988). Nonetheless, it is this East Asian formulation of the developmental state that has come to dominate subsequent studies of the developmental state model (Radice 2008).

This emergence of the East Asian formulation as the dominant model is a consequence of the post-Cold War emergence of East Asia as a major economic bloc. Indeed, it was only when political scientists sought to understand the rapid economic development experienced by East Asian nations during the 1970s, that the developmental state model took on its current conceptual and epistemological form. The conceptual form of the developmental state model that will inform the discussions in the rest of this book, and which will be theoretically expanded in its later chapters, is largely derived from this East Asian formulation of the model.

Given its point position in the 'flying geese' pattern of regional economic development, Japan became the archetypal Asian developmental state of the time (Korhonen 1994, Kojima 2000, Kasahara 2013), with many early studies of the developmental state model essentially covering case studies of Japanese economic development. This is evident in Trimberger's (1978) study on the extent of relative autonomy in the bureaucratic state apparatuses of Japan, Turkey, Egypt and Peru. Similarly, Johnson's (1982) seminal work *MITI and the Japanese Miracle* emphasizes the role of Japan's Ministry of International Trade and Industry (MITI) in driving Japanese economic growth.

It was also in Johnson's work that the term 'developmental state' was first coined. Furthermore, it was not so much Japan's stellar economic performance alone, but the fact that its economic rise was predicated upon extensive state management of the domestic economy – a phenomenon absent in Western market economies – that captured the interest of these scholars (Tan 2005, p. 3).

This renewed focus on state-led economic development in East Asia, with its emphasis on the central role of economic bureaucracies, led to further efforts to conceptually clarify and elucidate the ways in which other Asian developmental states govern and develop their economies (White 1984, Evans 1985, 1989, Wade 1990, Öniş 1991). At the heart of this spate of theoretical development was the growing recognition of the central role of politics and political institutions in the activities of Asian developmental states (Deyo 1987, Moon and Prasad 1994, Leftwich 1995).

Yet amid such theorizing on the developmental state model, economic development in Asia, not simply in Japan, continued unabated. This provided scholars of the developmental state with opportunities for both empirical research and theory testing, as these emerging Asian economies increasingly took on the form of the developmental state. This was particularly the case with Korea, which was rapidly industrializing and emerging as 'Asia's next giant' (Amsden 1992, Woo-Cumings 1999, Minns 2001, Kang 2002).

Indeed, the political and institutional bases of Korea's 'economic miracle' bear a strong resemblance to the archetypal developmental state, such as a strong state that is insulated from societal pressures, the driving role of economic bureaucracies such as the Economic Planning Board (EPB), close linkages between the state and major industrialists, among others (Luedde-Neurath 1988, Minns 2001). It should also be noted that the emergence of these institutional trappings of the developmental state model in Korea is by no means a matter of sheer coincidence.

It has, for instance, been argued that the origins of Korea's developmental state can be traced to the Japanese occupation of 1910–1945, with Japanese colonial influence resulting in the emergence of a dominant and authoritarian state that was capable of controlling and transforming Korean society as well as strong production-oriented alliances between the state and dominant, often capitalist, classes (Kohli 1994). The emergence of Korea's developmental state, in other words, bears both the imprints of general trends in East Asian economic development and the Japanese developmental state, the latter imparted with no small amount of pain and humiliation.

Aside from Korea, Taiwan's rapid industrialization and its burgeoning science and technology sector would also result in greater interest in Taiwan's developmental state (Levi-Faur 1998, Chu 2002, Wu 2007, Greene 2009). Like Japan, the Taiwanese state played an outsized role in driving economic development through policy initiatives that served to enhance the country's comparative advantages, such as land reform, encouraging import substitution and export promotion, selecting and supporting leading sectors, introducing labour-saving automation and facilitating financial liberalization (Wade 1988, pp. 41–45).

In both cases of Taiwan and Korea, rapid economic growth has often been misattributed to the effects of a free market, when in reality economic development has remained very much state-driven, with state interventions often implemented through market means (Luedde-Neurath 1988, Wade 1988). Joining Korea and Taiwan as Asian developmental states are Hong Kong and Singapore, with the four collectively known as the 'Asian Tigers' – a quartet of emerging East Asian developmental states. Chapters 3 and 4 will examine the two cases of Singapore and Hong Kong.

Having begun the process of 'opening up' its economy and surviving the 1997 Asian Financial Crisis relatively unscathed, China emerged as another important proponent of the developmental state model (Tan 2005). While its approach to economic development and governance prior to 1979 tended to resemble the Soviet model of total state domination over markets, the introduction of private property ownership and relatively freer markets with economic liberalization led to China's adoption of the developmental state approach, i.e. state-led development within the framework of free markets.

Despite the empirical beginnings of the developmental state model, with early studies on the developmental state driven by empirical studies of developmental states such as Japan, Korea and Taiwan rather than theory building or development, the developmental state model has since become a 'permanent fixture in the political economy of development' (Yeung 2017, pp. 2–3) and a 'stylized fact: the thing itself, a fixity in real-world politics' (Boyd and Ngo 2005, pp. 2–3). Furthermore, the developmental state is no longer solely applicable to East Asia, nor are its elements present or relevant only in developing economies.

As I will discuss further below, the emergence of new developmental states as well as a growing adoption of developmental state elements among developed market economies that have hitherto been seen as proponents of 'free market' liberalism suggest that the influence of the developmental state model is far greater than initially thought. Furthermore, the developmental state's ability to persist in the face of globalization and economic liberalization suggests a strong capacity among these states to innovate and adapt in response to changes in the global economic landscape. This adaptive and transformative ability of development states is an important, and often neglected, aspect that will be discussed throughout this book.

Regardless of their geographical origins, what unites all developmental states is an overwhelming focus on industrial policy as a means of generating economic growth and ensuring the dominance of the state over both socio-political and economic realms. Indeed, it has been noted that a defining characteristic of a developmental state is the government's role in coordinating national industrial transformation, which often includes acting as direct producer (Tan 2005). As Low (2001a, p. 413) has noted, there is an 'intrinsic, implicit correlation between a developmental state and industrial policy'. However, the developmental state's role in industrial policy is often more subtle and nuanced than the simple provision of goods and services.

Rather, it often relies on the provision of subsidies, incentives, and cheap credits to encourage the participation of private firms and entrepreneurs in its industrialization programme (Amsden 1992, Yeung 2017, p. 3). Industrial policy is hence 'not an alternative to the market' but the state's efforts in altering market incentives to influence the behaviour of producers, consumers and investors (Low 2001a, p. 413). The emphasis is therefore very much on coordinating the allocation of capital and other resources across domestic sectors and pooling a society's limited resources in targeted high-growth industries (Tan 2005, p. 163). Through such coordination and direction of resources, developmental states are often seen as 'picking winners' from among firms and industries, rather than being the primary provider of goods and services.

In the context of the Japanese developmental state, industrial policy has been described as a government's efforts at 'development, guidance, and supervision of industry' (Johnson 1995, p. 64). Such subtle means of directing and managing industrial transformation and development resonates with another major theoretical construct in development studies – the 'regulatory state' (Majone 1994, 1997, 1999). Indeed, linkages between the regulatory state and developmental state are already being explored, especially in light of the increasing use of regulatory policy instruments by developmental states such as China and Indonesia, among others, to achieve developmental policy goals and objectives (Jayasuriya 2005, Hsueh 2011, Jarvis 2012).

However, and as Chalmers has pointed out, industrial policy does not necessarily mean the 'tired old cliché' of 'picking winners', but rather a reorientation of the economic policy focus from consumer to producer economics, and a modifying of comparative advantages to concentrate on industries with a high human capital content (Johnson 1995, pp. 64–65). Given that the basic measure and focus of producer economics tends to be savings and investments, industrial policy, as (re)defined in terms of producer economics, involves the channelling of a nation's pool of savings to the right industries and ensuring consolidation of firms' interests and incentives around the state's industrial policies (Fingleton 1990, Johnson 1995, p. 66).

The developmental state model, in short, has emerged from its empirical beginnings to become a major theoretical fixture in the study of economic development, with subsequent theorizing, albeit much of it still based on key empirical studies such as Japan or Korea, resulting in a relatively consolidated concept and notion of what constitutes a developmental state, and the characteristics or elements that make up an ideal or archetypal developmental state. These characteristics and components of the developmental state model are discussed next.

Components and characteristics

Having provided a historical overview of the conceptual development and evolution of the developmental state model, I will now delve into the specific elements and components that make up a typical developmental state. While multiple conceptual interpretations and variations of the developmental state model have been proffered by scholars seeking to understand and describe the developmental state (White and Wade 1988, Evans 1989, Öniş 1991, Johnson 1995, Woo-Cumings 1999), this book draws from the seminal work of Adrian Leftwich (1995), whose interpretation of the developmental state stands out for both its accuracy and parsimony.

According to Leftwich, the developmental state model can be defined by six major components:

- i A developmental elite
- ii A powerful, competent and insulated economic bureaucracy
- iii Relative autonomy of the state
- iv The effective management of non-state economic interests
- v A weak and subordinated civil society
- vi Performance legitimacy

Developmental elite

At the core of every developmental state is the existence of a developmental elite comprising a 'small cadre of developmentally-determined senior politicians and bureaucrats, usually close to the executive head of government who was instrumental in establishing the developmental regime and its culture' (Leftwich 1995, p. 405). According to Johnson (1987, p. 142), the various roles of a typical developmental elite includes creating political stability, maintaining an equal distribution of resources or benefits to prevent class or sectorial exploitation, setting national goals and standards that tend to be internationally oriented, and creating and politically insulating a bureaucratic elite capable of administering and managing the developmental state's policy processes.

It is this core of developmental elites that informs and drives the policy agenda of the developmental state, by translating their desire for economic development into policy initiatives and pushing for the implementation of these initiatives. Importantly, the centrality of this developmental elite within a developmental state's political and policy apparatuses, as well as its proximity to the executive head of government, imbues it with significant influence over the types of policies to be implemented and the level of resources to be channelled towards these policies.

The notion of a developmental elite is by no means unique to the developmental state model. Political scientists have long noted the presence of select groups of highly influential political and bureaucratic actors who are able to almost unilaterally determine the policy directions and dominate policy processes. These policy elites have variously been referred to as 'iron triangles' (Cater 1964), 'issue networks' (Heclo 1978), 'policy networks' (Kenis and Schneider 1991, Atkinson and Coleman 1992, Rhodes 1997, Carpenter 2001, Howlett 2002), policy regimes (Wilson 2000, Jochim and May 2010), or 'policy communities' (Jordan and Richardson 1983, Atkinson and Coleman 1992, Lindquist 1992, Birkland 1996).

Of greater relevance to our discussion here is the 'policy subsystems' approach that has been taken to describe the groups of state and non-state actors who determine policy outcomes (Baumgartner and Jones 1991, Howlett and Ramesh 1995, 1998), whether through political influence (Baumgartner and Jones 1991, Howlett et al. 2009, Woo 2015a) or the legitimacy that is associated with the possession of either technical or policy knowledge (Adler and Haas 1992, Haas 1992, Voss and Simons 2013, Mukherjee and Howlett 2015, Béland and Howlett 2016). More importantly, policy subsystems can be formed around a set of shared beliefs (Sabatier 1988, Jenkins-Smith and Sabatier 1994, Weible et al. 2009).

Such belief-driven policy subsystems, or 'advocacy coalitions', have proven particularly useful in understanding the East Asian developmental state, with the developmental elite often formed around a shared set of beliefs that not only prioritize the need for economic growth and development, but emphasize the causal linkages between development-oriented policy initiatives or instruments and policy objectives of economic development (Woo 2015a, Woo and Howlett 2015, Woo 2016). Whether policy subsystems, policy networks, or iron triangles, these various concepts allude, in most cases, to the presence of a policy elite that is capable of defining the policy agenda and determining policy decisions.

In the context of developing Asian economies, this policy elite has often placed a strong focus on economic development, thereby making them developmental elites. While the developmental elite determines, to a significant extent, economic policies, they are not necessarily involved in the day-to-day implementation of these policies. Rather, they tend to create a bureaucratic elite that possesses the technical expertise and capabilities required to administer and implement economic policies; more importantly, the developmental elite ensures the political insulation of its bureaucrats, such that they can carry out their tasks technocratically, free from political pressure (Johnson 1987, p. 142). This economic bureaucracy is discussed next.

Economic bureaucracy

Taking point position in the functioning and operations of a developmental state is the economic bureaucracy. Tasked with shaping and leading economic development, economic bureaucracies have been described as 'core centres of strategic economic direction in developmental states', with their ability to organize and manage critical interactions between state and economy facilitated by their positions of power and authority, possession of technical competence, as well as insulation from socio-political pressures (Leftwich 1995, pp. 411–414) – in essence operating as an 'economic general staff' (Wade 1990, p. 196).

Such economic bureaucracies are also commonly known in the literature as 'pilot agencies' (Johnson 1982, p. 26). I will use the terms 'economic bureaucracy' and 'pilot agency' interchangeably in the rest of this book. Regardless of terminology, the activities and policies of developmental states are driven by such economic bureaucracies or pilot agencies that coordinate the policy efforts, and consolidate the resources, of the various agencies and organizations involved in economic development policy.

It is important to note that an economic bureaucracy is often not entirely separate or distinct from the developmental elite. This is especially the case for developmental states like Singapore, where there is a relatively high level of movement between the civil service and the political elite (Hamilton-Hart 2000), or China, where both civil servants and corporate leaders are frequently members of the ruling political party through its cadre system, with the party often drawing potential party leaders from the civil service (Elman 1991, Chan and Suizhou 2007, Brødsgaard 2012). In both cases, this close intermingling of the economic bureaucracy and political elite coincides with a highly depoliticized population, a point that is elaborated below and in the next chapter.

However, it is Japan's MITI that is often seen as the quintessential economic bureaucracy, largely by virtue of its approximation of an ideal Weberian bureaucracy that is characterized by long-term career paths, established rules and norms of operation and behaviour, meritocratic promotion of personnel, among others, as well as other factors unique to Japan, such as the presence of informal networks that ensure bureaucratic coherence and state–industry linkages or the ability of state agencies to attract top graduates (Evans 1989, p. 573).

As the example of Japan's MITI, along with similar agencies such as Singapore's Economic Development Board, has shown, the economic bureaucracy occupies a central position in the policy processes and political milieu of a developmental state. However, this is not to say that the success of a developmental state depends entirely on its economic bureaucracy. For instance, Chibber (2002) has argued that the efficacy of a developmental state's economic bureaucracy, in terms of fostering economic development, also depends very much on the overall internal cohesiveness of the state, defined in terms of the strength of interagency relations, with the economic bureaucracy embedded within such interagency relations.

There is therefore a need for the economic bureaucracy to be embedded within cohesive ties with other public agencies and organizations as well as private and societal actors. This latter point is especially important, given the fact that the economic bureaucracy, along with the developmental state writ large, is embedded within the socio-political and cultural structures of the nation-state, with economic development often shaped by ideologies of nationalism within an 'imagined community' of people (Hsu 2017).

Hence while the economic bureaucracy plays a key role in directing and driving development-oriented policies, it is also embedded within the broader socio-cultural milieu of the city or nation within which it exists. The 'embeddedness' of the economic bureaucracy, and developmental state, within these dense webs of social, cultural and political relations represents the third major element of a developmental state: embedded autonomy. I will now discuss this third component of the developmental state model.

Embedded autonomy

At the heart of the economic bureaucracy's role, as well as the roles of other relevant public agencies in driving economic development, is the notion of 'embedded autonomy'. First introduced by Peter B Evans in his 1995 work *Embedded Autonomy: States & Industrial Transformation,* embedded autonomy refers to developmental states' simultaneous autonomy from and embeddedness within society (Evans 1995). Two key elements make up embedded autonomy: social embeddedness and institutional autonomy. Both of these elements are both crucial for the functioning of a developmental state, especially in terms of ensuring that public officials are not captured by private interests but at the same time are able to discipline firms that do not align with national economic interests (Block and Negoita 2016).

Institutional autonomy is a crucial element that insulates a developmental state's public agencies and officials from unnecessary interference in their policy activities. Autonomy therefore has something to do with the 'strength' or ability of the state to resist socio-political pressures from the non-state sector. Indeed, much attention has been paid to the developmental state's ability or 'capacity' to deliver its development-oriented policy outcomes (Evans 1989). This state-centric focus on capacity both draws from and serves to further a growing research agenda on state capacity (Rondinelli and Cheema 2003, Hameiri 2007, Besley and Persson 2010, Savoia and Sen 2012) and more recently, policy capacity (Painter and Pierre 2005, Gleeson et al. 2011, Wu et al. 2015).

At the heart of state capacity, and hence institutional autonomy, is the 'internal coherence' of a developmental state's institutions, often defined in terms of an ideal Weberian bureaucracy, and which are imbued with what is known as 'bureaucratic rationality' (Evans 1989, 1995, Chibber 2002). This began with Chalmers, who saw Japan's MITI as an ideal Weberian bureaucracy, and hence a driving force behind Japan's developmental state model (Johnson 1982). As Riain (2000, p. 164) has noted, developmental states 'retain their autonomy due to the presence of a classic Weberian bureaucracy – based on meritocratic recruitment and promotion and norms of objective, procedural rationality'.

It is also important to note that while institutional autonomy facilitates the policy activities of the economic bureaucracy, it is also through the seizure of state power and de-politicization of the existing bureaucratic structures by an emergent developmental elite that such autonomy can be achieved in the first place (Leftwich 1995, p. 409). Furthermore, the consolidation of the developmental elite's power and autonomy is often achieved within formal democratic processes, often through the influence and actions of a single dominant party (Leftwich 1995, p. 410). The institutional autonomy of a developmental state's bureaucracy is therefore strongly linked to its political dominance and legitimacy.

Aside from institutional autonomy and bureaucratic rationality, developmental states also rely on their embeddedness within a dense web of ties with firms and other non-state actors in order to coordinate economic activities and fulfil developmental policy objectives (Evans 1989, pp. 575–581, Öniş 1991, pp. 123–124, Leftwich 1995, p. 408). Indeed, a developmental state's ability to implement its development-oriented policies hinges on its reputation and credibility in the eyes of the private sector, particularly in terms of the state's willingness to invest productively, manage private economic interests, deliver economic performance, and suppress any threats that civil society may pose to investment stability and economic growth (Huff 1999, pp. 216–217). This suggests a significant level of complicity in the private sector, in terms of their being vested in and hence supportive of the state's efforts at driving economic development.

More importantly, such complicity suggests a more nuanced approach to economic governance that involves persuasion rather than pure coercion, since the interests of the state and the private sector are often intertwined. As Chapters 3 and 4 will show, advanced developmental states that feature highly liberalized and open economies more often than not require the presence and participation of the private sector to achieve the high levels of economic growth desired, while private sector firms require the support of the state, whether in terms of providing subsidies and incentives or establishing public and economic infrastructure, to thrive. As Huff (1999, p. 217) notes:

> By convincing the private sector of development of its true intention, which would lead to more private sector investment and therefore more economic growth, the state can establish an equilibrium of high growth and secure a better outcome not just for the private sector but also for itself, provided it has a long enough horizon and values the future benefits of successful economic development sufficiently highly.

Furthermore, a shift among many developmental states towards a knowledge-based and innovation-driven economy has served to emphasize the importance of embedded autonomy in ensuring growth and development in this new economic landscape. Given the growing importance of technological transfer and capacity building for global competitiveness, public agencies are increasingly embedded within 'collaborative public spaces' that allow these agencies to connect firms with research institutions and laboratories, whether state- or privately owned, in the process facilitating the sharing of new technologies and ideas among technology agencies, firms and individuals (Lester and Piore 2006, Block and Negoita 2016).

As I will discuss in the rest of this book, such 'networked' understandings of embedded autonomy are particularly relevant to smart cities such as Singapore and Hong Kong, with embedded autonomy becoming an even more crucial element of managing and governing an increasingly networked and technologically driven economy. While traditional notions of embedded autonomy had emphasized the role of the state as *driver* of economic growth, the new knowledge-based economy requires the state to instead act as a *catalyst* of technological innovation and entrepreneurship. This conceptual shift in understanding of embedded autonomy will be discussed in Chapter 6.

From a conceptual point of view, the notion that policymakers and other societal actors can be 'embedded' within such webs of ties or relations draws from earlier work by sociologists and political scientists who had sought to understand the ways in which economies, political systems, and policy processes tend to be embedded or 'nested' within their broader socio-political contexts, and how these impact policymaking (Granovetter 1985, Ostrom 1990, 1998, Tsebelis 1991, Hollingsworth 1998, Howlett 2009). More recent work on 'policy relations' has related such state–society relations with policy co-creation and other collaborative approaches to policymaking (Ansell and Gash 2008, Poocharoen and Ting 2015, Woo 2015a, 2015b, 2016, Woo and Howlett 2015).

Taken on their own, therefore, embeddedness and autonomy are by no means unique to the developmental state model. As the brief discussion above has shown, these are concepts that have received a substantial amount of attention among scholars and researchers of political economy and the policy sciences. However, it is the confluence of the two – embeddedness and autonomy – that defines a developmental state.

As Evans (1995, p. 12) has argued, '[o]nly when embeddedness and autonomy are joined together can a state be called developmental'. Hence while the organizations that make up a developmental state approximate Weberian bureaucracies in their meritocratic recruitment and 'corporate coherence' and are hence able to maintain their autonomy or insulation from societal influence, these organizations are nonetheless deeply embedded within state–society ties that provide institutionalized channels for the negotiation of goals and policies (Evans 1995, p. 12).

Indeed, there is emerging interest in the ability of states to manage socio-political relations, and in doing so build up 'political' or 'legitimation' capacities (Jackman 1993, Dunlop 2015, Pal and Clark 2015, Woo et al. 2015). In these studies, there is strong focus on the embedded nature of state capacity, and how the development of political capacities is crucial for the formation and management of the state–society ties necessary for effective economic governance and policymaking (Woo et al. 2016). An important aspect of such political capacities involves the management of non-state economic interests as well as civil society. These are discussed in the next section.

Management of non-state economic interests

The political influence of the developmental elite and internal coherence of the economic bureaucracy, mediated by embedded autonomy, has allowed developmental states to effectively manage non-state economic interests, often directing such economic activity towards national developmental goals. This dominance of the state over non-state economic interests stems from the fact that in many of Asia's developmental states, state power and autonomy, especially in terms of the political and institutional configurations discussed above, were established before domestic or foreign capital were able to gain any influence (Leftwich 1995, pp. 416–417).

As a consequence, most, if not all, of the developmental states in Asia were from the start able to determine the 'industrial division of labour', defining the roles that transnational capital could (and could not) play (Evans 1987, p. 215). Indeed, the successful development of many Asian developmental states has hinged upon the state's ability to attract foreign capital, and at the same time ensure the alignment of foreign firms' business activities with the state's domestic economic development goals and priorities (Amsden 1985, Haggard and Cheng 1987, Mardon 1990, Dent 2003).

As I will discuss in Chapter 3, this alignment of foreign economic interests with state economic priorities was particularly crucial for Singapore's early development, with the newly independent city-state 'leapfrogging' the region by attracting foreign multinational companies, when most other postcolonial Southeast Asian states were deeply resistant to the presence of foreign economic interests (Low 2001b). However, the management of foreign economic interests is not unique to Singapore. In almost all the developmental states that have since emerged in Asia, there have been strong efforts to attract foreign firms and manage the state's relationships with these firms.

Such efforts have often taken on the form of 'economic diplomacy' or 'economic statecraft', with governments of many developmental states seeking to establish close relations with foreign capital (Haggard and Cheng 1987, Dent 2003) or even other states (Pekkanen et al. 2007, Bräutigam and Xiaoyang 2012), in a bid to reap the economic gains that may accrue from the investments and business activities that often accompany the participation of foreign firms and governments in the domestic economy. There is therefore a strong element of diplomacy and relationship management, with the success of the development state dependent on its ability to manage networks of socio-political relations.

Such diplomacy and relationship management requires the developmental state to expand its repertoire of capabilities from the technocratic skills or capabilities to include political or 'legitimation' capacities that may allow it to leverage on its socio-political relations to facilitate economy policy-making (Woo et al. 2015). For instance, the developmental state's ability to manage non-state economic interests has been attributed to the presence of 'operationally autonomous state managers' who are able to 'orchestrate a changing balance of markets, networks, government resources, and national solidarity to pursue national goals' (Jessop 2016).

Furthermore, economic liberalization has led to a growing need for more subtle means through which states can manage firms and other economic interests. This is particularly relevant to small open economies such as Singapore and Hong Kong, where the state, by virtue of its relatively small size, is less able to control or discipline global firms. In such small developmental states, there has been a shift towards regulatory regimes that employ much less direct regulatory instruments that, while providing firms with operational autonomy, nonetheless enhances state capacity by defining and circumscribing the sphere of firms' activities (Painter and Wong 2007, Woo 2016).

Despite caricatures of the developmental state as top-down and state-centric apparatuses driven by authoritarian governments possessing strong influence over firms (often described in the literature as 'crony capitalism'), the reality is much more nuanced and complex. Given the need to attract globally mobile multinational firms in an increasingly globalized economy, developmental states are increasingly relying on tools of persuasion, rather than coercion, in order to establish themselves as hubs of economic activity (Woo 2016). This renegotiation of power relations between the developmental state and global capital, however, is not replicated in the realm of civil society. I will next discuss the limited role of civil society in the developmental state.

Civil society

As the discussions on the developmental elite and economic bureaucracy have made clear, the developmental state is very much insulated from the lobbying efforts and influence of many non-state socio-political forces. More importantly, such political insulation requires, and is predicated upon, a weak civil society. As Pekkanen (2004) has noted, a weak or quiescent civil society sector is central to the success of key developmental states such as Japan. Such weakness or quiescence in civil society may be a matter of historical contingency or deliberate design.

For instance, Leftwich (1995, p. 415) has noted that many of Asia's developmental states tend to have emerged from socio-political contexts where civil society is already weak or oppressed. This is largely due to the low levels of economic development that existed at the inception of many of these states, with the consequence being the lack of an influential or sufficiently resourced social class or grouping that could initiate the formation of civil society. Such extant weakness in civil society tends to be reified by the introduction of the developmental state, with the developmental elite and economic bureaucracy retaining extensive control over political and policy processes.

In many cases, such control over political and policy processes has been extended to civil society, most notably in the form of 'infrastructural power', which allows developmental states to penetrate and control the activities of civil society, hence ensuring the sustenance of a strong state (Mann 1984). This has often included the use of legal-regulatory impediments such as internal security legislation and agencies (Leftwich 1995, p. 415, Rodan 2003, George 2007). Such control over civil society has in some cases been reinforced by the introduction of state-sponsored civil society organizations, with Indonesia being a case in point (Robison 1985).

While such efforts at maintaining a weak civil society has allowed most of Asia's developmental states to flourish and succeed in the absence of any substantial political resistance, the growing affluence of many of these developmental states has paradoxically prompted a proliferation of civil society organizations and growing political plurality, giving rise to new challenges for policymakers and political leaders (Pekkanen 2004). As Chapter 5 will discuss, the introduction of smart city modalities of governance and civic engagement has served to catalyze the emergence of civil society.

This has required a re-articulation of the developmental state, especially in terms of the avenues through which it engages civil society. This is discussed in Chapter 6. Furthermore, this need to maintain a weak civil society in order for a developmental state to succeed economically is itself contestable. In his study of the developmental state in Israel, Taiwan, and Korea, Levi-Faur (1998) shows how similar processes and outcomes of state-guided economic development can occur despite differences in political regimes and institutions.

Hence beyond such structural and visible exercise of power and influence, such as controlling civil society or maintaining embedded autonomy, there is also a need to examine the ideological bases upon which developmental states establish and justify their rule. This is discussed in the next section on performance legitimacy.

Performance legitimacy

The discussion thus far has painted a picture of a highly centralized developmental state that has been able to stimulate economic growth through the actions of a politically insulated developmental elite and economic bureaucracy, with this such political insulation often achieved through the control or repression of civil society. Yet despite such political repression, and the public protests that this has often evoked, developmental states have been able to retain their rule and legitimacy by ensuring a good distribution of benefits accruing from the high growth rates that they have managed to achieve (Leftwich 1995, p. 419).

This drawing of legitimacy from the state's ability to perform in its tasks of stimulating economic growth and the overall provision of public goods has been described in the existing developmental state literature as 'performance legitimacy' (Johnson 1982, p. 4, Leftwich 1995, Woo-Cumings 1999, Stubbs 2011, p. 154, Ortmann 2012, p. 340). It is this focus on delivering 'concrete goals' such as economic growth, social stability and 'good governance', among others, that has allowed developmental states to retain their legitimacy without the need for democratic processes, with China being a strong case in point (Zhu 2011).

The derivation of political legitimacy from economic performance is also strongly related to issues of reputation, with the legitimacy of a developmental state strongly dependent on its reputation for delivering economic performance, especially in the eyes of the private sector (Huff 1999). As I have discussed in an earlier section on embedded autonomy, the government's reputation for ensuring economic growth and distributing of economic advantages to firms contributes immensely to its ability to implement its economic policies, unopposed by industry and societal interests.

Performance legitimacy is hence key to maintaining the developmental state's credibility as driver of national economic development and provider of public goods, hence ensuring public support for the state and political legitimacy for its rule and policies without the concomitant need for democratic representation, although democratic processes do exist in almost all developmental states. This last point is an important one to keep in mind. Despite their reputation for authoritarianism, the exercise of state power by developmental states is in reality rooted within democratic process and/or the rule of law (Leftwich 1993, Trubek 2009, Whiting 2017).

Hence while developmental states tend to maintain a strong dominance over policy and political processes through the actions and activities of its developmental elite and economic bureaucracy, the ballot box nonetheless remains an important, and often the only, way for political elites to enter public office, with rule of law the medium through which developmental policies are implemented and enforced. As this section has discussed, the seeming contradiction that arises from such political dominance or even oppression amidst the rule of law and democratic processes is resolved when performance legitimacy is taken into consideration.

In introducing a 'performance' or developmental element to political legitimacy, performance legitimacy ironically requires the developmental elite to maintain a certain level of policy competency, in terms of guaranteeing a certain level of economic growth or ensuring the smooth delivery of public services. While performance legitimacy ensures and justifies the dominance of a political elite that is capable of ensuring economic growth and social stability, the converse is also true. In other words, there is a rapid loss of legitimacy and power for political leaders who fail to ensure an acceptable level of economic growth, with the resignation of Indonesia's Suharto in the aftermath of the 1997 Asian Financial Crisis being a case in point.

Rather than working against democratic or legal processes, performance legitimacy changes these processes by making policy performance or competency the sole measure of a government's efficacy and its right to rule. The exercise of authoritarian state power by many developmental states, in other words, is legitimated by developmental or performance considerations, with political elites obtaining public office through democratic and legal institutions and remaining in office by virtue of their ability to deliver on developmental objectives.

This makes performance legitimacy the key ideological basis of all the other components of the developmental state that I have discussed above, since it provides the developmental state with the legal-political basis for its dominance over the policy process and civil society; yet at the same time, it also provides firms and citizens with a measurable criteria for evaluating and empowering their governments. There is therefore a need to understand the five components of the developmental state that has been discussed in this section as an integrated whole.

Epistemological challenges

Having provided an extensive discussion of the components and elements of the developmental state model, it is also important to note that there may be limitations in the conception of the developmental state that I have provided above. This is especially the case, given that the developmental state, both as theoretical concept and empirical reality, is in a constant state of flux, buffeted by global economic forces and adapting to shifts in the global political economy (Chu 2002, 2016, Stubbs 2011, Hsu 2017).

While such conceptual and empirical shifts in the Asian developmental state are discussed in Chapter 6, I will now provide a brief discussion of two emerging conceptual and epistemological challenges to the developmental state model:

- The emergence of non-Asian developmental states
- A perceived decline of the developmental state

The growing adoption of the developmental state model among developing economies outside of Asia raises questions over whether there is an *Asian* developmental state. Or is the developmental state model much more universal and generalizable than initially thought? If so, is it possible to separate current understandings of the developmental state model from its origins? The second epistemological challenge pertaining to the decline of the developmental state is more severe, as it questions the overall viability of the developmental state, both as policy model and subject of scholarly enquiry. I will discuss these challenges next.

The rise of the non-Asian developmental state

While the developmental state model has provided the policy and ideological ballast for economic governance and development in East Asia, so much so that the developmental state model is often prefixed with 'East Asian', there has also been an emergence of non-Asian developmental states, most notably African and Latin American states. Although most of these states are not situated in East Asia, they nonetheless possess the trappings of a typical developmental state, albeit with notable differences in political and socio-cultural contextual variables.

While it is well beyond the scope of this book to delve into these 'non-Asian' developmental states, their unique appropriation of the developmental state model to a non-Asian socio-political context warrants a brief discussion of these new emerging developmental states and their implications for theoretical development.

The combination of political authoritarianism and a desire for rapid economic development has led to the adoption of the developmental state model in major African states such as Rwanda (Mkandawire 2001, Sandbrook 2005, Mann and Berry 2016). While the success of the East Asian developmental state, in terms of generating rapid economic growth and development, may have provided many of these developing nations with a role model, others have noted a more direct ideological transfer of the developmental state model through collaborations between East Asian nations such as Korea and China with emerging African states (Shaw et al. 2007, Brautigam 2009, Kalinowski and Park 2016).

Yet despite this proliferation of a developmental state rhetoric in Africa and other emerging economies, there are qualitative differences between the Asian or East Asian conception of the developmental state and these new and emerging developmental states. For instance, the domination of a political elite in African states such as Angola has hindered the structural development needed for a full transformation from 'petro-developmental state' to developmental state, with local elites continuing to hold and appropriate national assets (Ovadia 2017). As discussed above, the Asian developmental state tends to promote free markets, exercising state authority through market mechanisms, rather than through direct political manipulation or coercion.

Aside from these developing economies in Africa and Latin America, the developmental state model, or at least elements of it, has been found in developed market economies as well. For instance, Block (2008) has noted the presence of a 'hidden developmental state' in the US, with these developmental elements of US economic policy allowing the federal government to finance and support the commercialization of new technologies by the private sector. Again, these differ markedly from the Asian developmental states, which exercise their authority and influence over market outcomes in plain sight, with industry and business actors frequently complicit with the state, often through informal linkages and networks.

As the discussion thus far has shown, there are substantial differences between the traditional Asian developmental state and these emerging attempts to incorporate parts and aspects of the developmental state model in both emerging and developed economies outside of Asia.

While the developmental state model has gained significant traction among non-Asian developing economies (albeit with some modifications and caveats), there are also emerging views that the developmental state, faced with severe challenges in the form of government failures and economic liberalization, is really in a state of decline. I will address these views in the following section.

Decline of the developmental state?

While the 'East Asian Miracle' that had taken place from the 1970s to the 1990s had driven scholarly research on the developmental state model and emphasized its strengths, shifts in the global political economy have also resulted in a conceptual erosion of the developmental state, giving rise to other theories of the state, such as the 'regulatory state' (Majone 1997, Jayasuriya 2005, Hsueh 2011, Jarvis 2012). This conceptual erosion of the developmental state largely stemmed from the 1997 Asian Financial Crisis and 2008 Global Financial Crisis, both of which question the viability of state economic intervention in light of massive government failures (Pang 2000, Jomo 2003, Stubbs 2009, 2011, Wade 2010).

Aside from this crisis-driven conceptual erosion, global trends of economic liberalization and political democratization have also eroded the power and capabilities of developmental states (Kim 1999). This is particularly the case for states seeking to develop 'catch-up industries', since the changes in the global trade regime have made it much more difficult to establish import barriers (Block and Negoita 2016, p. 58). This makes the 'import-substitution' strategies that were employed by many early Asian development states to protect domestic industries much less feasible, with domestic firms required to compete globally.

These impacts of economic globalization and liberalization are exacerbated by the technological and organizational shifts that have accompanied globalization, which have led to a reshuffle of inter-firm relations as well as state-firm relations, with the result being a 'strategic coupling' of firms to global production networks that are governed by inter-firm relations rather than states (Yeung 2014, 2016). As a consequence, inter-firm dynamics are beginning to trump state-led initiatives as a critical condition of economic development (Yeung 2014).

Furthermore, the challenges faced by the developmental state model are not simply limited to shifts in empirical reality; there are conceptual weaknesses or limitations in the model as well. Gainsborough (2009) has identified three key weaknesses or limitations in the developmental state model as a theory of the state. First, the model takes a Weberian conception of the state, which may not necessarily be applicable to all states. Second, it relies on Cold War-era understandings of global power structures. Lastly, it assumes and perpetuates an artificial separation between state and society.

However, the developmental state model has also been associated with a significant amount of path dependency, with the trajectory of institutional development within a developmental state often rigid and not amenable to change (Pierson 2000, Tan 2005). As a result, developmental states tend to remain developmental states, even after these states have attained advanced economy status. This is obvious in states such as Japan and Singapore, both of which continue to feature strong state intervention in the domestic economy despite being advanced economies.

While financial crises, such as the 1997 Asian Financial Crisis or the 2008 Global Financial Crisis, had to some extent undermined confidence in the developmental state, the state has in almost all instances rebounded from these crises to reinstate its central position in economic development and governance, with the result being a continued dominance of the developmental state model, particularly among developing economies (Levi-Faur 1998, Block 2008, Evans 2010, Howlett and Lejano 2013, Howlett et al. 2015).

The strongest validation of the developmental state model is perhaps its continued persistence in major East Asian economies such as Japan and China, leading some to conclude that reports of the developmental state model's death are 'premature' (Beeson 2009). Indeed, and as Chapter 5 on the 'digitization' of the Hong Kong and Singaporean developmental states will show, the developmental state is not so much 'dead' as it is adapting to new political economic conditions. Rather than signalling its decline, such adaptations to new technological and economic realities indicate a certain resilience in the developmental state model.

It has been noted that the key reason for the longevity of the developmental state is the ability of many developmental states to adjust and adapt to shifting global economic forces. For instance, a need for globally competitive domestic firms has led developmental states to take on a more decentralized network approach in encouraging greater flexibility and innovation among domestic firms, rather than relying on import-substitution or direct financing as means of developing and nurturing national 'champions' (Riain 2000, Yeung 2016).

At a more fundamental level, Weiss (2000) has found a shift among major developmental states from a form of developmentalism that is driven by a need to 'catch up' to a more transformative process of 'continual upgrading' of the industrial economy. As a consequence, and as Weiss concludes, developmental states are not 'normalizing' towards an Anglo-Saxon neoliberal norm of free markets and passive states, but instead adapting, dismantling, and innovating in response to global economic shifts.

As their economies develop and diversify, the mechanisms and policy instruments that are implemented by developmental states may shift or adapt. As Chapters 5 and 6 show, the emergence of a knowledge-based and digital economy in developmental states such as Hong Kong and Singapore has necessitated a shift towards more sophisticated and subtle means of state intervention in the domestic economy.

Conclusion

This chapter has provided an extensive overview of the developmental state model, discussing its historical development and delineating the various elements and components that make up a typical developmental state. It has also addressed emerging epistemological challenges to the Asian developmental state, especially in terms of the emergence of non-Asian developmental states and a perceived decline of the developmental state. While these two challenges raise real concerns over the relevance and generalizability of the developmental state model, the conclusion that I have drawn in this chapter has been one of adaptive resilience rather than outright decline.

However, it is not enough to say that the developmental state is highly adaptable, or that the death knells sounded by its critics and detractors are but a figment of our imagination. Rather, there is a need to grapple objectively with these issues, and more importantly situate this conceptual notion of this 'adaptive' developmental state that I have alluded to above in empirical reality. The following chapters will aim to do this by focusing on the cases of Singapore and Hong Kong, and examining the ways in which these two developmental states have adapted and evolved in response to emerging technological and economic changes.

References

Adler, E. and Haas, P.M., 1992. Conclusion: epistemic communities, world order, and the creation of a reflective research program. *International Organization*, 46 (1), 367–390.

Amsden, A., 1985. The State and Taiwan's Economic Development. *In*: P. Evans, D. Rueschemeyer, and T. Skocpol, eds. *Bringing the State Back In*. Cambridge, U.K.: Cambridge University Press.

Amsden, A.H., 1992. *Asia's Next Giant: South Korea and Late Industrialization*. New York; Oxford: Oxford University Press.

Ansell, C. and Gash, A., 2008. Collaborative Governance in Theory and Practice. *Journal of Public Administration Research and Theory*, 18 (4), 543–571.

Atkinson, M.M. and Coleman, W.D., 1992. Policy Networks, Policy Communities and the Problems of Governance. *Governance*, 5 (2), 154–180.

Baumgartner, F.R. and Jones, B.D., 1991. Agenda Dynamics and Policy Subsystems. *The Journal of Politics*, 53 (4), 1044–1074.

Beeson, M., 2009. Developmental States in East Asia: A Comparison of the Japanese and Chinese Experiences. *Asian Perspective*, 33 (2), 5–39.

Béland, D. and Howlett, M., 2016. How Solutions Chase Problems: Instrument Constituencies in the Policy Process. *Governance*, 29 (3), 393–409.

Besley, T. and Persson, T., 2010. State Capacity, Conflict, and Development. *Econometrica*, 78 (1), 1–34.

Birkland, T., 1996. Natural Disasters as Focusing Events: Policy Communities and Political Response. *International journal of mass emergencies and disasters*, 14 (2), 221–243.

Block, F., 2008. Swimming Against the Current: The Rise of a Hidden Developmental State in the United States. *Politics & Society*, 36 (2), 169–206.

Block, F. and Negoita, M., 2016. Beyond Embedded Autonomy: Conceptualizing the Work of Developmental States. *In*: Y. Chu, ed. *The Asian Developmental State: Reexaminations and New Departures*. New York, N.Y.: Palgrave Macmillan, 57–72.

Boyd, R. and Ngo, T.-W., 2005. Emancipating the political economy of Asia from the growth paradigm. *In*: R. Boyd and T.-W. Ngo, eds. *Asian States: Beyond the Developmental Perspective*. London: Routledge.

Brautigam, D., 2009. *The Dragon's Gift: The Real Story of China in Africa*. Oxford, U.K.: OUP Oxford.

Bräutigam, D. and Xiaoyang, T., 2012. Economic statecraft in China's new overseas special economic zones: soft power, business or resource security? *International Affairs*, 88 (4), 799–816.

Brødsgaard, K.E., 2012. Politics and Business Group Formation in China: The Party in Control? *The China Quarterly*, 211, 624–648.

Carpenter, D.P., 2001. *The forging of bureaucratic autonomy: reputations, networks, and policy innovation in executive agencies, 1862–1928*. Princeton, N.J.: Princeton University Press.

Cater, D., 1964. *Power in Washington: A Critical Look at Today's Struggle to Govern in the Nation's Capital*. New York: Random House.

Chan, H.S. and Suizhou, E.L., 2007. Civil Service Law in the People's Republic of China: A Return to Cadre Personnel Management. *Public Administration Review*, 67 (3), 383–398.

Chibber, V., 2002. Bureaucratic Rationality and the Developmental State. *American Journal of Sociology*, 107 (4), 951–989.

Chu, Y., 2002. Re-engineering the Developmental State in an Age of Globalization: Taiwan in Defiance of Neo-liberalism. *China Review*, 2 (1), 29–59.

Chu, Y., 2016. The Asian Developmental State: Ideas and Debates. *In*: Y. Chu, ed. *The Asian Developmental State*. New York: Palgrave Macmillan US, 1–25.

Dent, C., 2003. Transnational capital, the state and foreign economic policy: Singapore, South Korea and Taiwan. *Review of International Political Economy*, 10 (2), 246–277.

Deyo, F.C., ed., 1987. *The Political Economy of the New Asian Industrialism*. Ithaca, N.Y.: Cornell University Press.

Dunlop, C.A., 2015. Organizational political capacity as learning. *Policy and Society*, 34 (3–4), 259–270.

Elman, B.A., 1991. Political, Social, and Cultural Reproduction via Civil Service Examinations in Late Imperial China. *The Journal of Asian Studies*, 50 (1), 7–28.

Evans, P.B., 1985. Transnational Linkages and the Economic Role of the State: An Analysis of Developing and Industrialized Nations in the Post-World War II

Period. *In*: P.B. Evans, D. Rueschemeyer, and T. Skocpol, eds. *Bringing the State Back In*. Cambridge: Cambridge University Press, 192–226.

Evans, P.B., 1987. Class, State and Dependency in East Asia: Lessons for Latin Americanists. *In*: F.C. Deyo, ed. *The Political Economy of the New Asian Industrialism*. Ithaca, N.Y.: Cornell University Press, 203–226.

Evans, P.B., 1989. Predatory, developmental, and other apparatuses: A comparative political economy perspective on the Third World state. *Sociological Forum*, 4 (4), 561–587.

Evans, P.B., 1995. *Embedded Autonomy: States & Industrial Transformation*. First Edition. Princeton, N.J: Princeton University Press.

Evans, P.B., 2010. Constructing the 21st Century Developmental State: Potentialities and Pitfalls. *In*: O. Edigheji, ed. *Constructing a Democratic Developmental State in South Africa: Potentials and Challenges*. Cape Town, South Africa: HSRC Press, 37–58.

Fingleton, E., 1990. *The Gaijin and Gyosei Shido*.

Gainsborough, M., 2009. The (Neglected) Statist Bias and the Developmental State: the case of Singapore and Vietnam. *Third World Quarterly*, 30 (7), 1317–1328.

George, C., 2007. Consolidating authoritarian rule: calibrated coercion in Singapore. *The Pacific Review*, 20 (2), 127–145.

Gleeson, D., Legge, D., O'Neill, D., and Pfeffer, M., 2011. Negotiating Tensions in Developing Organizational Policy Capacity: Comparative Lessons to be Drawn. *Journal of Comparative Policy Analysis: Research and Practice*, 13 (3), 237–263.

Granovetter, M., 1985. Economic Action and Social Structure: The Problem of Embeddedness. *American Journal of Sociology*, 91 (3), 481–510.

Greene, J.M., 2009. *The Origins of the Developmental State in Taiwan: Science Policy and the Quest for Modernization*. Cambridge, M.A.: Harvard University Press.

Haas, P.M., 1992. Introduction: epistemic communities and international policy co-ordination. *International Organization*, 46 (1), 1–35.

Haggard, S. and Cheng, T., 1987. State and foreign capital in the East Asian NICs. *In*: F.C. Deyo, ed. *The political economy of the new Asian industrialism*. Ithaca, N.Y.: Cornell University Press, 84–135.

Hameiri, S., 2007. Failed states or a failed paradigm? State capacity and the limits of institutionalism. *Journal of International Relations and Development*, 10 (2), 122–149.

Hamilton-Hart, N., 2000. The Singapore state revisited. *The Pacific Review*, 13 (2), 195–216.

Heclo, H., 1978. Issue networks and the Executive Establishment. *In*: King Anthony, ed. *The new American Political System*. Washington, D.C.: American Enterprise Institute, 87–124.

Hollingsworth, R.J., 1998. Territoriality in Modern Societies: The Spatial and Institutional Nestedness of National Economies. *In*: P.D.S. Immerfall, ed. *Territoriality in the Globalizing Society*. Springer Berlin Heidelberg, 17–37.

Howlett, M., 2002. Do Networks Matter? Linking Policy Network Structure to Policy Outcomes: Evidence from Four Canadian Policy Sectors 1990–2000. *Canadian Journal of Political Science/Revue canadienne de science politique*, 35 (2), 235–267.

Howlett, M., 2009. Governance modes, policy regimes and operational plans: A multi-level nested model of policy instrument choice and policy design. *Policy Sciences*, 42 (1), 73–89.

Howlett, M. and Lejano, R.P., 2013. Tales From the Crypt The Rise and Fall (and Rebirth?) of Policy Design. *Administration & Society*, 45 (3), 357–381.

Howlett, M., Mukherjee, I., and Woo, J.J., 2015. From Tools to Toolkits in Policy Design Studies: The New Design Orientation and Policy Formulation Research. *Policy and Politics*, 43 (2), 291–311.

Howlett, M. and Ramesh, M., 1995. *Studying public policy: Policy cycles and policy subsystems*. 1st ed. Oxford: Oxford University Press.

Howlett, M. and Ramesh, M., 1998. Policy Subsystem Configurations and Policy Change: Operationalizing the Postpositivist Analysis of the Politics of the Policy process. *Policy Studies Journal*, 26 (3), 466–481.

Howlett, M., Ramesh, M., and Perl, A., 2009. *Studying Public Policy: Policy Cycles and Policy Subsystems*. 3rd ed. Oxford: Oxford University Press.

Hsu, J., 2017. State transformation and the evolution of economic nationalism in the East Asian developmental state: the Taiwanese semiconductor industry as case study. *Transactions of the Institute of British Geographers*, 1–13.

Hsueh, R., 2011. *China's Regulatory State: A New Strategy for Globalization*. Cornell University Press.

Huff, W.G., 1999. Turning the Corner in Singapore's Developmental State? *Asian Survey*, 39 (2), 214–242.

Jackman, R.W., 1993. *Power Without Force: The Political Capacity of Nation-states*. Michigan: University of Michigan Press.

Jarvis, D.S.L., 2012. The Regulatory State in Developing Countries: Can It Exist and Do We Want It? The Case of the Indonesian Power Sector. *Journal of Contemporary Asia*, 42 (3), 464–492.

Jayasuriya, K., 2005. Beyond institutional fetishism: From the developmental to the regulatory state. *New Political Economy*, 10 (3), 381–387.

Jenkins-Smith, H.C. and Sabatier, P.A., 1994. Evaluating the Advocacy Coalition Framework. *Journal of Public Policy*, 14 (2), 175–203.

Jessop, B., 2016. The Developmental State in an Era of Finance-Dominated Accumulation. *In*: Y. Chu, ed. *The Asian Developmental State*. Palgrave Macmillan US, 27–55.

Jochim, A.E. and May, P.J., 2010. Beyond Subsystems: Policy Regimes and Governance. *Policy Studies Journal*, 38 (2), 303–327.

Johnson, C., 1987. Political Institutions and Economic Performance: The Government-Business Relationship in Japan, South Korea and Taiwan. *In*: F.C. Deyo, ed. *The Political Economy of the New Asian Industrialism*. Ithaca: Cornell University Press, 136–164.

Johnson, C., 1995. *Japan: Who Governs?: The Rise of the Developmental State*. New York: W. W. Norton & Company.

Johnson, C.A., 1982. *MITI and the Japanese Miracle: The Growth of Industrial Policy, 1925–1975*. 1st ed. Stanford, California: Stanford University Press.

Jomo, K.S., 2003. *Southeast Asian Paper Tigers?* London: Routledge.

Jordan, A.G. and Richardson, J.J., 1983. Policy Communities: The British and European Policy Style. *Policy Studies Journal*, 11 (4), 603–615.

Kalinowski, T. and Park, M.J., 2016. South Korean Development Cooperation in Africa: The Legacy of a Developmental State. *Africa Spectrum*, 51 (3), 61–75.

Kang, D.C., 2002. Bad Loans to Good Friends: Money Politics and the Developmental State in South Korea. *International Organization*, 56 (1), 177–207.

Kasahara, S., 2013. *The Asian Developmental State and the Flying Geese Paradigm*. Washington, D.C.: United Nations, UNCTAD Discussion Paper No. 213.

Kenis, P. and Schneider, V., 1991. Policy networks and policy analysis: Scrutinizing a new analytical toolbox. *In*: B. Marin and R. Mayntz, eds. *Policy networks: Empirical evidence and theoretical considerations.* Boulder, C.O.: Westview Press, 25–62.

Kim, Y.T., 1999. Neoliberalism and the decline of the developmental state. *Journal of Contemporary Asia*, 29 (4), 441–461.

Kohli, A., 1994. Where do high growth political economies come from? The Japanese lineage of Korea's 'developmental state'. *World Development*, 22 (9), 1269–1293.

Kojima, K., 2000. The 'flying geese' model of Asian economic development: origin, theoretical extensions, and regional policy implications. *Journal of Asian Economics*, 11 (4), 375–401.

Korhonen, P., 1994. The Theory of the Flying Geese Pattern of Development and Its Interpretations. *Journal of Peace Research*, 31 (1), 93–108.

Leftwich, A., 1993. Governance, democracy and development in the Third World. *Third World Quarterly*, 14 (3), 605–624.

Leftwich, A., 1995. Bringing politics back in: Towards a model of the developmental state. *Journal of Development Studies*, 31 (3), 400–427.

Lester, R.K. and Piore, M.J., 2006. *Innovation—The Missing Dimension.* Cambridge, M.A.: Harvard University Press.

Levi-Faur, D., 1998. The developmental state: Israel, South Korea, and Taiwan compared. *Studies in Comparative International Development*, 33 (1), 65–93.

Lindquist, E.A., 1992. Public managers and policy communities: learning to meet new challenges. *Canadian Public Administration*, 35 (2), 127–159.

Low, L., 2001a. The Singapore developmental state in the new economy and polity. *The Pacific Review*, 14 (3), 411–441.

Low, L., 2001b. *The Political Economy of a City-State: Government-Made Singapore.* Oxford: Oxford University Press.

Luedde-Neurath, R., 1988. State Intervention and Export-oriented Development in South Korea. *In*: G. White, ed. *Developmental States in East Asia.* London, U.K.: Palgrave Macmillan, 68–112.

Majone, G., 1994. The rise of the regulatory state in Europe. *West European Politics*, 17 (3), 77–101.

Majone, G., 1997. From the Positive to the Regulatory State: Causes and Consequences of Changes in the Mode of Governance. *Journal of Public Policy*, 17 (2), 139–167.

Majone, G., 1999. The regulatory state and its legitimacy problems. *West European Politics*, 22 (1), 1–24.

Mann, L. and Berry, M., 2016. Understanding the Political Motivations That Shape Rwanda's Emergent Developmental State. *New Political Economy*, 21 (1), 119–144.

Mann, M., 1984. The autonomous power of the state: its origins, mechanisms and results. *European Journal of Sociology / Archives Européennes de Sociologie*, 25 (2), 185–213.

Mardon, R., 1990. The State and The Effective Control of Foreign Capital: The Case of South Korea. *World Politics*, 43 (1), 111–138.

Minns, J., 2001. Of miracles and models: The rise and decline of the developmental state in South Korea. *Third World Quarterly*, 22 (6), 1025–1043.

Mkandawire, T., 2001. Thinking about developmental states in Africa. *Cambridge Journal of Economics*, 25 (3), 289–314.

Moon, C.-I. and Prasad, R., 1994. Beyond the Developmental State: Networks, Politics, and Institutions. *Governance*, 7 (4), 360–386.

Mukherjee, I. and Howlett, M., 2015. Who Is a Stream? Epistemic Communities, Instrument Constituencies and Advocacy Coalitions in Public Policy-Making. *Politics and Governance*, 3 (4), 68–71.

Öniş, Z., 1991. The Logic of the Developmental State. *Comparative Politics*, 24 (1), 109–126.

Ortmann, S., 2012. The 'Beijing consensus' and the 'Singapore model': unmasking the myth of an alternative authoritarian state-capitalist model. *Journal of Chinese Economic and Business Studies*, 10 (4), 337–359.

Ostrom, E., 1990. *Governing the commons: the evolution of institutions for collective action*. Cambridge: Cambridge University Press.

Ostrom, E., 1998. Scales, Polycentricity, Incentives: Designing Complexity to Govern Complexity. *In*: L.D. Guruswamy and J. McNeely, eds. *Protection of Global Diversity: Converging Strategies*. Durham, N.C.: Duke University Press, 149–167.

Ovadia, J., 2017. State-led industrial development, structural transformation and elite-led plunder: Angola (2002–2013) as a developmental state. *Development Policy Review*, n/a-n/a.

Painter, M. and Pierre, J., 2005. Unpacking policy capacity: issues and themes. *In*: M. Painter and J. Pierre, eds. *Challenges to State Policy Capacity: Global Trends and Comparative Perspectives*. Basingstoke: Palgrave Macmillan, 1–18.

Painter, M. and Wong, S., 2007. The telecommunications regulatory regimes in Hong Kong and Singapore: when direct state intervention meets indirect policy instruments. *The Pacific Review*, 20 (2), 173–195.

Pal, L.A. and Clark, I.D., 2015. Making reform stick: Political acumen as an element of political capacity for policy change and innovation. *Policy and Society*, 34 (3–4), 247–257.

Pang, E.-S., 2000. The Financial Crisis of 1997–98 and the End of the Asian Developmental State. *Contemporary Southeast Asia*, 22 (3), 570–593.

Pekkanen, R., 2004. After the Developmental State: Civil Society in Japan. *Journal of East Asian Studies*, 4 (3), 363–388.

Pekkanen, S.M., Solís, M., and Katada, S.N., 2007. Trading Gains for Control: International Trade Forums and Japanese Economic Diplomacy. *International Studies Quarterly*, 51 (4), 945–970.

Pierson, P., 2000. Increasing Returns, Path Dependence, and the Study of Politics. *The American Political Science Review*, 94 (2), 251–267.

Poocharoen, O. and Ting, B., 2015. Collaboration, Co-Production, Networks: Convergence of theories. *Public Management Review*, 17 (4), 587–614.

Radice, H., 2008. The Developmental State under Global Neoliberalism. *Third World Quarterly*, 29 (6), 1153–1174.

Rhodes, R.A.W., 1997. *Understanding governance: policy networks, governance, reflexivity, and accountability*. London: Open University Press.

Riain, S.O., 2000. The Flexible Developmental State: Globalization, Information Technology, and the 'Celtic Tiger'. *Politics & Society*, 28 (2), 157–193.

Robison, R., 1985. Class, capital and the state in New Order Indonesia. *In*: R. Higgott and P. Kegan, eds. *Southeast Asia: essays in the political economy of structural change*. London: Routledge, 295–335.

Rodan, G., 2003. Embracing electronic media but suppressing civil society: Authoritarian consolidation in Singapore. *The Pacific Review*, 16 (4), 503–524.

Rondinelli, D.A. and Cheema, G.S., 2003. *Reinventing Government for the Twenty-First Century: State Capacity in a Globalizing Society*. Bloomfield, C.T.: Kumarian Press.

Sabatier, P.A., 1988. An advocacy coalition framework of policy change and the role of policy-oriented learning therein. *Policy Sciences*, 21 (2–3), 129–168.

Sandbrook, R., 2005. Origins of the Democratic Developmental State: Interrogating Mauritius. *Canadian Journal of African Studies / Revue canadienne des études africaines*, 39 (3), 549–581.

Savoia, A. and Sen, K., 2012. *Measurement and Evolution of State Capacity: Exploring a Lesser Known Aspect of Governance*. Manchester, U.K.: Effective States and Inclusive Development Research Centre (ESID), Effective States and Inclusive Development Research Centre Working Paper No. 10.

Shaw, T.M., Cooper, A.F., and Antkiewicz, A., 2007. Global and/or regional development at the start of the 21st century? China, India and (South) Africa. *Third World Quarterly*, 28 (7), 1255–1270.

Stubbs, R., 2009. What ever happened to the East Asian Developmental State? The unfolding debate. *The Pacific Review*, 22 (1), 1–22.

Stubbs, R., 2011. The East Asian developmental state and the Great Recession: evolving contesting coalitions. *Contemporary Politics*, 17 (2), 151–166.

Tan, L., 2005. *The Paradox of Catching Up – Rethinking State-Led Economic Development*. London, U.K.: Palgrave Macmillan.

Trimberger, E.K., 1978. *Revolution from Above: Military Bureaucrats and Development in Japan, Turkey, Egypt, and Peru*. New Brunswick, N.J: Transaction Publishers.

Trubek, D.M., 2009. The Political Economy of the Rule of Law: The Challenge of the New Developmental State. *Hague Journal on the Rule of Law*, 1 (1), 28–32.

Tsebelis, G., 1991. *Nested Games: Rational Choice in Comparative Politics*. Berkeley, C.A.: University of California Press.

Voss, J.-P. and Simons, A., 2013. *Instrument constituencies and the supply-side of policy innovation*. Singapore: Lee Kuan Yew School of Public Policy, National University of Singapore, Paper presented at International Workshop: Designing Optimal Policy Mixes: Principles and Methods.

Wade, R., 1988. State Intervention in 'Outward-looking' Development: Neoclassical Theory and Taiwanese Practice. *In*: G. White, ed. *Developmental States in East Asia*. Palgrave Macmillan UK, 30–67.

Wade, R., 1990. *Governing the Market: Economic Theory and the Role of Government in East Asian Industrialization*. New Jersey: Princeton University Press.

Wade, R., 2010. After the Crisis: Industrial Policy and the Developmental State in Low-Income Countries. *Global Policy*, 1 (2), 150–161.

Weible, C.M., Sabatier, P.A., and McQueen, K., 2009. Themes and Variations: Taking Stock of the Advocacy Coalition Framework. *Policy Studies Journal*, 37 (1), 121–140.

Weiss, L., 2000. Developmental states in transition: adapting, dismantling, innovating, not 'normalizing'. *The Pacific Review*, 13 (1), 21–55.

White, G., 1984. Developmental states and socialist industrialisation in the third world. *The Journal of Development Studies*, 21 (1), 97–120.

White, G. and Wade, R., 1988. Developmental States and Markets in East Asia: An Introduction. *In*: G. White, ed. *Developmental States in East Asia*. Palgrave Macmillan UK, 1–29.

Whiting, S.H., 2017. Authoritarian 'Rule of Law' and Regime Legitimacy. *Comparative Political Studies*, 10414016688008.

Wilson, C.A., 2000. Policy Regimes and Policy Change. *Journal of Public Policy*, 20 (3), 247–274.

Woo, J.J., 2015a. Policy Relations and Policy Subsystems: Financial policy in Hong Kong and Singapore. *International Journal of Public Administration*, 38 (8), 553–561.

Woo, J.J., 2015b. Beyond the Neoliberal orthodoxy: Alternative financial policy regimes in Asia's financial centres. *Critical Policy Studies*, 9 (3), 297–316.

Woo, J.J., 2016. *Business and Politics in Asia's Key Financial Centres - Hong Kong, Singapore and Shanghai.* 1st ed. Singapore: Springer.

Woo, J.J. and Howlett, M., 2015. Explaining dynamics without change: a critical subsector approach to financial policy making. *Journal of Asian Public Policy*, 8 (3), 312–328.

Woo, J.J., Ramesh, M., and Howlett, M., 2015. Legitimation Capacity: System-Level Resources and Political Skills in Public Policy. *Policy & Society*, 34 (3–4), 271–283.

Woo, J.J., Ramesh, M., Howlett, M., and Coban, M.K., 2016. Dynamics of global financial governance: Constraints, opportunities, and capacities in Asia. *Policy and Society*, 35 (3), 269–282.

Woo-Cumings, M., 1999. *The Developmental State.* Ithaca, N.Y: Cornell University Press.

Wu, X., Ramesh, M., and Howlett, M., 2015. Blending Skill and Resources Across Multiple Levels of Activity: Competences, Capabilities and the Policy Capacities of Government. *Policy & Society*, 34 (3–4), 165–171.

Wu, Y.-S., 2007. Taiwan's Developmental State: After the Economic and Political Turmoil. *Asian Survey*, 47 (6), 977–1001.

Yeung, H.W., 2014. Governing the market in a globalizing era: Developmental states, global production networks and inter-firm dynamics in East Asia. *Review of International Political Economy*, 21 (1), 70–101.

Yeung, H.W., 2016. *Strategic Coupling: East Asian Industrial Transformation in the New Global Economy.* Ithaca, N.Y.: Cornell University Press.

Yeung, H.W., 2017. State-led development reconsidered: the political economy of state transformation in East Asia since the 1990s. *Cambridge Journal of Regions, Economy and Society*, 10 (1), 83–98.

Zhu, Y., 2011. 'Performance Legitimacy' and China's Political Adaptation Strategy. *Journal of Chinese Political Science*, 16 (2), 123–140.

3 Singapore Inc.

Despite its relatively short span of history, Singapore has established itself as one of the world's most competitive economies. It is ranked second on the World Economic Forum's Global Competitiveness Index, trailing only Switzerland and ahead of third-ranked United States (Schwab 2017). Similarly, IMD's World Competitiveness Yearbook ranks Singapore third among the world's most competitive economies (IMD 2017) while the World Bank considers Singapore the second easiest place to do business in the world (World Bank Group 2017). Its GDP per capita of US $52,888.70 (current prices) also places it among the world's most affluent countries (World Bank 2016a).

Yet at the same time, Singapore is ranked 151 on the World Press Freedom Index (Reporters Without Borders 2017) and 74th on the Economist Intelligence Unit's Democracy Index (Economist Intelligence Unit 2016), with the latter report labelling the city-state a 'flawed economy'. As discussed in Chapter 2, this combination of rapid economic growth and political control, albeit with some semblance of democratic processes, is characteristic of many developmental states. Singapore's elite-driven politics and its weak civil society further serve to reiterate its developmental state identity (Hamilton-Hart 2000, Lee 2002, Tan 2008).

This strong role of the Singaporean state in guiding economic and political development, along with its strong emphasis on attaining economic growth, has led Low (2001a, p. 412) to argue that Singapore's developmental state is 'embodied as Singapore Inc., with its social, political, and economic development "government-made" through extensive state intervention and circumscription' (Low 2003, 2006). At the same time, political and administrative reforms have also been enacted to ensure the adaptability of the Singaporean developmental state to shifting political economic circumstances (Haque 2004, Lee and Haque 2006, Singh 2012, Guo and Woo 2016, Tan 2016a).

Hence while Singapore retains the trappings of a typical developmental state, it has also introduced important policy and political reforms that have contributed to its persistence as a developmental state.

This chapter will provide a comprehensive overview of Singapore's role and identity as a developmental state. It will discuss Singapore's historical development and the historical contingencies and variables that have contributed to its formation as a developmental state, examine the developmental nature of its approach to economic governance and industrial policy, delineate the various components and elements of its developmental state, and address the various challenges and reforms that have emerged over the years. I will begin with a broad overview of Singapore's historical development.

History: the making of a developmental state

Located on the tip of the Malay Peninsula, commercial and economic activities have existed in Singapore from as early as 1298–1299, when early settlements in what was then known as *Temasek* ('Sea Town') and later *Singapura* ('Lion City') grew, on the back of growing trade and migration, to form a vibrant port city (Perry 2017, p. 11, Singapore Tourism Board 2017). This connection to maritime trade and commerce would continue to characterize economic development in modern Singapore, with its founding by Sir Stamford Raffles in 1819 leading to its transformation into a major entrepôt for the British empire.

This British rule was interrupted only by a tumultuous Japanese invasion during the Second World War, but ultimately ended in 1963 on the back of anti-colonialist sentiments (Perry 2017, pp. 150–155). In light of such growing sentiments, the British government granted Singapore self-government, with the exception of foreign policy and defence, in 1959. This shift to self-government would prove to be a key turning point for Singapore, with the People's Action Party (PAP), led by Lee Kuan Yew, winning the 1959 election by a landslide and henceforth establishing the PAP's dominance in Singapore's political and economic life (The Economist 2015).

Following a short-lived merger with Malaysia that was marked by violent race riots and conflicts with the Malaysian federal government over special privileges that were granted to Malaysia's ethnic-Malay majority, Singapore formally gained independence in 1965. These conflicts with Malaysia, along with the Japanese invasion and the 1963–1966 *Konfrontasi* conflict with Indonesia that had culminated in bombings in Singapore, gave rise to a 'siege mentality' among Singapore's political leaders, imbuing the city-state's policy and political discourse with a deep sense of vulnerability and survivalism (Leifer 2000). This sense of vulnerability would, as parts of this chapter will discuss, also permeate Singapore's developmental efforts.

Having gained independence at the expense of its natural Malaysian hinterland, Singapore's political leaders found themselves faced with a pressing need to provide its population with employment and security. This was exacerbated by an earlier-than-expected withdrawal of British forces from Singapore, not so much due to the loss of British defence forces but the fact that the British military bases were contributing to over 20 per cent of Singapore's gross national product and employed about 25,000 workers (National Library Board Singapore 2017). Singapore's independence and the loss of the British military bases would nonetheless serve to stimulate fundamental shifts in Singapore's economic policy direction.

Faced with the loss of the economic security that a natural hinterland and the British empire had provided, the Singapore government initiated a shift from import-substitution to export-oriented industrialization (Low 2001b, p. 43). More importantly, this shift in economic policy direction emphasized attracting multinational corporations (MNCs) to establish their operations in Singapore, at a time when its neighbouring countries were reluctant to do so due to their colonial experiences and fears of neocolonial exploitation (Lee 2000, Low 2001b, p. 44). Not only did this allow Singapore to, in the words of its founding Prime Minister Lee Kuan Yew, 'leapfrog the region' by attracting these MNCs to manufacture their products in Singapore and export these products (Lee 2000, p. 57), but it also allowed for a transfer of technology and expertise to domestic firms and workers (Swee 1996).

This shift towards an outward-oriented and export-driven approach to industry development can partly be attributed to the inputs of Dr Albert Winsemius, a Dutch industrial economist from the United Nations who was invited to visit Singapore in 1960 and provide recommendations for its economic development (Lee 2000, UNDP 2015, pp. 49–50). Serving as its chief economic advisor from 1961 to 1984, Winsemius was credited for Singapore's emergence as an air and sea transport hub as well as its transformation into a leading financial centre – all of which served to support its increasingly outward-oriented and export-driven approach to economic development (National Library Board 2009, Woo 2016a, p. 75).

Then-Foreign Minister S. Rajaratnam best summarizes Singapore's outward-oriented approach to economic development in an oft-cited speech:

> But once you see Singapore as a Global City the problem of hinterland becomes unimportant because for a Global City the world is its hinterland. This is no hopeful theory. Our shipping statistics show clearly that the world is our hinterland. In 1959 some 9,500 ships brought 14 million tons of cargo into Singapore. Some 10 years later, in 1970, the number of ships had doubled and the cargo trebled. The ships came from all parts of the world, carrying goods to and from all parts of the world.
>
> (Rajaratnam 1972)

Pre-dating the modern literature on 'global cities' (Taylor 2000, Sassen 2001, 2011), Rajaratnam's vision of a global city would serve as a key defining principle of Singapore's subsequent economic development, driving its continual desire to groom industries that can produce 'exportable' goods and services, hence allowing it to connect with, and derive economic gains from, its global hinterland (Woo 2016a, 2016b). This focus on becoming a global city would eventually allow Singapore to attain its current position as third most competitive global financial centre in the world (Yeandle 2016).

Aside from this outward-oriented global city strategy, economic development in Singapore can also be characterized by its state-centric and pragmatic approach to economic policy, or what is known as 'strategic pragmatism'. Like the global city strategy, the notion of strategic pragmatism originated from one of Singapore's early founding leaders, namely its Minister of Finance Dr Goh Keng Swee (Schein 1996). Strategic pragmatism fundamentally refers to a dual-pronged approach of establishing a coherent master vision or strategy and developing the 'practical intelligence' to implement this strategy effectively (Schein 1996, p. 175).

Strategic pragmatism has been described by a former head of Singapore's civil service as 'strategic in thinking and pragmatic in execution' (Ngiam 2010, p. 28). As the following section will show, strategic pragmatism represents a key ideological foundation of Singapore's industrial policy and economic governance, defining and driving its efforts at 'niche creation'. Suffice to say, niche creation and the strategic pragmatism that underpins it are both predicated upon the presence of a strong state that is capable of articulating and implementing its policy objectives.

In the case of Singapore, this strong state exists in the form of the PAP, which has not only established its dominance at the ballot box, but also permeated all spheres of political and economic life in Singapore, whether through its control over both civil society and the public service or by virtue of its policy competency (Chan 1971, Tan 2016a). In either case, PAP-governed Singapore exhibits many of the elements and components of a typical developmental state that were described in Chapter 2. A more in-depth discussion of the various components of Singapore's developmental state will be described below.

These two ideological foundations – outward-oriented globalism and strategic pragmatism – continue to animate Singapore's economic governance, driving the city-state's economic and industrial transformation in the decades after its independence. This is evident in its rapid industrialization in the 1970s, internationalization and financialization of its markets and economy through the 1980s and 1990s and more recently, its shift to a knowledge-based economy (Woo 2016b, 2017). In light of these successful economic transformations, I will now discuss Singapore's approach to economic development and industrial policy in greater depth.

Economic development and industrial policy

As discussed above, Singapore's approach to economic development and industrial policy is driven by two key ideological foundations: outward-oriented globalism and strategic pragmatism. In both instances, the state has played a central role in defining the policy agenda, establishing broad strategic directions, formulating policy initiatives, and finally implementing these policies. While this central role of the state will be discussed at greater length in the next section on the various components of Singapore's developmental state, I will now provide a broad picture of Singapore's approach to economic development and industrial policy.

Singapore's efforts to internationalize its economy and leverage its 'global hinterland' has proven to be highly successful, with the city-state becoming a leading global city. It is currently ranked the third most competitive global financial centre in the world by the Global Financial Centres Index (Yeandle 2016) and holds the sixth position on ETH's Index of Globalization 2016, having been ranked first in the world for economic globalization. According to the latest World Bank data, Singapore's exports of goods and services as a percentage of its GDP stand at 176.5 per cent (World Bank 2016b), while its net inflow of foreign direct investment (FDI) as a percentage of GDP is at 22.3 per cent (World Bank 2016c).

These figures represent huge strides in economic globalization, since according to the same data, exports of goods and services as a percentage of GDP were merely 123 per cent in 1965 and net inflows of FDI as a percentage of GDP only 13.1 per cent as recently as 1995. More than simply a result of regional economic expansion – although this has proven fortuitous to Singapore's internationalization efforts as well – Singapore's rapid economic globalization is a consequence of the state's efforts to manage and leverage on global political economic forces for its economic development goals (Ramesh 1995, Yeung 2000, Koh 2007, Woo 2017, p. 1).

Aside from its early efforts at attracting MNCs, it is also important to note that Singapore's 'global shift' had from the 1990s involved a 'regionalization strategy' that involves the development of industrial parks in selected cities across the Asia-Pacific region and subsequently encouraging Singaporean firms and businesses to locate production on these Singapore-developed business parks (Yeung 2000, Pereira 2005, Inkpen and Pien 2006).

However, and given its relative lack of private entrepreneurship, the Singaporean state had to take on an entrepreneurial role, with its regionalization strategy spearheaded by government-linked companies (GLCs) – which are essentially state-owned enterprises – and the government taking the first steps in opening up overseas business opportunities for private firms, often by negotiating the institutional framework within which firms can regionalize their operations (Wai-chung Yeung 1998).

This is most obvious in the government-to-government economic cooperation frameworks that were established between China and Singapore, such as Suzhou Industrial Park, Tianjin Eco-City, and the Chongqing Connectivity Initiative (Pereira 2004, Inkpen and Pien 2006, Hu et al. 2015, Koh 2016). More recent examples include collaborations with India to develop its new smart city Amaravati (Ravishankar 2016), as well as a swathe of agreements with Africa, including an avoidance of double tax agreement with Ethiopia, an investment treaty with Mozambique, and an air services agreement with Nigeria (Soh 2017), among others.

In all instances, Singapore's efforts to develop an external wing to its economy have involved government-to-government negotiations, with the result being the formation of economic and regulatory institutional frameworks that facilitate the entry of Singaporean GLCs and private capitalists into these newly opened markets. As is the case with the development of its domestic market, Singapore's efforts at expanding into other regional and global markets are state-driven. This introduces an external and diplomatic element to Singapore's developmental state model, which will be discussed later in this book. This state-driven and business-oriented approach to market expansion is related to the second aspect of Singapore's approach to economic development and industrial policy: strategic pragmatism.

One consequence of the PAP's longevity in office is its ability to make long-range plans, often through future-oriented economic planning committees such as the Economic Review Committee or the Future Economy Committee (Economic Review Committee 2003, Committee on the Future of Economy Secretariat 2015). While the Economic Review Committee, particularly its 1985 iteration, was responsible for charting Singapore's future trajectory as a global financial centre and wealth management hub (Lee and Vertinsky 1988, p. 162), the Future Economy Committee has emphasized the digitization of Singapore's economy and enhancing productivity (Committee on the Future Economy 2017).

Aside from these committees, strategic planning in Singapore has increasingly involved the use of strategic futures and scenario planning (Habegger 2010, Centre for Strategic Futures 2015a). Aside from the Centre for Strategic Futures, a centralized strategic futures unit housed under the Prime Minister's Office, strategic planning involves a range of decentralized strategic futures units embedded within the various levels of Singapore's government and public administration (Centre for Strategic Futures 2015a, 2015b). These institutions and approaches reflect a strong emphasis by the Singaporean state on long-term strategic planning.

This strategic element of economic governance and policymaking is complemented by Singapore's public administration, which is renowned for its transparency and efficiency in policy implementation (Quah 1995, 2010, 2013, 2013, Aoki 2015a). More than process efficiency, such policy effectiveness has also often been associated with Singapore's pragmatic approach to policymaking that eschews pre-fixed ideological positions in favour of adaptability and outcome orientation (Quah 2010, Tan 2012, Jones 2016). In the words of former Prime Minister Lee Kuan Yew:

> We are pragmatists. We don't stick to an ideology. Does it work? Let's try it and if it does work, fine, let's continue it. If it doesn't work, toss it out, try another one. We are not enamored with any ideology.
>
> (Lee 2007)

An important implication of such policy pragmatism is the government's willingness, and even desire, to incorporate private sector management styles, in what is often known as 'New Public Management' (NPM) reforms, into its policy processes, with the aim of introducing greater efficiency into public service delivery (Haque 2002, Lee and Haque 2006, Sarker 2006, Aoki 2015b). Other public administration reforms aimed at improving efficiency in public service delivery include the e-government drive (Chan et al. 2008, Jones 2016) as well as more recent efforts to digitize public services in the Smart Nation initiative (Smart Nation Programme Office 2017).

More than an outright rejection of ideology, however, pragmatism has been seen as an ideological tool that allows the PAP government to link Singapore's economic success to its ability to attract global capital, hence reifying the political dominance of a meritocratic and technocratic PAP, albeit in partnership with global capital (Tan 2008). As I will discuss below, such pragmatism, and the meritocracy that is often associated with it, is crucial in defining and supporting the government's performance legitimacy. There are therefore two layers of pragmatism in Singapore's approach to economic development.

First, Singapore practises pragmatism in its public administration and policy processes, with policy reforms enacted in response to policy needs, especially as it pertains to efficiency in public service delivery. Pragmatism, in this conception, is therefore a description of what is essentially an outcome-focused approach to policymaking. Second, and on a more fundamental level, pragmatism also occupies a central ideological position in Singapore's governing milieu. In this second understanding, pragmatism becomes an ideological tool through which the government is able to maintain its political dominance and, as I will discuss further below, provide a performance-based legitimation for its rule.

Taken together, this coupling of Singapore's long-range strategic approach to economic planning with its policy implementation capacities corresponds with the 'strategic in thinking and pragmatic in execution' characterization of its strategic pragmatism doctrine (Ngiam 2010, p. 28). Such strategic pragmatism is particularly evident in Singapore's ongoing efforts to identify and develop potential growth areas or 'niches' (Lee and Vertinsky 1988, Ngiam 2010, Monetary Authority of Singapore 2011, Woo 2016a). Such 'niche creation' has given rise to important drivers of growth such as the financial services sector, electronics, and more recently, big data.

While there are semblances between such 'niche creation' and the process of picking 'winners' or 'national champions' that is prevalent among many developmental states (Yeung 2014), Singapore's approach to niche creation places a stronger focus on establishing and sustaining a conducive 'enabling environment' within which businesses can thrive, although more direct and developmental forms of state interventions have been employed as well, such as directing state resources or investments towards selected industries or the establishment of GLCs (Woo 2015a, 2016a). Such efforts at niche creation also, as I have alluded to above, tend to involve economic planning committees such as the Economic Review Committee and Future Economy Committee.

More importantly, such committees tend to include both state and industry actors. This inclusion of industry representatives leads to a final point on strategic pragmatism. While the Singaporean state remains dominant in its political and policy processes, there is also a significant extent of industry participation in its economic policy processes. Through the abovementioned economic planning committees, along with other policy advisory committees as well as informal channels of communications between policymakers and businesses, there is a significant extent of 'policy co-creation' in Singapore's economic governance, with the inputs of businesses and industry actors often affecting policy decisions (Woo 2015b, 2016a).

Like niche creation, there are both strategic and pragmatic elements to policy co-creation. By incorporating the inputs and feedback of industry partners, Singapore's policymakers are often able to adjust their policies and regulations in response to industry needs and concerns; this allows them to, on the one hand, provide industries with the economic infrastructure and environment required for their operational needs and, on the other, pre-empt any potential issues with regulatory compliance, hence reducing compliance costs for businesses and ensuring that regulations are relevant to industry needs (Woo 2016a, 2016b).

In sum, Singapore's approach to economic governance and industrial policy can be characterized by two ideological foundations: globalism and strategic pragmatism. While globalism ensures that Singapore's economic governance is outward-oriented, with economic diplomacy playing an important role in developing an 'external wing' to the city-state's economy, strategic pragmatism allows it to orient its economic policies towards long-term strategic needs, while at the same time ensuring pragmatic efficiency in short- and medium-term policy implementation processes. Strategic pragmatism in turn involves policy activities such as niche creation and policy co-creation. Having discussed these ideological and procedural foundations of Singapore's approach to economic development and industrial policy, I will now turn my attention to the various components and elements that make up its developmental state.

Components of Singapore's developmental state

Given its state-centric nature, Singapore's economic success has been described as 'government-made' (Low 2001b), although its increasing business orientation and the inclusion of private sector management practices have subsequently led to its characterization as 'Singapore Inc.' (Haley et al. 1996, Low 2003, Aoki and Tay 2015). As has often been noted, this state-driven and business-oriented approach to economic governance represents important aspects of Singapore's developmental state model, along with others.

This section will discuss the various components and elements of Singapore's developmental state.

Developmental elite

Like most developmental states, economic governance and policymaking in Singapore is driven by a development-oriented political and policy elite, or developmental elite. As discussed above, the ruling PAP forms the core of Singapore's developmental elite, although it also includes other public and private actors. Having won all elections since independence, often with a sizeable margin, the PAP retains a significant influence over the composition of Singapore's government and cabinet. This is due to Singapore's majoritarian parliamentary system, a legacy of the British Westminster system, which requires the majority ruling party to form the government of the day.

Aside from such majoritarian rule however, observers have noted that the PAP's political dominance also stems from the various adaptations that have been introduced to Singapore's parliamentary system, such as 'group representation constituencies' (GRCs), which requires voters to select a slate of candidates or the 'non-constituency members of parliament' (NCMPs), who are drawn from the 'best' losing constituency, among others (Singh 2012, Guo and Woo 2016). While GRCs were introduced to ensure minority representation, with each GRC required to include at least one candidate from an ethnic minority, the NCMP scheme was established to introduce diversity to parliamentary debates, especially with insufficient, weak opposition presence.

However, it has often been argued that campaigning for GRCs requires a significant amount of resources, while NCMPs may serve to pre-empt, and even dilute, public desire for opposition presence in parliament (Tan 2013). In any case, these parliamentary innovations have, intentionally or otherwise, provided the PAP with a significant advantage. Others have identified the Singapore government's control over the media, curbs to freedom of speech and expression, as well as the use of legal instruments to address opposition and dissent as important means through which the PAP has secured, and continues to maintain, its dominance over political and economic life in Singapore (Barr 2006, George 2007, Lee 2010, George 2012). However, Singapore's developmental elite is not solely comprised of the PAP.

Rather, the developmental elite, also often referred to as the 'governing elite', includes members of the political elite, the bureaucracy (which includes the civil service and other quasi-governmental bodies), and major industry actors (Hamilton-Hart 2000, 2002). While most major policy decisions tend to be made by Singapore's political leaders, the public service plays a crucial role in policy implementation. The public service is made up of the civil service, represented by the various ministries that are tasked with overseeing policy implementation within a specialized policy domain, and a range of semi-autonomous statutory boards that operate under the purview of specific ministries, and hence play an important role as policy agents (Quah 2010, Woo 2014).

For instance, the Housing Development Board, which is tasked with building and maintaining Singapore's public housing estates, is housed under the Ministry of National Development (MND), along with other statutory boards such as the Agri-Food & Veterinary Authority, Building and Construction Authority, Council for Estate Agencies, National Parks, and Urban Redevelopment Authority. These statutory boards serve to support the MND's role in land use and urban planning, which encompasses the development of both urban spaces and communities (Ministry of National Development 2016). Other statutory boards are similarly housed under, and hence support the roles and functions of, relevant ministries.

This role of the public service in Singapore's developmental elite is accentuated by the tendency of public servants to enter political life (Guo and Woo 2016, p. 5, Krishnadas 2016), in some instances rising to the ministerial level. Current key appointment holders include Prime Minister Lee Hsien Loong (who was a Brigadier-General in the army), Deputy Prime Minister Tharman Shanmugaratnam (formerly from the Monetary Authority of Singapore), Deputy Prime Minister Teo Chee Hean (Navy), and Finance Minister Heng Swee Kiat (Monetary Authority of Singapore), among others. There are, in short, substantive linkages between the political elite and the public service.

Aside from the political elite and bureaucracy, and despite caricatures of state-centrism, however, Singapore's developmental elite includes private sector actors as well. These private sector industry actors tend to exercise their influence over policy processes and outcomes through less formal processes of 'policy co-creation', often bolstered by the government's desire to ensure a suitable policy environment and infrastructure within which businesses can thrive and hence contribute to national economic growth (Woo 2015b, 2015a, 2016a). As a consequence, Singapore's developmental elite includes select industry actors who are able to influence policy decisions, often towards development-oriented goals, through processes of policy co-creation. I will return to this point later in the section 'embedded autonomy'.

However, it is also important to note that Singapore's developmental elite is defined not so much by its composition or the nature of its membership, but by the goals and ideologies that bind its members together and hence drive its policy actions, such as developmentalism, meritocracy, pragmatism, and good governance (Chua 1997, Subramaniam 2001, Tan 2008, 2012, Jones 2016, Woo 2016a). As I have discussed in Chapter 2 and elsewhere, Singapore's developmental elite, in terms of both its membership composition and ontological foundations, is defined by policy goals and ideologies related to economic development (Woo 2015a, Woo and Howlett 2015, Woo 2016a, 2016b).

While the developmental elite plays a crucial role in continually emphasizing the need for economic development and influencing policy decisions and processes towards the attainment of developmental goals, the actual implementation of developmental policies tends to be carried out under the coordination of a pilot agency (or in the case of Singapore, a range of pilot agencies) that possess both the technical expertise and policy capacities necessary for leading economic development. I will now discuss these pilot agencies.

Pilot agency

Like most other developmental states, economic development in Singapore is led by a pilot agency that functions as lead agency and centralized policy coordinator. This pilot agency is the Economic Development Board (EDB), which was established in August 1961 as a 'one-stop agency so that an investor need not deal with a large number of departments and ministries' (Lee 2000, p. 58). The EDB's initial task was to focus on investment promotion, particularly in the four areas of ship breaking and repair, metal engineering, chemicals, and electrical equipment and appliances (Lee 2000, p. 59).

While the EDB was initially set up in 1961 as an investment promotion agency, it has subsequently taken on other developmental roles, such as addressing unemployment, manpower and human capital development, and industrial policy in general (Wai-chung Yeung 1998, p. 400). Today, the EDB is known as the 'lead government agency for planning and executing strategies to enhance Singapore's position as a global business centre. EDB dreams, designs and delivers solutions that create value for investors and companies in Singapore" (Economic Development Board 2016).

In 'dreaming, designing and delivering' solutions, the EDB's activities span the gamut of a typical policy cycle, including processes such as policy design and formulation, implementation, and evaluation. This makes the EDB the main policy agency for planning, designing, and implementing economic policies. Broadly defined, these policies involve attracting investments, exploring new growth areas, enhancing the business environment by working with government agencies involved in the provision of public infrastructure and public services, and maintaining Singapore's future competitiveness (Economic Development Board 2016).

Aside from attracting investments or enhancing the business environment, the EDB also plays a crucial role in channelling state resources towards industry development, especially through its corporate investment EDB Investments Private Limited, or EDBI. Specifically, EDBI 'invest(s) to shape the future industries of Singapore in the knowledge and innovation-intensive sectors of BioMedical Sciences, Information & Communication Technology, Smart & Sustainable Technology and select industry clusters', under its 'Strategic Growth Programme' (EDBI 2017). Aside from corporate investments, the EDB also invests in start-ups and entrepreneurs through initiatives such as the Start-up EnterprisE Development Scheme (SEEDS) and the Business Angel Scheme (BAS) (Economic Development Board 2015a).

Such investment activities complement the role of Singapore's Sovereign Wealth Funds, Temasek Private Limited and Government Investment

Corporation (GIC). Initially established in 1974 to own and manage investments and assets previously held by the government, Temasek has since become a fully corporatized return-seeking investor that nonetheless contributes to Singapore's economic position through its returns from investments (Wilson Ng 2010, Cummine 2015, Temasek 2017). Managing most of the Singapore government's financial assets, GIC's investment returns similarly contributes to government spending and reserves (GIC 2016).

The EDB also plays an important role in maintaining the Singapore government's reputation for economic development, especially through cultivating and maintaining state and industry relations with foreign MNCs (Huff 1999, pp. 224–225). This role is not simply restricted to establishing state–industry relations within Singapore. Indeed, the EDB has established offices and centres across the world, in order to engage foreign MNCs (Economic Development Board 2015a, 2015b). The EDB's role in fostering state–industry relations extends to its own organizational structure as well, with EDB directors often drawn from the private sector (Khorsheed 2017, p. 188).

However, the growing complexity of Singapore's economy and its industries also means that it may no longer be feasible for one pilot agency to possess all the capabilities and expertise necessary for managing the various facets and aspects of Singapore's increasingly diversified and digitized economy. Even if it were possible for such an all-encompassing pilot agency to exist, it is likely to be saddled with significant administrative inefficiency. The growing complexity and diversity of Singapore's economy has therefore prompted the formation of other public agencies that are tasked with leading the development of specific sectors.

This began with the establishment of the Monetary Authority of Singapore (MAS) in 1971 as the key agency in charge of both regulating and promoting Singapore's financial services sector. This essentially makes the MAS the pilot agency for financial sector development. This decision to establish a separate pilot agency for the financial services sector was predicated upon the need for specialized domain knowledge in promoting and governing the financial services sector (Woo 2016b, p. 29). Yet while the MAS possessed strong technical knowledge on finance, it nonetheless had to rely on EDB expertise and staff, often attached to the MAS on secondment, to provide it with knowledge and know-how on economic promotion (Koh 2013).

Similar agencies have since been established for other sectors, with these agencies operating as decentralized pilot agencies possessing specialized knowledge on the sector or industry that they are tasked with promoting and developing. This includes the Smart Nation and Digital Government Group, which leads Singapore's digital transformation and develops emerging 'smart' industries such as data analytics (Seow 2017) and the Infocomm Media Development Authority, which promotes and regulates Singapore's media and information and communication technology (ICT) sectors (Infocomm Media Development Authority 2016), among others. However, these agencies do not necessarily operate in silos. Rather, there is a significant extent of collaboration among these sectorial pilot agencies and the EDB, with the joint establishment of a data centre by the MAS, EDB and IBM, as part of the Smart Nation initiative, being a case in point (Tay 2016).

The growing diversity and complexity of Singapore's economy, driven by rapid economic liberalization and globalization, has therefore given rise to the formation of specialized pilot agencies that possess the domain knowledge required to promote and develop new and increasingly complex sectors such as financial services or data analytics. Hence while traditional conceptions of the developmental state model tend to emphasize the presence of a single pilot agency possessing control and oversight over national economic development, the case of Singapore shows that growing economic diversity and complexity may necessitate the decentralization of promotional functions, through the formation of sectorial pilot agencies for specific sectors.

Pilot agencies therefore exist at both the national and sectorial levels. Furthermore, and as I will discuss in later chapters, Singapore's transformation into a smart city also gives rise to new challenges to its pilot agencies. It is also important to note that while pilot agencies possess a significant extent of autonomy in promoting and guiding sectorial or national economic development, they also often operate in collaboration with other public agencies as well as industry and societal partners. Indeed, pilot agencies, whether at the national level or the sectorial level, are in reality embedded within a broader socio-political milieu and policy process. I will now discuss the embedded autonomy within which Singapore's developmental state exists and functions.

Embedded autonomy

The discussions so far have emphasized the role of the developmental elite and pilot agency in Singapore's developmental state approach to economic governance. Like most developmental states, this is a role that has required these two institutions – developmental elite and pilot agency – to be insulated from socio-political forces and pressures. Such political insulation of Singapore's political leaders and public officials has been widely discussed in studies of Singapore's developmental state as well as those dealing with its political system.

For instance, early studies by Chan (1971) argued that the Singaporean state has attained such a significant extent of autonomy from socio-political forces as to warrant its description as an 'administrative state' that is capable of implementing its policies in a mechanical and technocratic manner, free from political influence or pressure. Indeed, such political insulation of the state is seen to characterize all levels of political and bureaucratic institutions and processes (Barr 2006, Rodan 2009), culminating in the formation of a highly insulated and technocratic policy elite (Tan 2012) and contributing to 'economic hypergrowth' (Cheng 1987).

However, such observations of state autonomy through political insulation also tend to understate the role of the private sector in Singapore's policy processes. In line with emerging work on the private sector's growing role in, and influence over, national political and policy processes (Strange 1996, Haufler 2001, Cutler 2003), there is growing awareness of the close intermingling of private–public actors and interests that often occurs in Singapore's governing milieu. As Hamilton-Hart (2000, p. 197) has noted, 'non-state and government actors have become entwined in terms of their interests, roles and career paths'.

As Hamilton-Hart goes on to show, this entwining of public and private actors often occurs through extensive personnel movements between the public and private sectors, with individuals from the private sector often taking up senior positions in the civil service, and senior civil servants or political leaders taking up advisory or directorial positions within major firms (Hamilton-Hart 2000, pp. 198–202). Such intermingling of private and public sector roles and interest is further amplified by the establishment of GLCs, state-owned enterprises managed by both civil servants and individuals drawn from the private sector, and statutory boards, semi-autonomous agencies that are involved in the provision of public service.

Aside from such institutional and organizational intermingling of public and private sector personnel, however, are more extensive interactions between the public and private sectors, with public officials and political leaders often exercising their authority and performing their roles in collaboration with non-state actors. Despite caricatures of its authoritarian approach to economic governance and politics in general (Bell 1997, Sim 2006, Ortmann 2011), Singapore's approach to economic development in reality involves a relatively significant extent of private sector participation and influence.

For instance, it has been noted that almost all of Singapore's financial regulations undergo extensive private sector consultation, with the form and content of regulations often bearing the imprint of private sector interests and concerns (Menon 2013, Woo 2015a, 2016a). This is similarly the case for economic policy, often through consultative committees and mechanisms such as the above-mentioned Economic Review Committee. It is important, however, to note that the motives for the inclusion of private sector interests and concerns in economic policy are often themselves developmental in nature.

Specifically, the incorporation of private sector interests and feedback into economic policies and regulations contributes to the state's ability to understand and establish the infrastructure and incentives necessary for firms to thrive, and at the same time minimize costs of regulatory compliance for firms (Woo 2016a). As a consequence, such industry consultations tend to be state-driven, with private sector interests – though seen as crucial to Singapore's continued existence as a thriving business hub – often subsumed within the government's broader national economic interests. Regardless, the ongoing interactions between state and industry has given rise to strong 'policy relations' that contribute to policy co-creation between the Singapore government and its private sector partners (Woo 2015b).

Whether through intermingling of personnel or institutionalized channels of state-industry policy co-creation, the Singapore government exercises its authority and performs its policy functions through and within a dense web of policy relations with the private sector, even as it maintains a strong extent of insulation or autonomy from socio-political pressures and lobbying. The Singaporean state's autonomy, in other words, is embedded within a dense web of socio-political relations. As Khondker (2008, p. 48) notes, the 'Singapore state's autonomy enmeshed in a web of local structures is clearly an embedded autonomy'.

As the formation of such policy relations, and the extensive state–industry interactions that form these relations, show, Singapore's approach to economic governance and development involves much effort, on the part of the state, in managing non-state economic interests such as firms and businesses. This is especially the case given Singapore's strong reliance on global trade and finance as drivers of economic development. I will now proceed to discuss the Singaporean state's efforts at managing non-state economic interests.

Management of non-state economic interests

Upon its independence in 1965, Singapore found itself faced with the limitations of having a small domestic market, insufficient entrepreneurial activity and limited private capital. As discussed above, such economic limitations prompted the newly independent Singaporean state to rely on various developmental initiatives to spur economic growth and industrial development, particularly by encouraging export-led growth. This ran counter to the political-economic climate of the time, with its Southeast Asian neighbours driven by anti-colonialist sentiments to favour import substitution and protectionism.

More importantly, many of these initiatives have involved renegotiating the state's relationship with existing and emerging non-state economic interests. This is particularly the case with Singapore's early efforts at encouraging foreign MNCs to establish offices and operations within the city-state. While much of these efforts revolved around ensuring favourable business conditions such as establishing an efficient physical infrastructure, skilled workforce and robust regulatory infrastructure, the government also placed much focus on ensuring harmonious industrial relations and ensuring that firms' interests and business activities were aligned with the state's national interests (Goh 1997).

In almost all instances, the EDB acted as the main interface between the state and MNCs (Dent 2003, p. 255). This means that aside from its economic development policies, the EDB also played a crucial role in fostering and sustaining state–industry relations. Such a role has involved establishing overseas centres and offices, as well as dedicated departments for building foreign investor relations, such as a 'China Focus' Special Business Unit that was formed in 1990 (Economic Development Board 2015a).

Aside from encouraging foreign firms to establish business operations in Singapore, former Finance Minister Goh Keng Swee has noted that an important aspect of managing MNCs involved encouraging transfers of technology and expertise from MNCs to domestic firms, with the government playing an important role in establishing the conditions and infrastructure needed to facilitate such technological transfers (Goh 1996). Such technological transfers therefore provide another means of enhancing Singapore's economy through the presence and management of non-state economic interests such as MNCs.

As Singapore shifts towards a knowledge-based economy, university–industry–government relations have become increasingly crucial for fostering innovation and knowledge formation, especially among technology start-ups (Etzkowitz 2003, Lee and Win 2004). Indeed, and as I will further discuss in Chapters 5 and 6, Singapore's transformation into a smart city has given rise to new configurations of relations between the state and non-state organizations, with the government's approach to managing non-state economic interests shifting from simply providing firms with resources and direction to broader eco-system development and management.

Given Singapore's small size and limited market size, it is also important to note that the state's management of often-foreign economic entities tends to take on a foreign policy dimension. Indeed, much has been written about the Singapore government's role in 'economic diplomacy', whether this is in terms of the state's relations with foreign MNCs and businesses or other states (Dent 2001, 2003, Lim and Liang 2010). Indeed, state–industry and state–state relations tend to overlap and intermingle. For instance, it has been noted that the US's decision to negotiate a free trade agreement (FTA) with Singapore was based on the presence of strongly entrenched American corporate interests in the city-state (Dent 2003, p. 255).

The management of non-state economic interests, in other words, often impacts and sometimes enhances state-to-state diplomatic relations, with such inter-state relations giving rise to even closer state–industry relations. The US–Singapore FTA has therefore given rise to greater trade and investment activity between the two states, further expanding American corporate interests in Singapore (Office of the United States Trade Representative 2017). This is more often than not true of the various FTAs that Singapore has concluded with various major economic powers (Ministry of Trade and Industry 2011, International Enterprise Singapore 2017).

Yet despite the growing presence of foreign firms and MNCs in Singapore's political economic landscape, economic development remains state-driven, with non-state economic entities often dependent on the state's policies for their business interests (Hamilton-Hart 2002, Dent 2003, Woo 2016b). Furthermore, Singapore's export-centred and productionist-oriented approach to industrial relations and the management of non-state economic interests have also been associated with the containment or suppression of labour unions and civil society in general (Wilkinson and Leggett 1985, Leggett 1988, Kuruvilla 1996). This is discussed in the next section.

Civil society

Like many other developmental states, Singapore's civil society is relatively weak, often operating under state control and circumscription. Singapore's civil society has often been described as a 'state-sanctioned sphere of engagement' (Chua 1997, Leong et al. 2003, Lee 2011, Nasir and Turner 2013, Koh et al. 2017, p. 92). This is reflective of Singapore's status as an 'illiberal democracy' that is characterized by three defining features (Jones et al. 1995, Perry et al. 1997, pp. 80–81):

- A non-neutral state that intervenes in social affairs to promote its interpretation of national interest and views elections as a means of legitimizing its rule.
- The use of legal tools to circumscribe and specify the duties of citizens, with the legal system typically seen as a technical tool of governance.
- A managed civil society formed around specialized interests and operating within state-managed arenas.

This last feature – management and control of civil society – also means that illiberal democracies are essentially characterized as 'the existence of formal democratic procedures without politics' (Perry et al. 1997, p. 81). Hence while development states exercise strict control over civil society, at times with relatively draconian measures (Rodan 2003, Chong 2011), democratic procedures such as elections are paradoxically retained. As I will discuss further below, retaining such democratic procedures allows developmental states to maintain performance legitimacy as well as ensure stable leadership transitions.

Singapore's reputation as an illiberal democracy is also reflected in the Economist Intelligence Unit's Democracy Index, which ranks Singapore 74 out of 167 countries and labels it a 'flawed democracy' (Economist Intelligence Unit 2016). While the Democracy Index ranked Singapore favourably for the functioning of its government (7.50 points) and civil liberties (7.06 points), it gave the city-state low scores for its electoral process and pluralism (4.33 points), political participation (5.56 points), and political culture (6.25 points) (Economist Intelligence Unit 2016, Tham 2016).

However, it should be noted that the Singaporean state's control over civil society is often subtler than many other developing economies. This is especially the case as Singapore's population becomes increasingly educated, sophisticated, and attuned to global affairs through the Internet. Hence, rather than directly suppressing civil society activists, the Singaporean state has emphasized notions of 'civic society', such as civility, kindness and public orderliness, in order to forestall the potentially destabilizing political aspects and practices of civil society (Koh 1998, Lee 2002, p. 102).

The Singaporean state's control over civil society therefore increasingly relies on a less direct and more discursive approach that determines the boundaries within which civil society activities can (or cannot) exist. This often involves implicit 'out-of-bounds' markers that prompt self-censorship among civil society groups and the mainstream media, for fear of the potential penalties of transgressing these markers (Lyons 2011, Seng 2012). Such OB markers have also been described as a form of 'auto-regulative structure' that suppresses and regulates civil society discourse or activity through self-censorship (Lee 2002, p. 110).

However, such restrictions on civil society activity and discourse have loosened to some extent due to a growing liberalization of Singapore's media landscape, driven by an increasingly open Internet space (Sreekumar and Vadrevu 2013, Ortmann 2015). While this growing media space may have empowered, to some extent, civil society groups and even negatively impacted the PAP's performance in the 2011 general election, it has not substantially eroded the PAP's dominant position in Singapore's political landscape; rather, the ruling party has managed to leverage new media to consolidate its political dominance, as is evident in its strong performance in the 2015 general election (Tan *et al.* 2016).

In any case, state control over a weak civil society has been instrumental in facilitating strong economic growth in Singapore. Indeed, Perry et al. (1997, p. 7) argue that the 'ability of the government to exercise such tight control of society, and the basis on which the population accepts this direction, have been central to Singapore's economic success'. However, this acceptance of state control over civil society, and civic discourse in general, could not have been possible without the state's strong policy performance, and more importantly its ability to ensure strong economic growth. This growth-oriented and performance-driven aspect of the Singaporean state's governing legitimacy is discussed next.

Performance legitimacy

Having attained consistent and rapid economic growth over the short span of its history, the Singapore government, especially the ruling PAP, has established a reputation for its strong performance in economic development, as well as other policy domains. For instance, the PAP's election manifesto for the 2015 general election emphasized its policy achievements in the areas of the economy, healthcare, security, housing, as well as transport and infrastructure (Chew 2015). This emphasis on economic and policy performance is further buttressed by Singapore's depoliticized population (Chan 1971, Mauzy and Milne 2002), with citizens 'by and large more materialistic and less concerned with politics' (Wong and Huang 2010, p. 530).

As a consequence, evaluations of government performance tend to be made on the basis of economic performance, with the 'rough and tumble' of politics replaced by a technocratic 'administrative state' that governs on the basis of meritocracy and expertise (Chan 1971, Barr 2006, Tan 2008) and state–citizen relations defined by an instrumental logic of exchange (Wong and Huang 2010). As a key linchpin of its political and governing system, performance legitimacy allows Singapore's single-party state to retain its political legitimacy without the need to share power (Chua 2010). As Chua also notes, it is economic success, defined as the 'continuous translation of national economic success into an elevated material life for the population', and not authoritarianism, that has contributed to electoral support for the PAP.

Indeed, performance legitimacy is so entrenched within Singapore's political system that the PAP was able to achieve an electoral landslide victory during an economic crisis in 1980, with voters confident in the Party's ability to lead the country out of the crisis (Wong and Huang 2010, p. 530). This confidence in the government's ability to perform is also evident in other elections, such as the 2001 general election (which took place after the September 11 terrorist attacks in the United States). However, the flipside of performance legitimacy is that voter confidence can just as easily decrease with any perceived declines in policy performance.

This was evident in the 2011 general election, with the PAP experiencing a steep decline in vote-share due to public discontent over persistent public transport disruptions, excessive immigration, and rising income inequality (Cunha 2012, Tan 2014). In response, the PAP enacted a slew of policies to address these issues, with the result being a landslide victory in the 2015 general election (Tan 2016b). As this brief discussion has elucidated, policy performance, particularly regarding economic policy outcomes, is an important determinant of public support for the government, and consequently, electoral outcomes.

This focus on economic and policy performance is also strongly related to the PAP's core ideological foundations of pragmatism and meritocracy. While pragmatism entails adopting policies that allow the government to successfully achieve its desired policy goals and outcomes, regardless of their ideological bases and credentials (Schein 1996, Perry et al. 1997, p. 69, Tan 2012), meritocracy is related to the merit-based recruitment and promotion of public sector personnel within the bureaucracy, although this focus on merit has since flowed into the socio-political sphere as well, with political leaders and candidates often chosen on the basis of qualifications and career performance (Hamilton-Hart 2000, Tan 2008, Jones 2016).

Yet, and as the results of the 2011 general election show, political legitimacy is not necessarily a static phenomenon that, once established, permanently imbues a government with political legitimacy. Rather, there is a need to maintain performance legitimacy. As Huff (1999, p. 221) has argued, the Singapore government expended a significant amount of effort in economic reputation-building in the period immediately following its independence, especially through the formulation of economic programmes and infrastructure to establish credibility. Efforts at reputation-building also include managing public perceptions of being disadvantaged, to prevent such perceptions from weakening the state's legitimacy (Wong and Huang 2010).

Performance legitimacy therefore requires constant maintenance, whether in terms of ensuring an adequate level of policy performance or upholding a reputation for economic and policy performance, in order for it to retain its role in ensuring a developmental state's right to govern. There is therefore a strong capacity aspect in the maintenance of performance legitimacy, although, and as I will discuss in later chapters, such 'legitimation capacity' or policy capacity (Painter and Pierre 2005, Woo et al. 2015, Wu et al. 2015) is equally applicable to other elements of the developmental state.

Another important point to note is that performance legitimacy also requires some extent of democratization. As Mietzner (2017) has noted, unlike other developmental states that lack institutional mechanisms for leadership regeneration, such as Indonesia, performance legitimacy in Singapore was sustained by the presence of electoral processes that allow for stable leadership transition. This reduces the possibility of political instability, with any public discontent over weak or insufficient policy performance in the government reflected in electoral results rather than political upheaval.

Conclusion

This chapter has provided a comprehensive overview of Singapore's role and identity as an archetypal developmental state. In tracing its historic trajectory, I have sought to uncover the historical events and circumstances that have driven its initial emergence and subsequent success as a developmental state. Of particular significance is Singapore's ejection from the Malaysian Federation. Not only did this lead to Singapore's independence, but it also separated the already resource-poor city-state from its natural economic hinterland. This imbued its early leaders, as well as their successors, with a strong development focus.

Indeed, much of Singapore's economic history can be characterized by the state's efforts in identifying potential growth sectors and the various policy initiatives that tend to be implemented to develop these potential growth sectors. However, while such efforts at 'niche creation' tend to result in the formation of 'national champions', or domestic corporations formed with strong state support, in most developmental states, Singapore's limited domestic market and talent pool prompted the Singaporean state to focus instead on attracting MNCs to establish their operations within the city-state.

As I will argue in the next chapter, such state-driven internationalization can be found in Hong Kong as well, especially in its financial services sector. Indeed, and as I have argued elsewhere, this external-oriented approach to economic development is common among small states that are lacking in both natural resources and an economic hinterland (Guo and Woo 2016). And as I will argue in later chapters, this strong focus on economic internationalization also separates developmental *city-states* such as Hong Kong and Singapore from developmental *nation-states* such as Japan or South Korea.

Indeed, this difference also alludes to a lack of differentiation or gradation in existing understandings of developmental states, with city-states such as Hong Kong and Singapore examined alongside larger nation-states without sufficiently addressing the structural and political economic differences that may arise from such differences in size. As others have shown, small states are substantially different, especially in their economic openness and performance, political development, and policy orientation, from nation-states (Katzenstein 1985, Armstrong and Read 1998, Veenendaal and Corbett 2015).

This, along with other issues, suggests a need for further refinement of the developmental state concept. I attempt to do this in Chapter 6. It is therefore clear that the developmental state model is neither static nor unproblematic, in both its theoretical formulation and its empirical application by real-world developmental states. Rather, the notion and concept of a developmental state is constantly evolving, often in response to changes in both global and domestic political economic conditions or processes.

This is evident in Singapore's ongoing transformation into a smart city, which is discussed in Chapter 6. Yet even as Singapore embraces the digital economy and transforms itself into a smart city, it has retained most, if not all, of the various components and elements of the developmental state model that I have discussed above. Indeed, the brief overview above of the various components of Singapore's developmental state provides a useful starting point for identifying the specific areas in which Singapore has retained (or modified) its developmental state approach to economic governance.

Before delving into the conceptual modifications needed to ensure the developmental state model's relevance in light of growing digitization among developmental states, there is first a need to discuss the other case study of this book: Hong Kong. The next chapter will provide a comprehensive overview of Hong Kong's development, role and identity as a developmental state.

References

Aoki, N., 2015a. Let's Get Public Administration Right, But in What Sequence?: Lessons from Japan and Singapore. *Public Administration and Development*, 35 (3), 206–218.

Aoki, N., 2015b. Institutionalization of New Public Management: The case of Singapore's education system. *Public Management Review*, 17 (2), 165–186.

Aoki, N. and Tay, M., 2015. Managerialism Meets Regime: A Distinctively Singaporean Marriage? *Asian Journal of Political Science*, 23 (3), 346–365.

Armstrong, H.W. and Read, R., 1998. Trade and Growth in Small States: The Impact of Global Trade Liberalisation. *World Economy*, 21 (4), 563–585.

Barr, M.D., 2006. Beyond technocracy: The culture of elite governance in Lee Hsien Loong's Singapore. *Asian Studies Review*, 30 (1), 1–18.

Bell, D.A., 1997. A Communitarian Critique of Authoritarianism: The Case of Singapore. *Political Theory*, 25 (1), 6–32.

Centre for Strategic Futures, 2015a. A Short History of Futures Work in the Singapore Government [online]. Available from: http://www.csf.gov.sg/about-us/history [Accessed 2 March 2016].

Centre for Strategic Futures, 2015b. Our Approach [online]. Available from: http://www.csf.gov.sg/our-work/our-approach [Accessed 2 March 2016].

Chan, C.M.L., Lau, Y., and Pan, S.L., 2008. E-government implementation: A macro analysis of Singapore's e-government initiatives. *Government Information Quarterly*, 25 (2), 239–255.

Chan, H.C., 1971. *Singapore: The Politics of Survival, 1965–1967.* Oxford, U.K.: Oxford University Press.

Cheng, T., 1987. The Rise and Limits of the East Asian NICs. *Pacific Focus*, 2 (2), 51–75.

Chew, H.M., 2015. GE2015: PAP's manifesto sets out its achievements, challenges and vision. *The Straits Times*, 29 Aug.

Chong, T., 2011. Civil Society in Singapore: Popular Discourses and Concepts. *Sojourn: Journal of Social Issues in Southeast Asia*, 20 (2), 273–301.

Chua, B.-H., 1997. *Communitarian Ideology and Democracy in Singapore.* London, UK: Routledge.

Chua, B.H., 2010. The cultural logic of a capitalist single-party state, Singapore. *Postcolonial Studies*, 13 (4), 335–350.

Committee on the Future Economy, 2017. *Report of the Committee on the Future Economy.* Singapore: Government of Singapore.

Committee on the Future of Economy Secretariat, 2015. *Committee On The Future Economy To Review Singapore's Economic Strategies and Position Us For The Future.* Singapore: Ministry of Finance, Press Release.

Cummine, A., 2015. How Temasek has driven Singapore's development. *East Asia Forum.*

Cunha, D.D., 2012. *Breakthrough: Roadmap for Singapore's Political Future.* Singapore: Straits Times Press Reference.

Cutler, A.C., 2003. *Private power and global authority: transnational merchant law in the global political economy.* Cambridge: Cambridge Univ. Press.

Dent, C., 2003. Transnational capital, the state and foreign economic policy: Singapore, South Korea and Taiwan. *Review of International Political Economy*, 10 (2), 246–277.

Dent, C.M., 2001. Singapore's Foreign Economic Policy: The Pursuit of Economic Security. *Contemporary Southeast Asia*, 23 (1), 1–23.

Economic Development Board, 2015a. Our History [online]. *Singapore Economic Development Board – Investing Business in Singapore.* Available from: https://www.edb.gov.sg/content/edb/en/about-edb/company-information/our-history.html [Accessed 27 Jun 2017].

Economic Development Board, 2015b. Global Offices [online]. *Singapore Economic Development Board – Investing Business in Singapore.* Available from: https://www.edb.gov.sg/content/edb/en/contact-edb/meet-our-global-team.html [Accessed 27 Jun 2017].

Economic Development Board, 2016. Vision, Mission, and Core Values – What We Do [online]. *Singapore Economic Development Board – Investing Business in Singapore.* Available from: https://www.edb.gov.sg/content/edb/en/about-edb/our-strategy/what-we-do.html [Accessed 11 Jun 2017].

Economic Review Committee, 2003. *New Challenges, Fresh Goals: Towards a Dynamic Global City*. Singapore: Ministry of Trade and Industry.

Economist Intelligence Unit, 2016. *Democracy Index 2016*. London, UK: Economist Intelligence Unit.

EDBI, 2017. About EDBI [online]. Available from: http://www.edbi.com/ [Accessed 27 Jun 2017].

Etzkowitz, H., 2003. Innovation in Innovation: The Triple Helix of University–Industry–Government Relations. *Social Science Information*, 42 (3), 293–337.

George, C., 2007. Consolidating authoritarian rule: calibrated coercion in Singapore. *The Pacific Review*, 20 (2), 127–145.

George, C., 2012. *Freedom from the press: journalism and state power in Singapore*. Singapore: NUS Press.

GIC, 2016. Shaping Singapore [online]. Available from: http://www.gic.com.sg/shaping-singapore [Accessed 27 Jun 2017].

Goh, C.T., 1997. *Shaping our Future: Thinking Schools, Learning Natio.*

Goh, K.S., 1996. The Technology Ladder in Development: the Singapore case. *Asian-Pacific Economic Literature*, 10 (1), 1–12.

Guo, Y. and Woo, J.J., 2016. *Singapore and Switzerland: Secrets to Small State Success*. New Jersey: World Scientific Publishing Co.

Habegger, B., 2010. Strategic foresight in public policy: Reviewing the experiences of the UK, Singapore, and the Netherlands. *Futures*, 42 (1), 49–58.

Haley, U.C.V., Low, L., and Toh, M., 1996. Singapore Incorporated: reinterpreting Singapore's business environments through a corporate metaphor. *Management Decision*, 34 (9), 17–28.

Hamilton-Hart, N., 2000. The Singapore state revisited. *The Pacific Review*, 13 (2), 195–216.

Hamilton-Hart, N., 2002. *Asian States, Asian Bankers: Central Banking in Southeast Asia*. New York: Cornell University Press.

Haque, M.S., 2002. Structures of New Public Management in Malaysia and Singapore: Alternative Views. *The Journal of Comparative Asian Development*, 1 (1), 71–86.

Haque, M.S., 2004. Governance and Bureaucracy in Singapore: Contemporary Reforms and Implications. *International Political Science Review*, 25 (2), 227–240.

Haufler, V., 2001. *A public role for the private sector: industry self-regulation in a global economy*. Washington: Carnegie Endowment for International Peace.

Hu, M.-C., Wu, C.-Y., and Shih, T., 2015. Creating a new socio-technical regime in China: Evidence from the Sino-Singapore Tianjin Eco-City. *Futures*, 70, 1–12.

Huff, W.G., 1999. Turning the Corner in Singapore's Developmental State? *Asian Survey*, 39 (2), 214–242.

IMD, 2017. *World Competitiveness Yearbook 2017*. Lausanne, Switzerland: IMD.

Infocomm Media Development Authority, 2016. Sectors [online]. *Infocomm Media Development Authority*. Available from: http://www.imda.gov.sg/industry-development/sectors [Accessed 28 Jun 2017].

Inkpen, A.C. and Pien, W., 2006. An Examination of Collaboration and Knowledge Transfer: China–Singapore Suzhou Industrial Park. *Journal of Management Studies*, 43 (4), 779–811.

International Enterprise Singapore, 2017. Singapore FTAs [online]. *International Enterprise Singapore*. Available from: https://www.iesingapore.gov.sg/Trade-From-

Singapore/International-Agreements/free-trade-agreements/Singapore-FTA [Accessed 13 Jul 2017].

Jones, D., Jayasuriya, K., Bell, D.A., and Brown, D., 1995. Towards a model of illiberal democracy. *In*: D.A. Bell, K. Jayasuriya, D. Jones, and D. Brown, eds. *Towards Illiberal Democracy in Pacific Asia.* Basingstoke, UK: Macmillan Press, 163–167.

Jones, D.S., 2016. Governance and Meritocracy: A Study of Policy Implementation in Singapore. *In*: J.S.T. Quah, ed. *The Role of the Public Bureaucracy in Policy Implementation in Five ASEAN Countries.* Cambridge: Cambridge University Press, 297–369.

Katzenstein, P.J., 1985. *Small States in World Markets: Industrial Policy in Europe.* Cornell University Press.

Khondker, H.H., 2008. Globalization and State Autonomy in Singapore. *Journal of Asian Social Science*, 36 (1), 35–56.

Khorsheed, M.S., 2017. Learning from Global Pacesetters to Build the Country Innovation Ecosystem. *Journal of the Knowledge Economy*, 8 (1), 177–196.

Koh, A., 2007. Living with Globalization Tactically: The Metapragmatics of Globalization in Singapore. *Sojourn: Journal of Social Issues in Southeast Asia*, 22 (2), 179–201.

Koh, C.Y., Wee, K., Goh, C., and Yeoh, B.S.A., 2017. Cultural mediation through vernacularization: framing rights claims through the day-off campaign for migrant domestic workers in Singapore. *International Migration*, 55 (3), 89–104.

Koh, J., 2016. Singapore and China's third G2G project gets underway in Chongqing [online]. *Channel NewsAsia.* Available from: http://www.channelnewsasia.com/news/business/singapore-and-china-s-third-g2g-project-gets-underway-in-chongqi-8213744 [Accessed 10 Jun 2017].

Koh, T.A., 1998. Civl or civic society? The S'pore ideal(1). *The Business Times*, 30 May, p. 12.

Koh, Y.G., 2013. Interview.

Krishnadas, D., 2016. *The Seduction of the Simple: Insights on Singapore's future directions.* Singapore: Marshall Cavendish International Asia Pte Ltd.

Kuruvilla, S., 1996. Linkages between Industrialization Strategies and Industrial Relations/Human Resource Policies: Singapore, Malaysia, the Philippines, and India. *ILR Review*, 49 (4), 635–657.

Lee, E.W.Y. and Haque, M.S., 2006. The New Public Management Reform and Governance in Asian NICs: A Comparison of Hong Kong and Singapore. *Governance*, 19 (4), 605–626.

Lee, J. and Win, H.N., 2004. Technology transfer between university research centers and industry in Singapore. *Technovation*, 24 (5), 433–442.

Lee, K.-H. and Vertinsky, I., 1988. Strategic Adjustment of International Financial Centres (IFCs) in Small Economies: A Comparative Study of Hong Kong and Singapore. *Journal of Business Administration*, 17 (1–2), 151–172.

Lee, K.Y., 2000. *From Third World to First: The Singapore Story: 1965–2000.* Singapore: Times Editions.

Lee, K.Y., 2007. 'Excerpts from an interview with Lee Kuan Yew', *New York Times.* Aug 29, 2007.

Lee, T., 2002. The Politics of Civil Society in Singapore. *Asian Studies Review*, 26 (1), 97–117.

Lee, T., 2010. *The Media, Cultural Control and Government in Singapore.* London: Taylor & Francis.

Lee, T., 2011. Gestural Politics: Civil Society in 'New' Singapore. *Sojourn: Journal of Social Issues in Southeast Asia*, 20 (2), 132–154.

Leggett, C., 1988. Industrial Relations and Enterprise Unionism in Singapore. *Labour & Industry: a journal of the social and economic relations of work*, 1 (2), 242–257.
Leifer, M., 2000. *Singapore's foreign policy: coping with vulnerability*. London: Routledge.
Leong, H.K., Ho, K.L., and Leong, 2003. *Shared Responsibilities, Unshared Power: The Politics of Policy-Making in Singapore*. Rev Exp edition. Singapore: Cavendish Square Publishing.
Lim, C.L. and Liang, M., 2010. *Economic Diplomacy: Essays and Reflections by Singapore's Negotiators*. Singapore: World Scientific Publishing Company.
Low, L., 2001a. The Singapore developmental state in the new economy and polity. *The Pacific Review*, 14 (3), 411–441.
Low, L., 2001b. *The Political Economy of a City-State: Government-Made Singapore*. Oxford: Oxford University Press.
Low, L., 2003. Singapore Inc: A success story. *South African Journal of International Affairs*, 10 (1), 49–63.
Low, L., 2006. *The Political Economy of a City-State Revised*. Singapore: Marshall Cavendish.
Lyons, L., 2011. Transient Workers Count Too?: The Intersection of Citizenship and Gender in Singapore's Civil Society. *Sojourn: Journal of Social Issues in Southeast Asia*, 20 (2), 208–248.
Mauzy, D.K. and Milne, R.S., 2002. *Singapore Politics Under the People's Action Party*. 1st ed. London; New York: Routledge.
Menon, R., 2013. Interview.
Mietzner, M., 2017. Authoritarian elections, state capacity, and performance legitimacy: Phases of regime consolidation and decline in Suharto's Indonesia. *International Political Science Review*, 192512116687139.
Ministry of National Development, 2016. Introduction [online]. *Ministry of National Development Website*. Available from: http://app.mnd.gov.sg/about-us/introduction [Accessed 17 Jun 2017].
Ministry of Trade and Industry, 2011. *Do Free Trade Agreements Matter? Evaluating the Impact of FTAs on Singapore's Domestic Exports of Goods*. Singapore: Ministry of Trade and Industry, Feature Article.
Monetary Authority of Singapore, 2011. *Sustaining Stability, Serving Singapore*. Singapore: Monetary Authority of Singapore.
Nasir, K.M. and Turner, B.S., 2013. Governing as gardening: reflections on soft authoritarianism in Singapore. *Citizenship Studies*, 17 (3–4), 339–352.
National Library Board, 2009. Albert Winsemius [online]. *National Library Board Website*. Available from: http://eresources.nlb.gov.sg/infopedia/articles/SIP_1457_2009-02-11.html [Accessed 10 Jun 2017].
National Library Board Singapore, 2017. British withdrawal from Singapore [online]. *National Library Board Website*. Available from: http://eresources.nlb.gov.sg/infopedia/articles/SIP_1001_2009-02-10.html [Accessed 9 Jun 2017].
Ngiam, T.D., 2010. *Dynamics of the Singapore Success Story: Insights by Ngiam Tong Dow*. 1st ed. Singapore: Cengage Learning Asia.
Ng, W., 2010. The evolution of sovereign wealth funds: Singapore's Temasek Holdings. *Journal of Financial Regulation and Compliance*, 18 (1), 6–14.
Office of the United States Trade Representative, 2017. Singapore [online]. *Office of the United States Trade Representative*. Available from: /countries-regions/southeast-asia-pacific/singapore [Accessed 12 Jul 2017].
Ortmann, S., 2011. Singapore: Authoritarian but Newly Competitive. *Journal of Democracy*, 22 (4), 153–164.

Ortmann, S., 2015. Political Change and Civil Society Coalitions in Singapore. *Government and Opposition*, 50 (1), 119–139.

Painter, M. and Pierre, J., 2005. Unpacking policy capacity: issues and themes. *In*: M. Painter and J. Pierre, eds. *Challenges to State Policy Capacity: Global Trends and Comparative Perspectives*. Basingstoke: Palgrave Macmillan, 1–18.

Pereira, A., 2005. Singapore's Regionalization Strategy. *Journal of the Asia Pacific Economy*, 10 (3), 380–396.

Pereira, A.A., 2004. The Suzhou industrial park experiment: the case of China–Singapore governmental collaboration. *Journal of Contemporary China*, 13 (38), 173–193.

Perry, J.C., 2017. *Singapore: Unlikely Power*. 1 edition. New York, N.Y.: Oxford University Press.

Perry, M., Kong, L., and Yeoh, B., 1997. *Singapore: a developmental city state*. Chichester: John Wiley and Sons.

Quah, J.S.T., 1995. Sustaining quality in the Singapore Civil Service. *Public Administration and Development*, 15 (3), 335–343.

Quah, J.S.T., 2010. *Public Administration Singapore-style*. Singapore: Emerald Group Publishing.

Quah, J.S.T., 2013. Ensuring good governance in Singapore: Is this experience transferable to other Asian countries? *International Journal of Public Sector Management*, 26 (5), 401–420.

Rajaratnam, S., 1972. *Singapore: Global City*.

Ramesh, M., 1995. Economic Globalization and Policy Choices. *Governance: An International Journal of Policy and Administration*, 8 (2), 243–260.

Ravishankar, S., 2016. From Singapore to Amaravati: the battle to build India's new state capital. *The Guardian*, 26 Jan.

Reporters Without Borders, 2017. *2017 World Press Freedom Index*. Paris, France: Reporters Without Borders.

Rodan, G., 2003. Embracing electronic media but suppressing civil society: Authoritarian consolidation in Singapore. *The Pacific Review*, 16 (4), 503–524.

Rodan, G., 2009. New Modes of Political Participation and Singapore's Nominated Members of Parliament. *Government and Opposition*, 44 (4), 438–462.

Sarker, A.E., 2006. New public management in developing countries: An analysis of success and failure with particular reference to Singapore and Bangladesh. *International Journal of Public Sector Management*, 19 (2), 180–203.

Sassen, S., 2001. *The Global City: New York, London, Tokyo*. 2nd ed. Princeton, N.J.: Princeton University Press.

Sassen, S.J., 2011. *Cities in a World Economy*. 4th ed. California: SAGE Publications, Inc.

Schein, E.H., 1996. *Strategic Pragmatism: The Culture of Singapore's Economic Development Board*. Massachusetts: The MIT Press.

Schwab, K., 2017. *Global Competitiveness Report 2016–2017*. Geneva, Switzerland: World Economic Forum.

Seng, C.Y., 2012. *Ob Marker: My Straits Times Story*. Singapore: Straits Times Press.

Seow, J., 2017. Boost for Smart Nation push with agencies under one roof, 25 Mar.

Sim, S.-F., 2006. Hegemonic authoritarianism and singapore: Economics, ideology and the Asian economic crisis. *Journal of Contemporary Asia*, 36 (2), 143–159.

Singapore Tourism Board, 2017. About Singapore [online]. *Your Singapore*. Available from: http://www.visitsingapore.com/travel-guide-tips/about-singapore.html [Accessed 8 Jun 2017].

Singh, B., 2012. *Politics and Governance in Singapore: An Introduction*. 2nd ed. Singapore: McGraw-Hill Education (Asia).

Smart Nation Programme Office, 2017. Smart Nation Initiatives [online]. *Smart Nation Singapore*. Available from: http://www.smartnation.sg/initiatives/ [Accessed 15 Feb 2017].

Soh, A., 2017. Singapore searches for growth in 10 promising African countries [online]. *The Business Times*. Available from: http://www.businesstimes.com.sg/government-economy/singapore-searches-for-growth-in-10-promising-african-countries [Accessed 10 Jun 2017].

Sreekumar, T.T. and Vadrevu, S., 2013. Subpolitics and Democracy: The Role of New Media in the 2011 General Elections in Singapore. *Science Technology & Society*, 18 (2), 231–249.

Strange, S., 1996. *The Retreat of the State: The Diffusion of Power in the World Economy*. Cambridge: Cambridge University Press.

Subramaniam, S., 2001. The Dual Narrative of 'Good Governance': Lessons for Understanding Political and Cultural Change in Malaysia and Singapore. *Contemporary Southeast Asia*, 23 (1), 65–80.

Swee, G.K., 1996. The Technology Ladder in Development: the Singapore case. *Asian-Pacific Economic Literature*, 10 (1), 1–12.

Tan, K.P., 2008. Meritocracy and Elitism in a Global City: Ideological Shifts in Singapore. *International Political Science Review / Revue internationale de science politique*, 29 (1), 7–27.

Tan, K.P., 2012. The Ideology of Pragmatism: Neo-liberal Globalisation and Political Authoritarianism in Singapore. *Journal of Contemporary Asia*, 42 (1), 67–92.

Tan, K.P., 2013. The Singapore Parliament: Representation, Effectiveness, and Control. *In*: Y. Zheng, L.F. Lye, and W. Hofmeister, eds. *Parliaments in Asia: Institutional Building and Political Development*. Oxford, UK: Routledge, 27–46.

Tan, K.P., 2016a. *Governing Global-City Singapore: Legacies and Futures After Lee Kuan Yew*. New York: Routledge.

Tan, K.P., 2016b. Singapore in 2015. *Asian Survey*, 56 (1), 108–114.

Tan, N., 2014. The 2011 general and presidential elections in Singapore. *Electoral Studies*.

Tan, T.H., Tng, Y.H., and Yeo, A., 2016. Normalization versus Equalization Effects of the Internet for Political Parties: Singapore's General Election 2015 as a Case Study. *In*: *2016 Conference for E-Democracy and Open Government (CeDEM)*. Presented at the 2016 Conference for E-Democracy and Open Government (CeDEM), 84–95.

Tay, V., 2016. IBM partners with EDB and MAS to establish data centre [online]. *Marketing Interactive*. Available from: http://www.marketing-interactive.com/ibm-partners-edb-mas-establish-data-centre/ [Accessed 28 Jun 2017].

Taylor, P.J., 2000. World cities and territorial states under conditions of contemporary globalization. *Political Geography*, 19 (1), 5–32.

Temasek, 2017. Corporate Profile – About Temasek [online]. *Temasek Holdings Pte Ltd*. Available from: http://www.temasek.com.sg/abouttemasek/corporateprofile [Accessed 27 Jun 2017].

Tham, R., 2016. Singapore improves marginally in EIU's Democracy Index. *TODAYonline*, 22 Jan.

The Economist, 2015. How Singapore gained its independence [online]. *The Economist*. Available from: http://www.economist.com/blogs/economist-explains/2015/03/economist-explains-22 [Accessed 8 Jun 2017].

UNDP, 2015. *UNDP and the making of Singapore's Public Service.* Singapore: UNDP Global Centre for Public Service Excellence.

Veenendaal, W.P. and Corbett, J., 2015. Why Small States Offer Important Answers to Large Questions. *Comparative Political Studies*, 48 (4), 527–549.

Wai-chung Yeung, H., 1998. The political economy of transnational corporations: a study of the regionalization of Singaporean firms. *Political Geography*, 17 (4), 389–416.

Wilkinson, B. and Leggett, C., 1985. Human and industrial relations in Singapore: the management of compliance. *Euro-Asia Business Review*, 4, 9–15.

Wong, B. and Huang, X., 2010. Political Legitimacy in Singapore. *Politics & Policy*, 38 (3), 523–543.

Woo, J.J., 2014. Singapore's policy style: statutory boards as policymaking units. *Journal of Asian Public Policy*, 8 (2), 120–133.

Woo, J.J., 2015a. Beyond the Neoliberal orthodoxy: Alternative financial policy regimes in Asia's financial centres. *Critical Policy Studies*, 9 (3), 297–316.

Woo, J.J., 2015b. Policy Relations and Policy Subsystems: Financial policy in Hong Kong and Singapore. *International Journal of Public Administration*, 38 (8), 553–561.

Woo, J.J., 2016a. *Business and Politics in Asia's Key Financial Centres – Hong Kong, Singapore and Shanghai.* 1st ed. Singapore: Springer.

Woo, J.J., 2016b. *Singapore as an International Financial Centre: History, Politics and Policy.* London: Palgrave Macmillan.

Woo, J.J., 2017. *3-in-1: Governing a Global Financial Centre.* Singapore: World Scientific.

Woo, J.J. and Howlett, M., 2015. Explaining dynamics without change: a critical subsector approach to financial policy making. *Journal of Asian Public Policy*, 8 (3), 312–328.

Woo, J.J., Ramesh, M., and Howlett, M., 2015. Legitimation Capacity: System-Level Resources and Political Skills in Public Policy. *Policy & Society*, 34 (3–4), 271–283.

World Bank, 2016a. GDP per capita (current US$) [online]. *World Bank Database.* Available from: http://data.worldbank.org/indicator/NY.GDP.PCAP.CD?locations=SG&view=chart [Accessed 23 Sep 2016].

World Bank, 2016b. *Exports of goods and services (% of GDP).* Washington, D.C.: World Bank.

World Bank, 2016c. Foreign direct investment, net inflows (% of GDP) | Data [online]. *World Bank Database.* Available from: http://data.worldbank.org/indicator/BX.KLT.DINV.WD.GD.ZS?locations=SG&view=chart [Accessed 21 Sep 2016].

World Bank Group, 2017. *Doing Business 2017: Equal Opportunity for All.* Washington, D.C.: World Bank.

Wu, X., Ramesh, M., and Howlett, M., 2015. Blending Skill and Resources Across Multiple Levels of Activity: Competences, Capabilities and the Policy Capacities of Government. *Policy & Society*, 34 (3–4), 165–171.

Yeandle, M., 2016. *Global Financial Centres Index 20.* London, UK: Z/Yen Group and China Development Institute.

Yeung, H.W., 2014. Governing the market in a globalizing era: Developmental states, global production networks and inter-firm dynamics in East Asia. *Review of International Political Economy*, 21 (1), 70–101.

Yeung, H.W.-C., 2000. State intervention and neoliberalism in the globalizing world economy: lessons from Singapore's regionalization programme. *The Pacific Review*, 13 (1), 133–162.

4 Hong Kong

Administrative developmental state

Like Singapore, Hong Kong has, despite its relatively small size, established itself as one of the world's most competitive economies.[1] It is ranked first on IMD's World Competitiveness Yearbook (IMD 2017) and ninth on the World Economic Forum's Global Competitiveness Index (Schwab 2017), while the World Bank places Hong Kong fourth on its ease of doing business ranking (World Bank Group 2017). As of 2016, Hong Kong's GDP per capita stands at US $43, 500 (Hong Kong Trade Development Council 2015).

Hong Kong's economic success is predicated upon its laissez-faire approach to economic governance which emphasizes free markets and open trade (Li 2012). Yet beneath this veneer of its highly liberalized and open economy, and as the rest of this chapter will elaborate, Hong Kong's approach to economic governance is very much in line with the Asian developmental state model. This is a result of both historical-political contingencies and developmental needs. As prominent scholar of Hong Kong's economic development Eliza Lee (1998, p. 626) has noted, 'a "developmental state" form has complemented the economic development of Hong Kong'.

Furthermore, such adherence to the developmental state model is not simply a matter of economics, but politics as well, with the Hong Kong state's significant level of political insulation. This is in part due to a lack of universal suffrage, often seen as exacerbated by growing Chinese influence over various facets of Hong Kong's socio-political landscape and institutions (Ortmann 2014, Russolillo 2017). Similar to Singapore, Hong Kong is considered a 'flawed democracy' in the Economist Intelligence Unit's Democracy Index (Economist Intelligence Unit 2016).

While it fares better on the World Press Freedom Index, having been ranked 74th (Reporters Without Borders 2017), there is widespread perception of declining press freedom in Hong Kong (Lam 2017). This combination of strong economic performance and political controls bears more than a faint resemblance to the developmental state model of economic development. However, there is a caveat. Unlike Singapore and other Asian developmental states, Hong Kong is not a state unto itself. Rather, it exists under Chinese rule.

However, and under China's One Country, Two Systems principle, Hong Kong nonetheless retains a significant extent of autonomy in economic governance. Together with its lack of universal suffrage, Hong Kong's highly insulated civil service has led to its characterization as an 'administrative state' that bears a strong resemblance to other Asian developmental states (Painter 2005). Others have also noted the presence of a 'sustained pro-development regime' (Wissink et al. 2017, p. 237), with the origins of Hong Kong's developmental state traced to its colonial history (Lee 1998). Hence despite its unique political and economic position as a highly autonomous global city operating under the rubrics of China's One Country, Two Systems principle, Hong Kong can be characterized as a highly advanced developmental state.

This chapter will provide a comprehensive discussion of Hong Kong's role and position as an Asian developmental state. It will begin with a broad overview of Hong Kong's historical development, focusing in particular on the historical trajectory of its formation as a developmental state. I will then examine the ways in which Hong Kong's developmental state has manifested in its approach to economic governance and industrial policy. This is followed by a more systematic discussion of the various components and elements of Hong Kong's developmental state. Finally, I will address emerging challenges to Hong Kong's developmental state model.

History: the beginnings of a developmental state

The origins of modern Hong Kong can be found in 'its nineteenth-century beginnings in the intersection of two large empires: on the one hand, the long-established civilization of the Qing Empire, and on the other hand, the burgeoning power of the British Empire' (Preston 2016, p. vi). Founded in 1842 as a British colonial outpost, Hong Kong would become a thriving entrepôt serving British trade interests.

Hong Kong's role as a major trading hub would give rise to the emergence of maritime-related financial services, such as shipping finance, and culminate in the city's transformation into a leading international financial centre in the early 1900s (Reed 1980, p. 28). Like Singapore, much of Hong Kong's legal institutions and economic infrastructure were established under British colonial rule. This presents significant similarities between the two cities' legal-regulatory systems. However, similarities between the two cities end here.

While the two cities share similar *forms* of legal-regulatory institutions, they differ significantly in terms of the policies that were enacted by these institutions. For instance, the policy and political autonomy of the Hong Kong state was a consequence of the colonial government's efforts at 'boundary maintenance' between state and society, combined with utilitarian and materialistic cultural tendencies within the population (Ngok 2016, p. 248). In contrast, and as discussed in the previous chapter, the autonomy of the Singaporean state largely arises from the political dominance of its ruling People's Action Party.

Nonetheless, the two cities share similar vulnerabilities to external political economic crises and events. In particular, Hong Kong's fortunes took a turn with the Japanese occupation of China in 1937 prior to and during the Second World War. The Japanese occupation of Hong Kong took place from 1941 to 1945, during which time Hong Kong's network of external economic relations fell apart and its stock of human capital dwindled with the large-scale deportations that were carried out by the Japanese (Mushkat and Mushkat 2016, p. 11).

While Hong Kong would recover from the war, with the re-emergence of global and regional trade giving rise to the agglomeration of trade-related financial services and driving the city's rise as a leading international centre (Schenk 2001, pp. 120–121), it remained vulnerable to external shocks. For instance, the Korean War and the Chinese Civil War resulted in severe disruptions to Hong Kong's exports, with UN sanctions on the People's Republic of China for siding with the Communist North resulting in a deterioration of its positions as an entrepôt for the Mainland; at the same time, massive inflows of refugees fleeing the Chinese Civil War swelled Hong Kong's population considerably (Mushkat and Mushkat 2016, p. 11).

Paradoxically, this influx of refugees would serve to drive Hong Kong's manufacturing sector, with an expanding pool of labour (both skilled and unskilled) as well as considerable flight capital from the Mainland facilitating the emergence of labour-intensive manufacturing and driving overall economic development in the territory for the subsequent two decades (Mushkat and Mushkat 2016, pp. 11–12). Such manufacturing-driven growth, coupled with a revival of trade activity, would subsequently fuel the rise of Hong Kong's services sector. Schenk (2001, p. 122) has noted that the emergence and subsequent development of Hong Kong's financial sector 'tracked the development of the economy'.

In other words, Hong Kong's financial services sector emerged as a natural offshoot of its broader economic development. However, and unlike Singapore, the emergence of financial services in Hong Kong did not follow a smooth and natural progression from manufacturing to services, with the financing and operational needs of the former giving rise to the later. Rather, Hong Kong's financial services sector emerged as a consequence of the relocation of manufacturing firms from Hong Kong to the Pearl River Delta during China's opening up in 1979 and the city's efforts to capitalize on China's nascent industrial and economic emergence by attracting Chinese capital and investments (Wissink et al. 2017, p. 234).

Indeed, this early entwinement of Hong Kong's economy with that of the Mainland has played a crucial role in driving the city's subsequent emergence as a leading global financial centre, with China's economic rise through the 1990s and 2000s driving the rapid expansion of Hong Kong's financial sector. While the 1997 Asian Financial Crisis and 2003 SARS (Severe Acute Respiratory Syndrome) epidemic exposed vulnerabilities associated with an over-reliance on finance and real estate as sources of revenue (Wissink et al. 2017, p. 234), Hong Kong would rebound from these challenges to regain its position as a leading Asian financial centre.

Economic development and industrial policy

Despite caricatures of Hong Kong's approach to economic governance as laissez-faire and driven by free market principles, the reality is that the Hong Kong government has provided a significant extent of support and direction for general macro-economic and social stability (Tsui-Auch 1998, p. 68). This is particularly the case in industrial policy, with the Hong Kong government playing a significant role in the territory's various rounds of industrial restructuring (Ho 2016).

Yet at the same time, it is important to emphasize that Hong Kong's approach to economic development and governance has involved a lower level of state intervention, especially when compared to Singapore. Rather, Hong Kong's position as a small open economy and the presence of strong entrepreneurial activity, driven by colonial-era institutional factors, obviated the need for costly state-owned enterprises and infusions of state capital (i.e. the 'Singapore miracle') and allowed Hong Kong to rely on less interventionist means of economic governance and development (Mushkat and Mushkat 2016, pp. 13–14).

This approach to economic development has often been described as 'positive non-interventionism' by former Hong Kong financial secretaries John J. Coperthwaite and Sir Philip Haddon-Cave (Schenk 2002, p. 332, Tsang 2006, Ho 2016, pp. 202–203). More than simply laissez-faire non-interventionism, however, positive non-interventionism connotes an *active* role for the government in managing Hong Kong's economy, with 'positive' referring to the active coordinative role of government and 'non-intervention' denoting the favouring of laissez-faire capitalism (Li 2012, p. 548).

Hence paradoxically, Hong Kong's adherence to free market principles requires extensive and active state intervention in ensuring the conditions necessary for free markets. This makes Hong Kong's laissez-faire economic policy a 'deliberate policy choice rather than merely an absence of policy' (Schenk 2002, p. 332). Nor is it due to the influence of business interests. As Tang (1999, p. 285) argues, 'Hong Kong's well established economic philosophy of "positive non-interventionism", was therefore an outcome of not simply a pro-business agenda, but also a deliberate choice by a colonial administration whose raison d'etre was almost completely commercial'.

It has also been noted that Hong Kong's motives for adopting positive non-interventionism are not merely commercial or economic in nature. Ngo (2000, p. 32) argues that the laissez faire ideal was appropriated and articulated by the Hong Kong state as a political mechanism for establishing 'substantive consent' among its ruling elite. I will discuss this further below. More than simply a reflection of laissez-faire, positive non-interventionism is therefore a means through which the government is able to enhance Hong Kong's economic advantage as well as ensure its political legitimacy.

Furthermore, the adoption of positive non-interventionism as economic governing principle also reflects a 'greater willingness by government than traditionally may have been the case to take steps to complement (e.g., accelerating investment in physical and social infrastructure) and support (e.g., the recent introduction of an elaborate competition law) the operation of market forces' (Mushkat and Mushkat 2016, p. 10). The introduction of positive non-interventionism therefore heralds a shift in Hong Kong's overall approach to economic governance towards a closer approximation of the developmental state model. As Tang (1999, p. 283) has noted,

> the notion of 'positive non-intervention' marked the transformation of Hong Kong from an administrative state to a provider state in response to both challenges to the legitimacy of the colonial regime and an expansion of public services and more active approach to physical and human capital investment.

In short, the institution of positive non-interventionism as economic development doctrine can be seen as a step towards greater market interventions by the Hong Kong state. In any case, this is a doctrine that requires considerable governmental restraint from market intervention, 'guided by a liberal economic ideology' (Tang 1999, p. 285). Hence there are two layers of interventionism in Hong Kong's positive non-interventionist approach to economic development. On the one hand, the doctrine connotes a greater willingness by the Hong Kong government to facilitate and complement market forces through overt policy interventions.

Yet on the other hand, positive non-interventionism also often involves deliberate efforts by the government to maintain the socio-economic and institutional conditions required for ensuring Hong Kong's free and open markets. This means, not without irony, that active state effort is required to ensure non-intervention, or at least prevent interventions that may distort or negatively impact Hong Kong's free markets. Given the significance of such free markets to Hong Kong's value proposition as a global financial centre, such active efforts at ensuring free and open markets are fundamentally driven by industrial policy needs and concerns (Woo 2015, 2016).

Furthermore, and perhaps more significantly, it is important to note how Hong Kong's approach to economic governance has shifted and changed after its handover from British to Chinese rule in 1997. Despite China's pledge to grant Hong Kong a significant extent of autonomy (barring foreign policy and defence) for the first 50 years after the handover, under its One Country, Two Systems principle, the reality is there have since been shifts in Hong Kong's approach to economic governance. Indeed, some of these shifts predate the handover.

For instance, Ngok (2016) has noted that the Chinese government had from the 1980s helped build a corporatist state in Hong Kong that laid the foundations for heavier sectorial interventions post-1997. An important implication of this is the increasingly close relations between the Chinese government and Hong Kong's business elites (Fong 2014). The handover has, in short, given rise to a more interventionist approach to economic governance and a greater role of the Chinese government. Furthermore, such post-handover shifts in governance are not restricted to the realm of economics, with shifts and challenges emerging in the realm of political governance as well. These will be discussed in a later section on Hong Kong's civil society.

Hong Kong's financial governance model has since evolved from 'positive non-intervention' to what former Chief Executive Donald Tsang has termed 'big market, small government' (Tsang 2006, 2013). The central belief of 'big market, small government' is that 'government will only do the things which the market does not do' (Tsang 2013). In light of the 2007 Global Financial Crisis, it is increasingly clear that many of the socio-economic services and functions that had hitherto been provided or performed by markets are now increasingly reverting to the state (Howlett and Lejano 2013, Howlett et al. 2015).

At a more fundamental level, Hong Kong's governing principle of 'big market, small government' involves 'highly selective intervention' on the part of the government in ensuring basic economic functionality, especially during crises or in the face of market failure (Glassburner and Riedel 1972, p. 61). This strong role of the state in ensuring market stability is itself an important means of maintaining Hong Kong's attractiveness as a place for business and investments, with economic freedom and market stability long being held up as key strengths or value propositions (Jao 1997, Schenk 2002, Woo 2016).

In short, Hong Kong's economic development and governance involves a significant extent of state intervention and management, although such interventions are much more subtle and calibrated when compared to Singapore. This is due in part to policy legacies of laissez-faire stemming from the city's British colonial history and, perhaps in large part, to a continued need to maintain market freedom and stability as key value propositions. This has significant implications for industrial planning and policy.

In terms of industrial policy, Hong Kong's economic openness has been used as an 'instrument for attracting inward capital in the form of foreign investment and external demand in the form of manufactured goods and services exports' (Li 2012, p. 40). It is for this reason that many analyses tend to characterize Hong Kong's industrial policy as that of laissez-faire. As Tsui-Auch (1998) and others (Painter 2005, Cheung 2008, Woo 2016) have noted, Hong Kong may well possess one of the freest markets in the world, its economic governance is by no means laissez-faire in nature.

Rather, Hong Kong's free markets are a matter of deliberate policy, driven by a need to maintain economic freedom and openness. Characterizations of a laissez-faire Hong Kong model, therefore, in many cases, confuse form for substance. While the form of the Hong Kong economy – its free markets – alludes to the laissez-faire approach of neoclassical economics, its substance – economic policies – suggest a different story of deliberate state interventions to maintain this economic freedom and, increasingly, direct market interventions that resemble those typically used by other developmental states to stimulate economic growth and industrial development.

This latter shift is perhaps most evident in Chief Executive Carrie Lam's 2017 Policy Address, where she introduced a whole array of policy measures to spur innovation and technological development, in a bid to grow Hong Kong's creative industries, with the government's R&D expenditure as a percentage of GDP expected to grow from 0.73 per cent to 1.5 per cent (Hong Kong Trade Development Council 2015). Hence, and as I will further elaborate in later chapters, Hong Kong's smart city policies tend to be highly developmental in nature.

Nor is such developmentalism restricted to smart city policies. Ms Lam's Policy Address also laid out policy initiatives aimed at trade and investment promotion, financial sector development and diversification, regional integration, and the enhancement of overall economic competitiveness (Hong Kong Trade Development Council 2015). Furthermore, development-oriented industrial policies pre-date Ms Lam's current policy directions. For instance, then-Chief Executive Leung Chun-yin's 2014 Policy Address emphasized an 'appropriately proactive' approach to economic development that involved active efforts to develop strategic sectors such as financial services, trade, maritime services, and logistics, among others (Government of Hong Kong Special Administrative Region 2014).

It is therefore clear that economic development and governance in Hong Kong have often involved extensive state interventions that are deeply reminiscent of the Asian developmental state model. Indeed, this proclivity for developmentalism has only intensified of late, with growing regional competition, especially from Singapore and Shanghai, necessitating interventionist and developmental approaches to industrial policy and market development. I will now proceed to discuss the various components of Hong Kong's developmental state.

Components of Hong Kong's developmental state

As this chapter has thus far elucidated, Hong Kong's approach to economic development and governance is very much in line with that of the Asian developmental state model. Despite its reputation as a proponent of free markets and a laissez-faire approach to economic development, Hong Kong is increasingly relying on developmental and interventionist policy measures to stimulate economic growth and development. Indeed, even its desire to ensure economic freedom is itself predicated upon a desire to enhance the city's attractiveness as a business destination.

For these reasons, and others, Hong Kong has often been characterized as a developmental state (Lee 1998, 2005, Tsui-Auch 1998, Ngok 2016) or a development-oriented 'administrative state' (Painter 2005, Cheung 2008). In the rest of this chapter, I will discuss and assess the various components of Hong Kong's developmental state. This will allow for a more systematic comparison of the developmental states of Hong Kong and Singapore, which will be presented in Chapter 6.

Developmental elite

An important consequence of Hong Kong's unique political system is its tendency to form a political and policy elite, particularly through the appointment of its political executive by a select group of approximately 1, 200 individuals, comprising representatives from business and finance, professionals, labour, social services and civil society, and politicians (The Economist 2017). Political elitism therefore begins from the very apex of Hong Kong's governing system – the appointment of its Chief Executive. Indeed, the level of authority wielded by the Chief Executive has led Lee to characterize Hong Kong's system of governance as a 'securely authoritarian, if not dictatorial, rule' (Lee 1999, p. 951).

Such rule by elites is furthermore replicated at other levels of government. For instance, it has been noted that Hong Kong is 'governed by bureaucrats under the control of a small appointed secretariat led by a chief executive' (MacCarthaigh et al. 2016, p. 498), with all of these individuals – whether bureaucrats, secretaries or the chief executive – appointed to their roles and offices, rather than through popular elections. Indeed, Hong Kong's economic success has been attributed to its 'bureaucratic dominance in an executive-led system' (Lee 1999, p. 943).

Hence the alignment of public officials and agencies under the political executive, combined with a high level of socio-political insulation among both political actors and the bureaucracy, has given rise to the formation of a highly consolidated governing elite. Furthermore, and by virtue of the strong focus on economic development and industrial policy that was discussed above, this elite group of policy and political actors can also be seen as Hong Kong's developmental elite – a select and exclusive group that drives and determines economic policy directions and strategies in the territory.

It is also important to note that membership in this developmental elite is not solely restricted to the public sector. As was the case in Singapore, business and industry actors often play a crucial role in influencing or determining economic and industrial policy, frequently through their infiltration of, or in some cases co-optation into, the developmental elite. Private sector membership in Hong Kong's developmental elite has occurred through several channels.

The first, and most significant, channel through which business interests have often been able to determine Hong Kong's political and policy processes is the Legislative Council (LegCo). In particular, business and professional interest groups are able to articulate their political preferences through 'functional constituencies' that are elected by the respective sectors' members (Loh 2006, Wong 2016). In contrast to geographical constituencies, which form the second component of the LegCo, functional constituencies tend to be dominated by business interests, with the influence of opposition democrats restricted to geographical constituencies (Wong 2017, p. 46).

Furthermore, Hong Kong's Basic Law stipulates that a simple majority from each of the constituencies is required for the passing of government bills or amendments; this conversely means that only half of one constituency is required to veto or block a bill, effectively amplifying the influence of functional constituency members, who tend to be elected from narrow constituencies (Wong 2017, p. 46). This role of the functional constituency in facilitating private sector membership in Hong Kong's developmental elite is not entirely new.

In the pre-handover period and prior to the introduction of functional constituencies, the colonial government frequently co-opted business elites by appointing them directly to either the Executive Council (ExCo) and Legco (Mushkat and Mushkat 2016, p. 17, Ngok 2016, p. 250). However, with pressures of decolonization and democratization emerging after the signing of the 1984 Sino-British Declaration, there was a need to establish a channel of elite co-optation that would suit the needs of both the British and Chinese governments, thereby formalizing elite co-optation through the establishment of functional constituencies (Ngok 2016, p. 250).

In short, functional constituencies have arguably introduced a certain extent of business influence over Hong Kong's economic policies, with business actors and interests granted a certain amount of access to Hong Kong's developmental elite. However, it is often easy to overstate this role of the private sector in Hong Kong's developmental elite, especially given caricatures of laissez-faire. Rather than private sector interests driving the state's developmental policies and agenda, the reverse could also be equally, if not more, true.

For instance, functional constituencies have been described by Leung as a 'means of elite co-optation, representing an 'attempt by the government, or the ruling party, to promote political stability by bringing potential dissent groups into the formal intermediate structure where different conflicting interests are represented' (Leung 1990, p. 143). In other words, functional constituencies allow the Hong Kong state to incorporate and co-op business interests into its developmental elite. This latter view of elite co-optation corresponds with a growing cognizance of Hong Kong's state-centric approach to economic governance.

Aside from the LegCo, the private sector's role and position in Hong Kong's developmental elite is reinforced by their membership in the Election Committee, which votes for the Chief Executive and typically includes property tycoons, lawmakers, professional bodies, business representatives and trade associations (Ngok 2016, p. 259, Lim 2017). As Ngok (2016, p. 258) has shown, the support of such sectorial representatives in the Election Commission is often reciprocated with strong commitment by the newly elected Chief Executive to appoint more sectorial representatives into future decision-making or consultative bodies, or even commit to enacting policies or institutions aimed at promoting sectorial growth.

Such direct linkages between business or sectorial interests and the Chief Executive therefore plays a significant role in encouraging the Chief Executive to, once elected into office, emphasize developmental goals. However, it is often also noted that members of the Election Committee tend to be pro-Beijing or, at the very least, unwilling to contest the Mainland's choice of Chief Executive (Lee 1999, Fong 2014, 2017, Lim 2017, Ngok 2017). Furthermore, the business-centred sectors of the Election Committee, such as the commercial and financial sector or the professions sector, are seen as part of Beijing's broader co-optation efforts (Wong 2017, p. 42).

This role of the Chinese central government introduces another layer of politics and governance that is missing in the city-state of Singapore. In particular, Hong Kong's developmental elite is highly pro-Beijing, whether due to the Hong Kong government's desire to integrate itself more deeply within China's One Country, Two Systems approach (Lo 2008), or strong ties between the Chinese government and Hong Kong's business elite and capitalist class (Fong 2014). Such strong ties between the Chinese government and Hong Kong's business elite further reinforce the view that private participation in Hong Kong's developmental elite arises from active efforts by the state, whether this is the Hong Kong government or the Chinese central government, to co-op these business interests into a state-driven developmental elite.

In sum, Hong Kong's economic development is driven by a developmental elite that, while largely dominated by the political executive and the bureaucracy, has increasingly incorporated and co-opted business and other non-state interests, often through institutionalized channels such as functional constituencies within its LegCo. However, and as I have noted elsewhere, such industry participation in Hong Kong's policy processes remains limited and circumscribed, with the government's emphasis on arms-length transactions with businesses ironically limiting business's ability to influence the policy process (Woo 2015, 2016). In other words, economic development in Hong Kong remains very much driven by the state.

Indeed, it has often been noted that economic development in Hong Kong frequently involves a significant extent of centralized state intervention and action (Glassburner and Riedel 1972, Lui and Chiu 1993, Schenk 2001, 2002, Li 2012). As the discussion above has shown, such state interventions have become increasingly overt and extensive, as the Hong Kong government seeks to maintain its economic competitiveness, especially with regard to the formation and development of new creative industries. However, it is also important to note that such interventions are often coordinated by a lead public agency, or in the parlance of the developmental state literature, a pilot agency. I will now turn my discussion to Hong Kong's developmental pilot agency.

Pilot agency

In line with the developmental state model, economic development in Hong Kong is led by a pilot agency that is tasked with economic governance and market promotion. In the case of Hong Kong, the Commerce and Economic

Development Bureau perform this role of the pilot agency. The Commerce and Economic Development Bureau is driven by five goals (Commerce and Economic Development Bureau 2011a):

- Enhancing Hong Kong's position as a leading international trade and business centre
- Fostering a business-friendly environment and attracting investments
- Positing Hong Kong as the premier telecommunications hub of Asia
- Promoting high value-added and creative activities.
- Ensuring closer economic integration between Hong Kong and the Pearl River Delta region

The Commerce and Economic Development Bureau also comprises the Commerce, Industry and Tourism Branch and the Communications and Creative Industries Branch. While the Commerce Industry and Tourism Branch is responsible for enhancing Hong Kong's external relations, fostering inward investments, protecting intellectual property, supporting industries and businesses, tourism promotion, and ensuring consumer protection and competition, the Communications and Creative Industries Branch focuses on broadcasting and film-related issues, developing the telecommunications and creative industries, as well as the 'control of obscene and indecent articles' (Commerce and Economic Development Bureau 2011b).

At this point, it is important to note that there are key differences in the pilot agencies of Hong Kong and Singapore. While Singapore's pilot agency, the Economic Development Board, operates as a statutory board or public agency that is focused solely on issues pertaining to economic promotion and development, the Commerce and Economic Development Bureau exists at the ministerial/departmental level (rather than agency level) and plays several non-developmental policy roles, such as media censorship and intellectual property protection.

In incorporating these roles, Hong Kong's Commerce and Economic Development Bureau differs from other overtly development-focused pilot agencies as well, such as Japan's Ministry of International Trade and Industry (now Ministry of Economy, Trade and Industry). Yet at the same time, the inclusion of these policy roles is in line with Hong Kong's approach to economic development, as discussed above. Given that much of this role has involved the fostering of a conducive and 'enabling' business environment, intellectual property protection and media censorship arguably ensures a media sphere that is both conducive to media corporations and protective of socio-cultural-political norms.

Nonetheless, the Commerce and Economic Development Bureau often employs very interventionist means of market promotion and economic development. For instance, the Communications and Creative Industries Branch has sought to support creative industries by organizing trade fairs and events for industries' players to explore business opportunities with the

Mainland and funding Hong Kong publishers directly; it has also since 2007 injected HK $540 million into the Film Development Fund, which serves to promote the development of the film industry (Communications and Creative Industries Branch 2017).

Similarly interventionist policy measures can be found in the repertoire of the Commerce, Industry and Tourism Branch, such as providing HK $200 million of funds to support the professional services sector, identifying and developing potential growth sectors, assisting Hong Kong enterprises in branding, upgrading and domestic sales through a HK $1 billion fund, and various small and medium enterprises (SME) funding schemes, among others (Commerce, Industry and Tourism Branch 2016). In short, the Commerce and Economic Development Bureau operates like a typical pilot agency in supporting and driving industry development.

However, the Commerce and Economic Development Bureau does not possess oversight of all developmental activities. Like Singapore, the governance and promotion of Hong Kong's financial services sector lies not in the ambit of the main economic development agency, but a separate and more specialized organization. In the case of Hong Kong, these roles are carried out by the Financial Services and the Treasury Bureau, with its constituent Financial Services Branch specifically tasked with consolidating and enhancing Hong Kong's status as an international financial centre (Financial Services and the Treasury Bureau 2003, 2013).

This is similar to the Monetary Authority of Singapore (MAS), which promotes and develops Singapore's financial services sector. Indeed, the complementary roles played by the Commerce and Economic Development Bureau and the Financial Services and Treasury Bureau in economic and financial sector development reflect a certain extent of pilot agency decentralization in Hong Kong's (as well as Singapore's) developmental state. This presence of multiple pilot agencies is discussed at greater length in Chapter 6.

Aside from these two Bureaus, the Innovation and Technology Bureau can also be seen as a pilot agency, through its role in developing Hong Kong as a knowledge-based economy and an innovation hub for technology, particularly through supporting sectorial development, talent development, investments in research and development, and facilitating cooperation among public agencies, start-ups, and other stakeholders (Innovation and Technology Bureau 2015). Hence, like Singapore, Hong Kong's emerging innovation and technology sector has necessitated the formation of a specialized pilot agency.

The roles of Hong Kong's Innovation and Technology Bureau and Singapore's Smart Nation and Digital Government Group in promoting and developing the two cities' 'smart' industries will be further discussed in Chapters 5 and 6. It is also important to note that the presence of multiple pilot agencies does not necessarily result in the emergence of policy siloes. In both instances, there is a significant extent of policy coordination and overlaps among these agencies. Such collaborative relations are administratively reflected in the placing of the Bureaus of Commerce and Economic Development, Financial Services and the Treasury, and Innovation and Technology under the oversight of the Financial Secretary.

Embedded autonomy

An important consequence of the lack of universal suffrage in Hong Kong is the high level of insulation that its government, particularly the civil service, enjoys from political and societal forces (Painter 2005). Given that the political executive is appointed by an elected committee, rather than elected through popular vote, the Hong Kong government is highly insulated from the influence and activities of lobby groups and other socio-political interests. Such policy autonomy can arguably be traced back to Hong Kong's colonial history, with the lack of electoral influence on its then-colonial government, ensuring high levels of state autonomy, albeit within the constraints of British rule (Tsui-Auch 1998).

Indeed, Hong Kong has long been caricatured as a 'bureaucratic polity' or 'administrative state' – with a strong emphasis on 'bureaucratic' and 'administrative' – that insulates the policy decision-making processes of both the political elite and the civil service from societal pressures and demands (Harris 1978, Lau and Liu 1984). Aside from political systemic factors, it has also been argued, albeit from a more anthropological perspective, that such insulation may stem from a political culture of 'utilitarianistic familism' that was prevalent among early Hong Kong Chinese, which emphasized material values and favoured the solving of social problems through familial networks (Lau 1984).

Regardless of its origins, this lack of socio-political pressure has resulted in a high level of continuity and stability in Hong Kong's bureaucracy, buttressed by the extensive political clout of civil servants, whether through their membership and participation in legislative bodies or their possession of technical domain knowledge (Cooper and Lui 1990), although the flipside of this is its 'seclusion' from the rest of society (Lau and Liu 1984). Such political insulation is reinforced by formal institutions such as LegCo, which limits the ability of popular powers to hold government accountable, reserving such powers instead for specific vested interests (Loh and Cullen 2005, Wissink et al. 2017, p. 231).

Furthermore, the socio-political insulation of Hong Kong's bureaucracy is strongly related to its 'positive non-interventionist' approach to economic governance. As Ngok (2016, p. 249) has noted, the colonial government's decision to encourage non-interventionism in its economic policy stance was not so much driven by free market ideologies; rather, it was devised to manage state-societal relations by turning down competing demands from both Chinese industrialists and British merchants for greater sectorial intervention. In other words, Hong Kong's laissez-faire approach to economic governance can be seen as a means through which bureaucratic insulation can be achieved, by enforcing arms-length transactions between state and business.

Owing to such bureaucratic stability, insularity and influence, Hong Kong's approach to governance and policy is often characterized as that of an 'administrative state' (Harris 1978, Painter 2005, Cheung 2008, Painter and Yee 2012). However, this is not to say that the state is entirely insulated from all business and societal elements. Indeed, and as Ngo (1999) has noted, business and industrial groups have often been able to (successfully) lobby the colonial government for subsidies. Nor are such activities restricted to colonial-era Hong Kong. Indeed, business and industrial groups continue to exercise considerable influence in determining sectorial development and intervention in Hong Kong (Ngok 2016).

Such overlaps between business and government also exist in more formal governing institutions, such as the Executive Council (Exco) and Legco, with heads of leading firms often taking up position within the Executive Council and industry constituencies represented within Legco (Enright et al. 1997, p. 33). Indeed, some have gone so far as to argue that both the Executive and Legislative Councils represent the interests of 'big business', rather than the popular majority (Goodstadt 2005, Loh and Cullen 2005, Wissink et al. 2017, p. 231). However, such assertions are, more often than not, difficult to prove, since they are based on analyses of institutional membership, rather than policy outcomes.

Indeed, and as I have noted elsewhere, the outcomes of policy deliberations and consultative sessions in Hong Kong tend to emphasize developmental policy needs rather than business or societal demands (Woo 2015, 2016). While such developmental needs may at times encourage greater efforts by the government to engage its industry partners, it does not necessarily translate to extensive social embeddedness or business capture. As Cheung (2008, p. 138) has noted, Hong Kong's existing political system, which emphasizes laissez-faire economic governance, continues to limit the government's ability to foster closer links with its industry partners.

This separation of state and business has also limited the Hong Kong state's ability to obtain sufficient political legitimacy for its policies (Cheung 2008, p. 138). However, it is also important to note that business actors and interests continue to maintain a presence within Hong Kong's governing mechanisms, even as their actual influence on policy decisions are difficult to assess. This combination of state insulation from socio-political pressure and presence of government-business overlaps suggests that Hong Kong possesses some embedded autonomy, although to a much lesser extent than that enjoyed by Singapore.

While the Hong Kong state, along with its constituent public agencies, possesses a significant extent of policy autonomy, it remains strongly embedded within its close relations with industry and business actors. Yet unlike Singapore, these government-business relations do not necessarily give rise to material impacts on policy decisions, nor is it common for Hong Kong's consultative mechanisms to amount to anything more than an exercise in informing citizens and business stakeholders of already-determined policy decisions. Indeed, such policy consultations often proceed with the government's pre-existing decisions, *despite* public resistance (Topping 2013).

However, it has also been noted that Hong Kong's embedded autonomy may have gone into decline after the handover. For instance, Cheng (2016, p. 455) has noted:

> One may argue that while the colonial bureaucracy in Hong Kong maintained close ties with the major business groups, especially the British groups, embedded autonomy was upheld. One may also argue that the extent of embedded autonomy maintained by the HKSAR government has been in decline since 1997.

This is partly due to changes in the mix of business and economic interests dominating Hong Kong's commercial landscape as well as post-handover adaptations to the territory's political institutions. These will be discussed further below.

With regard to the presence of embedded autonomy in Hong Kong, there appears to be a paradox. While Hong Kong's reputation for laissez-faire juxtaposes against Singapore's far more interventionist approach to economic development, its public institutions and agencies are more insulated and less accessible than those of Singapore. This paradox disappears when one considers the differences in political institutions of the two cities. Given its lack of universal suffrage, there is less need for the Hong Kong government to include business and societal interests in all of its policy decisions. In contrast, the Singaporean state needs to at least retain a semblance of public or sectorial participation in its policy deliberations, in order to retain its political legitimacy and right to rule, in the face of regulator general elections.

Management of non-state economic interests

As the discussion thus far has shown, business interests play an important role in Hong Kong's economic governance, whether through their membership and participation in Hong Kong's developmental elite or via institutional channels such as the LegCo. However, there are also some limits to the ability of non-state and business interests to influence or shape policies, given that the Hong Kong government and civil service are both relatively insulated from socio-political forces and lobbying efforts.

Yet at the same time, the presence of business interests in the LegCo functional constituencies as well as the role of corporate elites in electing Hong Kong's Chief Executive suggests a certain element of business influence or control over both political processes and policy outcomes. These two views – government autonomy versus business capture – have dominated and polarized existing scholarly work on government–business relations in Hong Kong (Ngo 2000, pp. 26–27). However, neither of these diametrically opposed views provides a complete picture of government–business relations in Hong Kong. Rather than extol the virtues of either view, it may be more useful to operate on the assumption that each view contains a grain of truth.

Business participation in Hong Kong's economic governance and policy processes began during its colonial era, with British-owned trading houses known as 'hongs' establishing trade relations with China through Hong Kong, in the process dominating the commercial landscape of the territory (Ngo 1999, 2000). While these British-owned 'hongs' would decline with the emergence of more competitive local entrepreneurs and enterprises as well as other non-British foreign corporate interests, non-state economic interests such as multinational corporations, domestic companies and entrepreneurs continue to dominate Hong Kong's economy.

Furthermore, and as I have discussed above, these economic interests have an outsized influence over Hong Kong's political landscape as well. Specifically, the business and economic elite's role in electing both the Chief Executive and functional representatives in Hong Kong's LegCo provides it with direct influence over the election of key policymakers and legislators. This political role of non-state economic interests has endured through the handover, with Chinese officials who were responsible for managing the transition from British to Chinese rule further entrenching the business elite in Hong Kong's political establishment, in a bid to dilute the political influence of the British colonial bureaucracy (Goodstadt 2000).

Such efforts have also led to business elites circumventing the Hong Kong government by bringing their concerns directly to Mainland authorities (Fong 2014), giving rise to greater complexity in Hong Kong's management of non-state economic interests. This is further complicated by the growing clout of, often politically connected, Chinese businesses in Hong Kong (Tang 1999). However, it is also easy to overstate the influence of the business elite.

Despite their strong presence in key political institutions such as LegCo or the Chief Executive Election Committee, the impacts of business elites on actual policy outcomes are difficult to measure. Furthermore, and as I have discussed above, the socio-political insulation of the Hong Kong government, along with its adherence to positive non-interventionism, means that business influence over day-to-day economic governance may be limited. Indeed, it has often been noted that the Hong Kong government tends to implement policies that are unpopular with business interests, often despite resistance from the business elite (Topping 2013, Woo 2016).

This suggests a relatively state-centric approach to the management of non-state economic interests, with the Hong Kong government defining the parameters within which business and economic elites are able to influence economic policies. However, this does not necessarily mean that state and business interests are at odds. According to Ngo (2000), the Hong Kong government manages business and public interests by forging a 'substantive consent' among the developmental elite that limits both bureaucratic and business influence by establishing boundaries around potential policy options.

Determined by bureaucratic practicability, economic affordability and political feasibility, these boundaries allow for the formation of socio-political consent around policy outcomes, rather than electoral or procedural arrangements (Ngo 2000, pp. 31–32). More importantly, this emphasis on substantive, rather than procedural, consent has allowed the Hong Kong state to retain its developmental focus through pro-business policies such as low business taxes, limited social welfare provisions, minimal labour protection, free enterprise and free capital flows, without needing to enact any preferential treatment for selected economic and business interests (Ngo 2000, p. 32).

In short, the Hong Kong government's approach to managing non-state economic interests is sectorial and outcome-focused. Given the Hong Kong government's desire to ensure strong economic growth by supporting businesses and industries, such an outcome-focused consensus within Hong Kong's developmental elite serves to achieve the goals of both the government and business elites. However, it also goes without saying that this emphasis on outcome over procedural consent can also disadvantage societal interests that rely on procedural democratic institutions, such as universal suffrage, to gain access to political leaders and policy processes.

The negative implications of emphasizing outcome over procedural consent have become increasingly evident, with mass protests and demonstrations such as the Yellow Umbrella movement increasingly focused on a desire for political reform. Yet despite this lack of universal suffrage, Hong Kong continues to enjoy high levels of civil liberties. I will discuss these societal interests, especially as they pertain to civil society organizations, in the following section.

Civil society

Despite its lack of universal suffrage and relatively limited state of democratization, Hong Kong possesses a vibrant civil society, civil liberties comparable to those in Western democracies, a relatively free press, and independent courts (Ma 2007, 2008). Indeed, this paradox of having a free civil society in the absence of democratization stands in contrast to Singapore, where civil society activity is more constrained despite the presence of universal suffrage and a popularly elected government.

When discussing Hong Kong's civil society, it is important to take note of the socio-political context. While a nascent civil society had existed during early British colonial rule, civil society organizations tended to exist solely within the Chinese migrant community and lacked the horizontal linkages necessary for political mobilization. However, growing Chinese nationalism from the entry of the People's Republic of China into the United Nations and the increasingly salient prospect of a future Chinese sovereign master gave rise to more organized efforts by civil society organizations to push for greater civil liberties and democratization (Ma 2008, pp. 160–161).

The signing of a Sino-British Joint Declaration in 1984 would further spark off democratization efforts, with the colonial government subsequently expanding civil liberties and encouraging citizen participation (Lo 2001). These efforts culminated in the formation of the Joint Committee for the Promotion of Democratic Government (JCPDG) in 1986, which would also form the basis for future democratization efforts in the early 1990s. As such, Hong Kong's vibrant civil society and extensive civil liberties were established during British colonial rule. Paradoxically, Ma (2008, p. 172) has noted that such extensive civil liberties had the effect of reducing the need for a unified opposition or any urgency for political reform.

However, all these would change after the handover. In particular, it has been noted that state–society relations declined after the handover, with the government slowing down the democratization process and policy processes becoming increasingly top-down (Cheung 2008, p. 128). Indeed, post-handover Hong Kong increasingly approximates an archetypal developmental state, with both the Hong Kong authorities and Chinese central government seeking to enact national security laws aimed at curbing civil unrest and potentially restricting civil society activity (Cheung 2017).

Correspondingly, civil society activity and social movements have increased in tandem with such growing restrictions on civil liberties (perceived or otherwise). Indeed, it was only in 2003, in response to the Hong Kong government's efforts to enact a national security law, that civic groups and activists increasingly perceived of themselves as part of 'civil society', often taking a more unified, proactive, and even aggressive approach to advance their collective interests (Chan and Chan 2017, pp. 135–136). Reflecting a loss of public confidence in the Tung Chee-hwa administration, the 2003 protests represented a marked shift from economically driven protest movements to a growing focus on political autonomy among protesters (Wong and Chan 2017).

This focus on political autonomy would flow into more recent protests such as the Umbrella Movement or Hong Kong Independence, both of which were driven by a desire for electoral reforms and political autonomy from the Mainland. Such protests and social movement have come to form a major part of civil society activity in Hong Kong. As Wong and Chan (2017) have noted, the type and nature of protests and civil disobedience that have emerged in Hong Kong are strongly related to the nature of civil society in the territory, as defined by the extent of state control and the level of society's desire for autonomy.

It is, however, also easy to overstate the impact of such antagonistic state–society relations on Hong Kong's overall civil society landscape or fall back on caricatures of authoritarianism in the emerging government restrictions over civil society activity. Rather, the reality is much more complex. For instance, it has been noted that despite its desire to restrict or even curb civil society movements, Beijing has sought instead to rely on more subtle methods such as co-optation or the creation of a parallel network of pro-government societal organizations, in order to maintain the image of a free Hong Kong (Ma 2008, p. 162).

Furthermore, not all civil society organizations are politically motivated. For instance, Chan and Chan have noted the proliferation of social enterprises between 2007 and 2017, with the Hong Kong government promoting such 'civil society in the service of others' by providing both monetary support and mentorship opportunities (Chan and Chan 2017, pp. 143–145). Social enterprises therefore represent a less antagonistic and less aggressive form of civil society, with these organizations playing an increasingly crucial role in social service delivery.

There are therefore two facets to Hong Kong's civil society. While politically motivated civil society organizations such as the Yellow Umbrella Movement are increasingly posing challenges to Hong Kong's developmental state by taking on a more aggressive and antagonistic stance, socially motivated civil society organizations such as social enterprises tend to operate in partnership with government agencies in enhancing social capital and providing social services (Chan and Chan 2017).

In both instances, there are significant implications for Hong Kong's developmental state. While social enterprises contribute to the aims and goals of the developmental state by assisting in the provision of social and public services and thereby alleviating potential fiscal constraints arising from the state's need to provide such services, protests and acts of civil disobedience tend to work against the developmental state by disrupting economic activities for political reasons and motivations. Hence in contrast to Singapore, the role of Hong Kong's civil society in its developmental state is much more complex.

While there are instances whereby civil society organizations have contributed to the government's social policy objectives, the overall picture is that of growing conflict amid antagonistic state–civil society relations (Chan and Chan 2017). More than simply a contest for political autonomy, such increasingly antagonistic relations reflect deeper underlying shifts in the government's basis for political legitimacy. More than simply a decline in performance legitimacy due to perceived policy failures, there has been a more fundamental shift from economically determined performance legitimacy towards notions of political determinism or social compact (Scott 2007, Chan and Chan 2017, Wong and Chan 2017).

Performance legitimacy

Like other developmental states, the Hong Kong state derives political legitimacy from its ability to 'perform' in the realm of economic policy, i.e. to consistently deliver high levels of economic growth. The origins of Hong

Kong's emphasis on performance legitimacy began from its colonial era, with the combination of materialistic and utilitarian cultural milieux and the colonial government's ability to deliver economic growth serving to reinforce an instrumental view of democracy that emphasized the attainment of pragmatic goals rather than citizen rights (Lau 1984, Ngok 2011, pp. 686–687, 2016). As Sing (1996, p. 346) has noted:

> Unlike many authoritarian governments elsewhere in the third world, Hong Kong's rulers were neither particularly inept or inherently corrupt, and their administration was not at all closely and irredeemably identified with economic failure. On the contrary, a good economic record and a gradually expanding welfare programme had in time come to generate a moderate degree of legitimacy for what remained a top-down, paternalistic administration.

At a more fundamental level, Hong Kong's unique political circumstances also form the basis for its political legitimacy. While its lack of universal suffrage prevents the formation of 'input democracy' and its concomitant sources of process legitimacy, Hong Kong's relatively transparent political institutions and the presence of extensive civil liberties make it an 'output democracy' that derives its political legitimacy from the state's ability to achieve results that are desired by the citizenry (Pierre et al. 2011, MacCarthaigh et al. 2016).

Furthermore, performance legitimacy in Hong Kong differs from Singapore in one important way. While the governments of both cities derive political legitimacy from their ability to consistently deliver high levels of economic growth, some element of the Hong Kong colonial government's performance legitimacy also derives from its willingness and ability to maintain high levels of civil liberties. This differs from many Asian developmental states, where the tendency is to restrict, rather than expand, civil liberties. As Sing (1996, p. 346) argues, the colonial government attained its political legitimacy 'by satisfying public demands for stability, prosperity and civil liberties'.

However, much of this would change after the handover, with the Hong Kong government, beginning with the Tung administration, rapidly losing legitimacy, giving rise to mass protests and civil unrest (Sing 2006, Scott 2007, Ngok 2011). While this loss in legitimacy can partly be attributed to the civil service's inability to respond to rising expectations among citizens, especially in terms of managing crises such as the 1997 Asian Financial Crisis or the 2003 SARS outbreak, defects in constitutional design, institutional constraints and fiscal limitations were also to blame (Scott 2000, pp. 33–36, Cheung 2004, p. 20).

For instance, the Basic Law that serves as the constitution for post-handover Hong Kong consolidated power in a political executive that is appointed by the developmental elite, at the same time setting up a relatively weak democratically elected legislature (Scott 2000, p. 30). Coupled with increasing politicization and the growing role of left-leaning democrats, these institutional deficiencies resulted in a 'disarticulation' of Hong Kong's political system, which in turn resulted in a decline in the government's legitimacy (Scott 2000).

Furthermore, Scott (1993) argues that post-handover adaptations to Hong Kong's political institutions did not sufficiently possess the legal validity, moral justifiability and public consent needed to retain output legitimacy. In other words, Hong Kong experienced a decline in its performance legitimacy after the handover, with Beijing's efforts to adapt or reform the territory's political institutions seen as a key catalyst for this decline in legitimacy.

Hence unlike the Singaporean state, which has over the years engaged in 'ideological work' with the aim of maintaining its performance legitimacy (Tan 2008, 2012), Hong Kong's post-handover efforts to reform or adapt its political institutions, ostensibly to bolster state authority or political legitimacy, may have paradoxically resulted in a decline in its performance legitimacy (Scott 1993, 2000, 2007, 2007, Sing 2008).

Aside from institutional deficiencies or policy failures, the erosion of performance legitimacy in Hong Kong has also been associated with broader social, political and economic shifts that emphasized post-materialist values as well as a less instrumental view of democracy that goes against the grain of Hong Kong's existing neo-liberal and economically driven model of governance (Ngok 2011). While these shifts are no doubt important, they are exogenous to the internal dynamics of Hong Kong's developmental state and hence will not factor heavily in this book's analysis.

Conclusion

This chapter has provided a comprehensive overview of Hong Kong's role and identity as a developmental state. Despite its reputation as one of the world's freest economies and a proponent of laissez-faire economic governing principles, there is more state intervention and centralization in Hong Kong's economic development than meets the eye. As the discussions in this chapter have shown, Hong Kong possesses all of the components of an archetypal developmental state, although variances exist within some of these components.

Like most developmental states, a developmental elite that comprises both public and private interests drives economic development in Hong Kong, with the implementation of development-oriented policy initiatives led by a pilot agency, in this case the Commerce and Economic Development Bureau. However, and like Singapore, the growing diversity and complexity of Hong Kong's economy has given rise to more specialized agencies that function as pilot agencies for specific industries and sectors. These include the Innovation and Technology Bureau for Hong Kong's knowledge-based economy, and the Services and the Treasury Bureau for its financial services sector.

More importantly, the roles and functions of the developmental elite and pilot agencies are guided by developmental state ideological constructs. For instance, the Hong Kong government governs on the basis of performance legitimacy, drawing political trust and support on the basis of its ability to deliver strong economic growth and consistent improvements to quality of life. However, and as I have discussed above, there has been a gradual degradation of this performance legitimacy, with growing politicization in the population giving rise to demands for political reform, often expressed through public protests.

This decay in performance legitimacy is somewhat related to the second ideological basis of Hong Kong's developmental state: embedded autonomy. While the practice of embedded autonomy had allowed Hong Kong's pilot agencies and policymakers to straddle a fine line between policy autonomy and close relations with economic and societal interests, the growing political clout of the business elite, often exercised through institutionalized means such as LegCo or the Chief Executive elections committee, has combined with Hong Kong's lack of universal suffrage to give rise to the view that the government may be more 'embedded' than 'autonomous'.

This growing perception of business capture, with the government seen as more representative of business interests rather than societal interests, is seen to have contributed to Hong Kong's declining performance legitimacy (Cheung 2004, Chan and Chan 2017, Fong 2017). Such ideological shifts have also affected the Hong Kong government's relations with non-state economic interests and civil society. With regard to non-state economic interests, an emphasis on an outcome-driven consensus between policy and business elites, rather than the procedural consensus that is typical of most democratic institutions, has further aligned political and business interests.

However, and as I have discussed above, this emphasis on outcome over procedural consent may have sparked public protests among quarters of Hong Kong society that feel left out of the government's political and policy processes (Cheng 2014, Hui and Lau 2015, Kaeding 2017, Lam and Cooper 2017). Given its desire to maintain socio-political stability and conduciveness of its business environment, the Hong Kong government has responded to such protests by ramping up its policing and enforcement efforts. This declining tolerance for civil protest has ironically spilled over onto other civil society organizations as well, despite Hong Kong's history of strong civil liberties.

It is now clear that despite its historical adherence to the developmental state model, economic governance and development in Hong Kong is rapidly shifting. While the developmental state model continues to hold sway among both policymakers and business elites, growing politicization and pressures for political reform have resulted in the decay of certain components of Hong Kong's developmental state. In both Hong Kong and Singapore, socio-political realities are stretching and challenging the conceptual boundaries of the developmental state approach. This suggests a need for a conceptual rethink or theoretical adjustment of the developmental state model. I attempt to address this in Chapter 6.

Aside from these socio-political realities, both Hong Kong and Singapore are facing deeper shifts in their economies. Specifically, the emergence of a knowledge-based and digital economy has given rise to a fundamental digital transformation, with both cities striving to become 'smart cities'. This digital transformation poses significant political-economic implications for both cities, giving rise to a need for both governments to reconfigure the institutional and ideological foundations of their developmental state approaches to economic governance.

I will discuss the digital transformation of Hong Kong and Singapore into leading smart cities in the next chapter. I will then address the implications of this digital transformation on the developmental state model in Chapter 6, with an emphasis on the experiences of Hong Kong and Singapore.

Note

1 Hong Kong occupies a land area of 1,105.7 square kilometres and has a population of approximately 7.3 million.

References

Chan, E. and Chan, J., 2017. Hong Kong 2007–2017: a backlash in civil society. *Asia Pacific Journal of Public Administration*, 39 (2), 135–152.

Cheng, J., 2016. Business-government nexus: the special case of Hong Kong. *Asian Education and Development Studies*, 5 (4), 454–467.

Cheng, J.Y.S., 2014. *New Trends of Political Participation in Hong Kong*. Hong Kong: City University of HK Press.

Cheung, A.B.L., 2004. Strong executive, weak policy capacity: The changing environment of policy-making in Hong Kong. *Asian Journal of Political Science*, 12 (1), 1–30.

Cheung, A.B.L., 2008. The story of two administrative states: state capacity in Hong Kong and Singapore. *The Pacific Review*, 21 (2), 121–145.

Cheung, T., 2017. 'Beijing will take action if city fails to enact national security law' [online]. *South China Morning Post*. Available from: http://www.scmp.com/news/hong-kong/politics/article/2120319/beijing-will-take-action-if-hong-kong-fails-enact-national [Accessed 17 Nov 2017].

Commerce and Economic Development Bureau, 2011a. Commerce and Economic Development Bureau – Mission [online]. *Government of the Hong Kong Special Administrative Region*. Available from: http://www.cedb.gov.hk/about/mission.htm [Accessed 18 Oct 2017].

Commerce and Economic Development Bureau, 2011b. Commerce and Economic Development Bureau – Home [online]. *Government of the Hong Kong Special Administrative Region*. Available from: http://www.cedb.gov.hk/about/index.htm [Accessed 18 Oct 2017].

Commerce, Industry and Tourism Branch, 2016. *Policy Initiatives of Commerce, Industry and Tourism Branch*. Hong Kong: Government of the Hong Kong Special Administrative Region.

Communications and Creative Industries Branch, 2017. *Policy Initiatives of Communications and Creative Industries Branch*. Hong Kong: Government of the Hong Kong Special Administrative Region.

Cooper, T.L. and Lui, T.L., 1990. Democracy and the Administrative State: The Case of Hong Kong. *Public Administration Review*, 50 (3), 332–344.

Economist Intelligence Unit, 2016. *Democracy Index 2016*. London, UK: Economist Intelligence Unit.

Enright, M., Scott, E., and Dodwell, D., 1997. *The Hong Kong Advantage*. 1st ed. Oxford: Oxford University Press.

Financial Services and the Treasury Bureau, 2003. Financial Services Branch – About Us [online]. *Government of the Hong Kong Special Administrative Region*. Available from: http://www.fstb.gov.hk/fsb/aboutus/welcome/index.htm [Accessed 19 Oct 2017].

Financial Services and the Treasury Bureau, 2013. Financial Services and the Treasury Bureau : Home [online]. *Government of the Hong Kong Special Administrative Region*. Available from: http://www.fstb.gov.hk/en/index.htm [Accessed 19 Oct 2017].

Fong, B., 2017. In-between liberal authoritarianism and electoral authoritarianism: Hong Kong's democratization under Chinese sovereignty, 1997–2016. *Democratization*, 24 (4), 724–750.

Fong, B.C.H., 2014. The Partnership between the Chinese Government and Hong Kong's Capitalist Class: Implications for HKSAR Governance, 1997–2012. *The China Quarterly*, 217, 195–220.

Glassburner, B. and Riedel, J., 1972. Government in the Economy of Hong Kong. *Economic Record*, 48 (1), 58–75.

Goodstadt, L.F., 2000. China and the Selection of Hong Kong's Post-Colonial Political Elite. *The China Quarterly*, 163, 721–741.

Goodstadt, L.F., 2005. *Uneasy Partners: The Conflict Between Public Interest and Private Profit in Hong Kong*. Hong Kong: Hong Kong University Press.

Government of Hong Kong Special Administrative Region, 2014. *Policy Address 2014*. Hong Kong: Government of the Hong Kong Special Administrative Region.

Harris, P.B., 1978. *Hong Kong: A Study in Bureaucratic Politics*. Hong Kong: Macmillan.

Ho, Y.-P., 2016. *Trade, Industrial Restructuring and Development in Hong Kong*. London: Macmillan.

Hong Kong Trade Development Council, 2015. *Economic and Trade Information on Hong Kong*. Hong Kong.

Howlett, M. and Lejano, R.P., 2013. Tales From the Crypt: The Rise and Fall (and Rebirth?) of Policy Design. *Administration & Society*, 45 (3), 357–381.

Howlett, M., Mukherjee, I., and Woo, J.J., 2015. From Tools to Toolkits in Policy Design Studies: The New Design Orientation and Policy Formulation Research. *Policy and Politics*, 43 (2), 291–311.

Hui, P.-K. and Lau, K.-C., 2015. 'Living in truth' versus realpolitik: limitations and potentials of the Umbrella Movement. *Inter-Asia Cultural Studies*, 16 (3), 348–366.

IMD, 2017. *World Competitiveness Yearbook 2017*. Lausanne, Switzerland: IMD.

Innovation and Technology Bureau, 2015. Innovation and Technology Bureau: Our Role [online]. *Government of the Hong Kong Special Administrative Region*. Available from: http://www.itb.gov.hk/en/about_us/role/ [Accessed 19 Oct 2017].

Jao, Y.C., 1997. *Hong Kong as an International Financial Centre: Evolution, Prospects and Policies.* Hong Kong: City University of Hong Kong Press.

Kaeding, M.P., 2017. The Rise of 'Localism' in Hong Kong. *Journal of Democracy*, 28 (1), 157–171.

Lam, J., 2017. Perception of Hong Kong press freedom improves slightly. *South China Morning Post*, 6 Apr.

Lam, W. and Cooper, L., 2017. *Citizenship, Identity and Social Movements in the New Hong Kong: Localism after the Umbrella Movement.* London: Routledge.

Lau, S. and Liu, Z., 1984. *Society and Politics in Hong Kong.* Chinese University Press.

Lau, S.-K., 1984. *Society and Politics in Hong Kong.* Hong Kong; New York: Palgrave Macmillan.

Lee, E.W.Y., 1998. The political economy of public sector reform in Hong Kong: The case of a colonial-developmental state, 64 (4), 625–641.

Lee, E.W.Y., 1999. Governing Post-Colonial Hong Kong: Institutional Incongruity, Governance Crisis, and Authoritarianism. *Asian Survey*, 39 (6), 940–959.

Lee, E.W.Y., 2005. The Politics of Welfare Developmentalism in Hong Kong. *In*: H.J. Kwon, ed. *Transforming the Developmental Welfare State in East Asia.* Palgrave Macmillan, London, 118–139.

Leung, J.Y.H., 1990. Functional Representation in Hong Kong: Institutionalization and Legitimization of the Business and Professional Elites. *Asian Journal of Public Administration*, 12 (2), 143–175.

Li, K.W., 2012. *Economic Freedom: Lessons of Hong Kong.* 1st ed. Singapore: World Scientific Publishing Company.

Lim, J., 2017. What you need to know about the Hong Kong Chief Executive Election [online]. *The Straits Times.* Available from: http://www.straitstimes.com/asia/east-asia/what-you-need-to-know-about-the-hong-kong-chief-executive-election [Accessed 11 Nov 2017].

Lo, S.-H., 2001. Citizenship and Participation in Hong Kong. *Citizenship Studies*, 5 (2), 127–142.

Lo, S.S., 2008. *The Dynamics of Beijing-Hong Kong Relations: A Model for Taiwan?* Hong Kong: Hong Kong University Press.

Loh, C., 2006. *Functional Constituencies: A Unique Feature of the Hong Kong Legislative Council.* Hong Kong: Hong Kong University Press.

Loh, C. and Cullen, R., 2005. Political Reform in Hong Kong: the Principal Officials Accountability System. The first year (2002–2003). *Journal of Contemporary China*, 14 (42), 153–176.

Lui, T.-L. and Chiu, S., 1993. Industrial Restructuring and Labour-Market Adjustment under Positive Noninterventionism: The Case of Hong Kong. *Environment and Planning A*, 25 (1), 63–79.

Ma, N., 2007. *Political Development in Hong Kong: State, Political Society, and Civil Society.* Hong Kong: Hong Kong University Press.

Ma, N., 2008. Civil Society and Democratization in Hong Kong: Paradox and Duality. *Taiwan Journal of Democray*, 4 (2), 155–175.

MacCarthaigh, M., Painter, M., and Yee, W.-H., 2016. Managing for Legitimacy: Agency Governance in Its 'Deep' Constitutional Context. *Public Administration Review*, 76 (3), 496–506.

Mushkat, M. and Mushkat, R., 2016. The Political Economy of Constitutional Incrementalism in Hong Kong. *Northwestern Interdisciplinary Law Review*, 9, 1–46.

Ngo, T.-W., ed., 1999. *Hong Kong's History: State and Society Under Colonial Rule.* London; New York: Routledge.

Ngo, T.-W., 2000. Changing Government–Business Relations and the Governance of Hong Kong. *In*: R. Ash, P. Ferdinand, B. Hook and R. Porter, eds. *Hong Kong in Transition*. London: Palgrave Macmillan, 26–41.

Ngok, M., 2011. Value Changes and Legitimacy Crisis in Post-industrial Hong Kong. *Asian Survey*, 51 (4), 683–712.

Ngok, M., 2016. The Making of a Corporatist State in Hong Kong: The Road to Sectoral Intervention. *Journal of Contemporary Asia*, 46 (2), 247–266.

Ngok, M., 2017. The China Factor in Hong Kong Elections: 1991 to 2016. *China Perspectives*, (3), 17.

Ortmann, S., 2014. *Beijing's growing influence over Hong Kong. East Asia Forum.*

Painter, M., 2005. Transforming the Administrative State: Reform in Hong Kong and the Future of the Developmental State. *Public Administration Review*, 65 (3), 335–346.

Painter, M. and Yee, W.-H., 2012. Agencies and policy in an administrative state: The case of Hong Kong. *Policy and Society*, 31 (3), 223–235.

Pierre, J., Røiseland, A., and Gustavsen, A., 2011. *Legitimacy by Performance in Democratic Systems? Preparing for Empirical Analysis.*

Preston, P.W., 2016. *The Politics of China–Hong Kong Relations: Living with Distant Masters*. Cheltenham, UK: Edward Elgar Publishing.

Reed, H.C., 1980. The Ascent of Tokyo as an International Financial Center. *Journal of International Business Studies*, 11 (3), 19–35.

Reporters Without Borders, 2017. *2017 World Press Freedom Index*. Paris, France: Reporters Without Borders.

Russolillo, S., 2017. 20 Years After Handover, China Looms Ever Larger Over Hong Kong Markets. *Wall Street Journal*, 29 Jun.

Schenk, C.R., 2001. Hong Kong as an International Financial Centre: Emergence and development 1945–1960. New York: Routledge.

Schenk, C.R., 2002. Banks and the emergence of Hong Kong as an international financial center. *Journal of International Financial Markets, Institutions and Money*, 12 (4–5), 321–340.

Schwab, K., 2017. *Global Competitiveness Report 2016–2017*. Geneva, Switzerland: World Economic Forum.

Scott, I., 1993. Legitimacy and its discontents: Hong Kong and the reversion to Chinese sovereignty. *Asian Journal of Political Science*, 1 (1), 55–75.

Scott, I., 2000. The Disarticulation of Hong Kong's Post-Handover Political System. *The China Journal*, (43), 29–53.

Scott, I., 2007. Legitimacy, Governance and Public Policy in Post-Handover Hong Kong. *Asia Pacific Journal of Public Administration*, 29 (1), 29–49.

Sing, M., 1996. Democratization and economic development: The anomalous case of Hong Kong. *Democratization*, 3 (3), 343–359.

Sing, M., 2006. The Legitimacy Problem and Democratic Reform in Hong Kong. *Journal of Contemporary China*, 15 (48), 517–532.

Sing, M., 2008. *Politics and Government in Hong Kong: Crisis Under Chinese Sovereignty*. London: Routledge.

Tan, K.P., 2008. Meritocracy and Elitism in a Global City: Ideological Shifts in Singapore. *International Political Science Review / Revue internationale de science politique*, 29 (1), 7–27.

Tan, K.P., 2012. The Ideology of Pragmatism: Neo-liberal Globalisation and Political Authoritarianism in Singapore. *Journal of Contemporary Asia*, 42 (1), 67–92.

Tang, J.T.H., 1999. Business as usual: The dynamics of government-business relations in the Hong Kong special administrative region. *Journal of Contemporary China*, 8 (21), 275–295.

The Economist, 2017. How Hong Kong picks its chief executives [online]. *The Economist*. Available from: https://www.economist.com/blogs/economist-explains/2017/03/economist-explains-19 [Accessed 9 June 2017].

Topping, S., 2013. Interview.

Tsang, D., 2006. *Big Market, Small Government*. Hong Kong: The Government of Hong Kong Special Administrative Region, Press Release.

Tsang, D., 2013. Interview.

Tsui-Auch, L.S., 1998. Has the Hong Kong Model Worked? Industrial Policy in Retrospect and Prospect. *Development and Change*, 29 (1), 55–79.

Wissink, B., Koh, S.Y., and Forrest, R., 2017. Tycoon City: Political Economy, Real Estate and the Super-Rich in Hong Kong. *In*: R. Forrest, S.Y. Koh and B. Wissink, eds. *Cities and the Super-Rich*. Palgrave Macmillan, New York, 229–252.

Wong, C., 2016. What Exactly Is Hong Kong's Legislative Council? [online]. *The Diplomat*. Available from: https://thediplomat.com/2016/09/what-exactly-is-hong-kongs-legislative-council/ [Accessed 6 Nov 2017].

Wong, M.Y.H., 2017. *Comparative Hong Kong Politics*. Singapore: Palgrave.

Wong, Y.C. and Chan, J.K.H., 2017. Civil disobedience movements in Hong Kong: a civil society perspective. *Asian Education and Development Studies*, 6 (4), 312–332.

Woo, J.J., 2015. Beyond the Neoliberal orthodoxy: Alternative financial policy regimes in Asia's financial centres. *Critical Policy Studies*, 9 (3), 297–316.

Woo, J.J., 2016. *Business and Politics in Asia's Key Financial Centres – Hong Kong, Singapore and Shanghai*. 1st ed. Singapore: Springer.

World Bank Group, 2017. *Doing Business 2017: Equal Opportunity for All*. Washington, D.C.: World Bank.

5 Becoming smart cities

According to Jessop (2016, pp. 27–28), the Asian Financial Crisis of 1997 had prompted a search among leading Asian developmental states for alternative economic and political strategies that could be employed to recalibrate the developmental state approach to economic development, with two main 'exit strategies' (from the hitherto export-oriented economic growth) identified: a knowledge-based economy and neoliberal financialization.

While financialization had, from the 1970s, driven Hong Kong's and Singapore's transformation into leading global financial centres (Carroll and Jarvis 2014, Woo 2016a, 2017a), a subsequent shift towards a knowledge-based economy has given rise to a digital transformation that has seen Hong Kong and Singapore vying to become leading smart cities that are capable of applying the latest digital and data technologies to their policy processes and industrial development.

Yet this digital transformation does not in any way supplant the earlier financial transformation of these two cities. Rather, there are key points of complementarity and intersections between the knowledge-based economy and financialization, with policymakers increasingly cognizant of the economic and technological possibilities associated with the emergence of a 'smart financial centre' (Menon 2015). Such complementarity between technology and finance alludes to a deeper point about the economic opportunities associated with the digital economy.

Indeed, both governments' efforts to transform their cities into smart cities are fundamentally rooted in a desire to strengthen the economy, whether by enhancing urban efficiency, stimulating innovation and productivity, or developing new digital industries such as data analytics or the Internet of things (Calder 2016, SPRING Singapore 2016, Watts and Purnell 2016, Woodhouse 2016, Chow 2017). This is evident in Singapore's Smart Nation initiative, as well as the nascent 'Smart Hong Kong' plan (Balakrishnan 2016, Office of the Government Chief Information Officer 2016a, Smart Nation Programme Office 2017).

Hence beneath the veneer of the smart city lies the developmental state model that has thus far driven economic development in both Hong Kong and Singapore, albeit with some modifications. This chapter will provide a broad overview of the two cities' smart city strategies, focusing in particular on the developmental foundations of these strategies. By establishing the two cities' smart city strategies within the context of the developmental state model, this chapter provides the empirical basis for Chapter 6, which will discuss the evolving conceptual bases of the 'smart developmental state'.

I will begin with a broad introduction to smart cities, providing a review of existing understandings of what constitutes a smart city and its impacts on policy and politics. Having established a clear and theoretically informed understanding of the smart city, I will then discuss the strategies and initiatives that underpin Singapore's smart city transformation, followed by a similar discussion on Hong Kong.

Smart cities

Both as concept and in practice, smart cities exist at the intersection of technology and urban complexity. More specifically, much of our current understanding of smart cities is predicated upon the possibility of using advanced ICT or data technology to address highly complex, and even intractable, urban policy problems. Fundamental to the concept of a smart city, therefore, is the assumption that complex, 'wicked' problems, especially urban transport, crime, healthcare, and education, among others, can be addressed through the use of data analytics and sensors that allow for more effective information collection (Batty 2013, Kitchin 2014, Perera et al. 2014, Goodspeed 2015, Stimmel 2015).

This notion of a smart city as a source of policy solutions has become increasingly prominent over the past decade, with cities across the world seeking to utilize data analytics to address urban and municipal issues (Batty 2013, Kitchin 2014, Townsend 2014, Goodspeed 2015, Stimmel 2015). This often involves the use of data-sharing platforms (Goldsmith and Crawford 2014, Misuraca et al. 2014, Noveck 2015), 'city dashboards' (Kitchin and McArdle 2016, Dameri 2017), as well as networks of sensors and digitally augmented appliances or objects, also known as the 'Internet of things' (Filipponi et al. 2010, Bakıcı *et al.* 2012, Gubbi et al. 2013, Perera et al. 2014, Zanella et al. 2014).

It is also important that the current discourse on smart cities did not emerge in a conceptual vacuum. Rather, it is built upon an existing body of work on the use of technological innovations, particularly advanced ICT, to address policy issues. This began with the notion of e-government, which has been defined by West (2004, p. 16) as the 'delivery of government information and services online through the Internet or other digital means'. Indeed, much of the e-government literature focuses on the delivery of public services through online mechanisms and platforms (Norris and Reddick 2013, Meijer and Bolívar 2016).

However, the emphasis on public service delivery also means that policy changes associated with e-government tend to be incremental in nature, with limited scope for citizen interaction or inputs (Norris and Reddick 2013, Meijer and Bolívar 2016). Indeed, West (2004, p. 24) has found that the implementation of e-government initiatives does not increase public trust or confidence in the government. While there have in some cases been some degree of systems integration in e-government, such efforts tend to retain a service delivery and functionality perspective by emphasizing a 'one-stop shopping' platform for citizens (Layne and Lee 2001).

However, growing demands by citizens to participate in policy and political processes would give rise to a broad systemic shift from 'government' to 'governance' among policy scholars and practitioners (Rhodes 1996, 1997, Weiss 2000, Newman et al. 2004, Ansell and Gash 2008, Duit and Galaz 2008, Colebatch 2009, Duit et al. 2010, Fukuyama 2013). This prompted the emergence of an 'e-governance' literature that seeks to incorporate notions of public participation and democratic processes (Chadwick 2003, Dawes 2008). What has emerged is a more inclusive understanding of how technology can be used to augment a government's policy processes.

For instance, Dawes (2008) defines e-governance as the 'use of information and communication technologies (ICTs) to support public services, government administration, democratic processes, and relationships among citizens, civil society, the private sector, and the state'. Hence aside from enhancing public service delivery, e-governance emphasizes the potential for greater public participation in governments' policy processes, whether through online consultations, involvement of users in the design and delivery of public services, or greater transparency and open-source collaboration within and among public organizations (Chadwick 2003).

Marche and McNiven (2003, p. 75) provide a concise explanation of this difference between e-government and e-governance by stating that:

> e-government is the provision of routine government information and transactions using electronic means, most notably those using Internet technologies, whether delivered at home, at work, or through public kiosks. E-governance is a technology-mediated relationship between citizens and their governments from the perspective of potential electronic deliberation over civic communication, over policy evolution, and in democratic expressions of citizen will.

Furthermore, Marche and McNiven have also associated e-government with policy implementation and e-governance with policy formulation and decision-making, observing that '[g]overnance stresses the ways in which decisions are made, while government stresses the way in which these decisions are carried out' (Marche and McNiven 2003, p. 75). In short, e-governance presents a shift towards greater citizen-centrism and participatory decision-making, from e-government's focus on public service delivery and policy implementation.

Yet despite its broader and more inclusive approach, others have noted that e-governance has made limited progress in enhancing democracy or facilitating institutional reform (Dawes 2008). Even in instances where governments are in favour of involving other actors and stakeholders in their policy decisions, proponents of e-governance have faced challenges in identifying or designing appropriate models for public–private partnership (Van der Meer and Van Winden 2003).

These limitations are due in part to e-governance's conceptual weaknesses and in part to the technological limitations that proponents of e-governance faced. The emergence of new technological innovations such as data analytics, machine learning, artificial intelligence and the Internet of things have since brought forth a shift from e-governance to 'smart' governance. However, much of this later literature is strongly rooted in the urban context, specifically smart cities.

This notion of a smart city as a source of policy solutions has become increasingly prominent over the past decade, with cities across the world seeking to utilize data analytics to address urban and municipal issues (Batty 2013, Kitchin 2014, Townsend 2014, Goodspeed 2015, Stimmel 2015). This often involves the use of data-sharing platforms (Goldsmith and Crawford 2014, Misuraca et al. 2014, Noveck 2015), 'city dashboards' (Kitchin and McArdle 2016, Dameri 2017), as well as networks of sensors and the Internet of things (Filipponi et al. 2010, Bakıcı *et al.* 2012, Gubbi et al. 2013, Perera et al. 2014, Zanella et al. 2014).

Yet despite this growing currency among policymakers, particularly in city or local-level governments, definitions of what exactly constitutes a smart city remain ambiguous (Cocchia 2014). Broadly speaking, current understandings of smart cities tend to focus on one of two directions (World Bank Group 2017):

- Efficient delivery of public services through the use of 'smart' technologies such as sensors, interconnected devices and data analytics
- The cultivation of better citizen–government relationships through technologically enabled citizen consultation and interactions as well as the use of open government data to co-create solutions

In both instances, what separates smart cities from e-governance or e-government is the pervasive use of sensors and advanced data collection methods to both enhance public service delivery and facilitate government–citizen relations. There are therefore technological, governmental and relational aspects to smart cities. This is elucidated in the work of Nam and Pardo (2011), who distinguish between the technological, human and institutional dimensions of a smart city.

Hollands (2008, pp. 307–310) provides a more comprehensive definition by arguing that a smart city comprises four key elements:

- The utilization of networked infrastructure to improve economic and political outcomes, as well as enable socio-cultural and urban development

- An underlying emphasis on business-led urban development, requiring an entrepreneurial, rather than managerial, approach to governance
- The presence of high-tech and creative industries such as digital media or arts and culture
- A concern with both social and environmental sustainability

In any case, a common denominator that underpins all these definitions of the smart city is the application of advanced communications and digital technologies to the resolution of urban or municipal policy issues. At the heart of such efforts is the smart city's ICT infrastructure. As Hollands has noted, ICTs undergird all the various networks that make up the smart city, whether transport, business services, or housing and other public services, and therefore 'lie at the core of the smart city idea' (Hollands 2008, p. 307).

In other words, having an efficient and reliable ICT infrastructure allows governments to establish the various inter-linked networks that make up the smart city. This is especially the case with the Internet, which allows for the online transactions that underpin much of a smart city's commercial and financial activities (Woo 2017a). However, smart city technology extends beyond ICT, which arguably forms the crux of e-government and e-governance as well. Rather, smart cities feature an extensive array of sensors, along with the computational capacity to sort, store, and process the data that is collected by these sensors.

In terms of hardware, smart cities are characterized by the pervasive use of sensors, often embedded within physical infrastructure and digital devices (Filipponi et al. 2010, Resch et al. 2012, Greco and Bencardino 2014, Ratti and Claudel 2016). This is complemented by the application of data analytics to process, visualize, and utilize the information and data that is collected by these sensors (Batty 2013, Kitchin 2014, Townsend 2014, Hashem et al. 2016). While such data is often owned and used by either public agencies or corporate entities, smart cities are also increasingly characterized by the presence of open data platforms that allow free public access to data, often for the purpose of encouraging innovation and co-creation of solutions among citizens (Janssen et al. 2012, Chan 2013, Goldsmith and Crawford 2014, Misuraca et al. 2014, Janssen et al. 2017).

More importantly, these technological innovations have fundamentally transformed urban life, especially with regard to the ways that citizens, businesses and governments interact with each other (Goldsmith and Crawford 2014, Townsend 2014, Ratti and Claudel 2016). Hence, and unlike its conceptual forebears, smart cities are not simply about the building of technological infrastructure and hardware, or the application of ICT to public service delivery. Rather, the pervasive use of sensors, application of advanced data collection and processing technologies, and the growing role of citizens and businesses in urban and industrial development suggest a far deeper urban and economic transformation than was the case with e-government or e-governance.

Such deep shifts in the socio-economic fabric of many smart cities have also often been accompanied by a sea change in governments' approach to urban policy and governance (Nam and Pardo 2011, Meijer and Bolívar 2016, Woo 2017b). For instance, the application of data analytics and 'senseable' technologies to policymaking has led to the emergence of the 'senseable' or 'responsive' city that features greater responsiveness in collecting policy feedback and addressing policy problems (Resch et al. 2012, Goldsmith and Crawford 2014, Greco and Bencardino 2014, Perera et al. 2014). This is particularly evident in the realm of urban policy, with municipal feedback applications such as the 311 app or Singapore's OneServices app providing policymakers with access to real-time citizen feedback.

More importantly, this emphasis on 'responsiveness' or 'sensing' places a closer interest on citizens and communities, with new digital tools and platforms facilitating civic engagement and policy collaboration with industry and societal actors (Bakıcı *et al.* 2012, Goldsmith and Crawford 2014, 2014, Townsend 2014). As Meijer and Bolivar point out, 'smart city governance is about crafting new forms of human collaboration through the use of ICTs to obtain better outcomes and more open governance processes' (Meijer and Bolívar 2016). Indeed, ICT has been seen as an enabling factor for smart city governance, by facilitating information sharing and integration among public agencies and citizens (Pereira et al. 2017).

Indeed, it is this focus on open collaboration and civic engagement that separates smart cities from e-government. While proponents of e-government have tended to take a state-centric and top-down approach to encouraging the use of advanced ICT by public agencies, smart cities emphasize instead public–private collaboration and policy co-creation, often through data sharing. Furthermore, there is an inherent urban-spatial aspect to smart city governance. As Roche (2014) has noted, a smart city is characterized by its 'ability to produce favorable conditions to get urban operators (citizens, organizations, private companies, etc.) actively involved into socio-spatial innovation dynamics'.

This collaborative approach also often suggests a certain extent of disruption in policy processes, with policy change often transformational and unpredictable, whereas e-government has been associated with incremental changes in policy processes and outcomes (Norris and Reddick 2013). Beyond policy change, smart cities have also been associated with a tendency for transformative changes in the overall urban governance process itself, often giving rise to administrative reform (Meijer and Bolívar 2016, Woo 2017b). In contrast, e-government is not typically seen as an instrument of administrative reform (Kraemer and King 2006), nor is it likely to give rise to any substantial shifts in governance processes (Torres, Pina, and Royo 2005).

Even in instances where e-government initiatives have given rise to administrative reform, such reforms tend to emphasize administrative decentralization and/or greater government oversight of key policy functions and activities (Ma et al. 2005). Indeed, e-government initiatives tend to be seen as an extension of government, being 'non-interactive and non-deliberative' and often associated with new public management (NPM) reforms (Schedler and Scharf 2001, Torres, Pina, and Acerete 2005, Torres, Pina, and Royo 2005). In emphasizing public–private collaboration and policy co-creation, smart cities represent a clear shift in public administration style, from the delivery-oriented NPM to a more collaborative, inclusive and citizen-centric style of public administration (Paskaleva 2011, Lee and Lee 2014, Dameri and Ricciardi 2017, Paskaleva et al. 2018).

In sum, the emergence of smart cities has given rise to new modalities of policy and governance. Specifically, smart city governance tends to take a more integrated approach that emphasizes responsiveness and transparency of a city's policy processes, rather than simply efficiency in public service delivery (Gil-Garcia 2012, Goldsmith and Crawford 2014, Noveck 2015, Meijer and Bolívar 2016). This emphasis on collaboration and responsiveness makes smart city governance conceptually distinct from e-government, which represents an extension of NPM approaches that emphasize public service efficiency and stronger governmental oversight of policy processes and outcomes.

As discussions below will also show, such shifts in policy and governance have also prompted broader administrative reforms, such as the creation of new institutions to foster public–private collaboration and lead the overall digitization of government. While such digitally augmented transformations in policy and governance processes have been well documented in the existing literature, much less has been said about the place and role of the developmental state amid smart city transformations. Given the rapid digitization of key Asian developmental states such as Hong Kong, Singapore, South Korea, and, to some extent, China, there is a need to address this gap in the literature.

While it has been argued that the developmental state has declined with the emergence of a 'networked state', these arguments begrudgingly acknowledge that key concepts and components of the developmental state remain relevant within these 'networked states' (Larson and Park 2014). Furthermore, much of the current discourse on smart cities has retained a strong emphasis on economic development, particularly the ways in which smart cities can boost economic growth (Ferguson 2013, Spencer 2015, Calder 2016, Shichiyakh et al. 2016). Certainly, economic development remains a key concern for policymakers in emerging smart cities such as Hong Kong, Singapore and Seoul.

In other words, the emergence of smart cities has not come at the detriment of the developmental state model. As I will discuss in the next chapter, emerging smart cities, particularly those situated in East Asia, have retained the key elements and components of the developmental states, albeit with some adaptations and modifications. Before proceeding to discuss these 'smart' adaptations to the developmental state model and their theoretical implications, I will first provide a broad overview of the smart cities of Singapore and Hong Kong.

Singapore

While Hong Kong and Singapore have expressed their ambition and desire to become smart cities, there is a broad consensus that Singapore's efforts have yielded a greater extent of success, whether in terms of policy effectiveness, size of digital economy, or performance on smart city rankings (Azhar and Zaharia 2016, Woodhouse 2016, Woo 2017c, Yeung and Singh 2017). Indeed, Singapore has been ranked the world's top smart city (Juniper Research 2016a, 2016b). As I will discuss below, Singapore's transformation into a smart city is a state-driven affair, with the government enacting various key initiatives to drive this transformation.

At the heart of Singapore's smart city transformation is the Smart Nation initiative, which was launched in 2014 to harness data and technological solutions for the purpose of addressing urban policy issues (Lee 2014). However, it is also important to note that Singapore's digital transformation predates the Smart Nation initiative. Beginning with a 'Civil Service Computerisation Programme' that was introduced in the late 1980s and followed by the 'IT 2000' strategic plan, e-Government Action Plans, iGov 2010 initiative, and 2015 eGov Masterplan that were implemented over the subsequent two decades (Soh et al. 1993, Arun and Yap 2000, GovTech Singapore 2017), the Singapore government has progressively digitized its policy processes. Figure 5.1 provides a timeline of these initiatives.

As Figure 5.1 shows, Singapore's digital transformation began in the 1980s, with efforts to progressively introduce advanced ICT tools and applications to its policy processes long pre-dating the Smart Nation initiative. However, these early initiatives tended to focus on increasing efficiency in public service delivery, especially through streamlining government websites or automating some aspects of public service delivery. Indeed, these early initiatives tended to involve incremental adoption of ICT to existing policy processes and institutions.

Such incremental approaches to digitizing public service delivery are broadly in line with NPM reforms, of which Singapore has been a key proponent (Haque 2002, Lee and Haque 2006, Aoki 2015). This often means automating, decentralizing and/or contracting out specific components

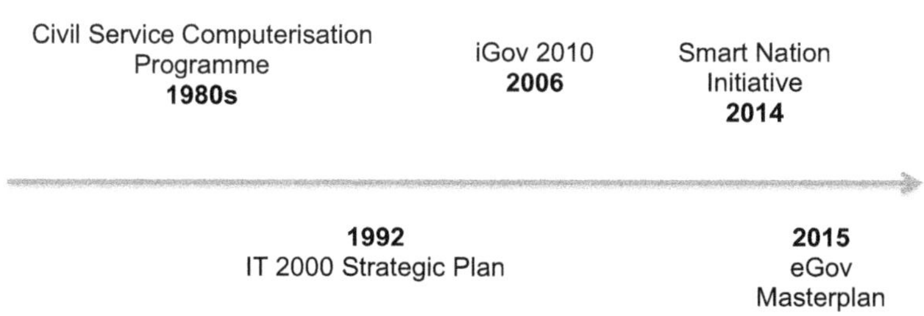

Figure 5.1 Singapore's digitization initiatives. Adapted from J.J. Woo (2017b), *Singapore's Smart Nation Initiative – A Policy and Organisational Perspective.*

of the policy process. Examples include the outsourcing of X-ray work by public hospitals and polyclinics to either local or foreign diagnostic companies through 'teleradiology' (Singapore General Hospital 2007) or the delivery of public services through websites or 'e-citizen' portals (Wong 2008), among others. Furthermore, it has also been noted that such early e-government initiatives limit pluralism (Sriramesh and Rivera-Sánchez 2006).

In contrast, the Smart Nation initiative is much more comprehensive, reflecting a broader 'digital transformation' that aims to digitize all aspects of urban life and foster government collaborations with non-state actors such as businesses, citizens, and NGOs (Smart Nation Programme Office 2016, Loke 2017). Launched in 2014, the Smart Nation initiative aims to harness data and technological solutions to address urban policy issues (Lee 2014). Broadly speaking, this involves extensive data collection efforts through sensors and cameras embedded across the city and the visualization of this data on Virtual Singapore, an online platform for real-time data visualization (Watts and Purnell 2016).

More specifically, the Smart Nation initiative is focused on five key policy domains (Smart Nation Programme Office 2017):

- Transport
- Health and enabled ageing
- Home and environment
- Business productivity
- Public sector service

Specific policy initiatives within these five domains are guided by a set of 'enablers' (Smart Nation Programme Office 2017, Woo 2017b, pp. 3–4):

- Facilitating smart solutions through test-bedding and research collaborations
- Nurturing a culture of experimentation and sustaining innovation
- Data sharing through the open data portal and Smart Nation Platform
- Investments in Research and Development (R&D)
- 'Living laboratories' for the development and piloting of technological solutions
- Growing an industry and start-up ecosystem
- Cyber-security and data privacy
- Building computational capabilities
- Educational programmes at various levels, including young children, secondary school students, and working professionals
- Upgrading programmes such as SkillsFuture
- A Smart Nation Fellowship Programme that invites experienced data scientists and engineers to work with the government to develop technological solutions

These enablers are essentially policy tools that are applied across the five domains. For instance, open data platforms have been applied to the development of urban transport solutions and public service delivery, while pilot trials have been utilized to develop technology solutions such as self-driving vehicles and smart home technologies (Smart Nation Programme Office 2017). More recently, the Singapore government has identified five 'strategic national projects' that could potentially form the foundation for the Smart Nation initiative (Smart Nation and Digital Government Office 2017):

- National Digital Identity framework: to facilitate secure digital transactions by citizens and businesses
- e-Payments drive: to encourage cashless payments and transactions
- Smart Nation Sensor Platform: to manage and accelerate the deployment of sensors and IOT (Internet of things) devices
- Smart Urban Mobility: to enhance public transportation through the use of data and digital technologies, including artificial intelligence and autonomous vehicles
- Moments of Life: which essentially aims to bundle and integrate public service delivery to citizens at key moments or milestones of their lives, reducing the need for citizens to transact with multiple government agencies

While these enablers and strategic national projects provide forward guidance for the Smart Nation initiative, the Singapore government has already begun implementing some elements of the initiative. For instance, the Monetary Authority of Singapore has established a regulatory sandbox that allows FinTech start-ups to test-run their products within a controlled environment, thereby reducing systemic risks to the financial sector (Monetary Authority of Singapore 2016, Yahya 2017). Various start-up incubators have also been established, both by government departments and research institutions such as universities, in order to encourage technological start-ups.

At the national level, the Singapore government has designated the Jurong Lake District (JLD) as its test bed for the Smart Nation initiative (Tham 2014). Led by the URA, the JLD aims to incorporate data analytics and sensor technologies to enable 'data-driven decision-making' among residents, businesses, facility managers and urban planners (Urban Redevelopment Authority 2017a). This complements other pilot areas that are situated within residential districts and which seek to introduce smart home technologies to citizens (Urban Redevelopment Authority 2016, Ng 2017). However, the JLD differs from these other pilot areas and test beds in both scale and scope.

More than simply a technological test bed, the JLD has been envisioned to become the largest commercial and regional centre outside Singapore's city centre (Urban Redevelopment Authority 2017b), with Smart Nation initiatives seen as a means to transforming the JLD into a hub for the future economy (Urban Redevelopment Authority 2017c). Encompassing public and private housing estates, two national universities, and a range of other educational and leisure facilities, the JLD can also be seen as a microcosm of what a smart city or smart nation could look like (Urban Redevelopment Authority 2017d).

This means that the JLD serves socio-economic goals, making it an integral component of Singapore's developmental state. As I will discuss further below, there are strong similarities between the JLD and Hong Kong's smart city test bed, the Kowloon East District. In both instances, test beds were used as a means for developing a secondary business district that can serve to drive economic growth, whether through encouraging data-augmented innovation or developing a data industry as a growth sector.

In any case, it is increasingly clear from the discussion thus far that Singapore's approach to digitization and smart city development is highly state-centric, with policy tools such as the Smart Nation enablers and policy objectives such as the strategic national projects designed and driven by the government, often through public agencies such as the Smart Nation and Digital Government Office and Government Technology Agency (GovTech). Indeed, these public agencies were formed for the specific purpose of driving the Smart Nation initiative.

Housed under the Smart Nation and Digital Government Group (SNDGG), the Smart Nation and Digital Government Office (SNDGO) and GovTech are tasked respectively with the formulation and implementation of Smart Nation initiatives. The SNDGO was formed through a consolidation of the Smart Nation Programme Office (which was housed within the Prime Minister's Office), the Ministry of Finance's Digital Government Directorate, and the Ministry of Communications and Information's Government Technology Policy department. In doing so, the SNDGO consolidates ICT and digital expertise from the various government departments.

Situated within the Prime Minister's Office, the SNDGG now serves to house the various agencies and experts that are involved in the Smart Nation initiative (Seow 2017). Figure 5.2 provides a diagrammatic representation of the SNDGG and its component units. Aside from the SNDGG, the Cyber Security Agency of Singapore (CSA) also plays a supporting role by developing Singapore's cybersecurity ecosystem, responding to cyber threats, and protecting critical sectors from cyberattacks (Cyber Security Agency Singapore 2017).

As I will discuss in Chapter 6, the SNDGG represents a pilot agency tasked with driving Singapore's digitization efforts. Furthermore, most of the Smart Nation enablers listed above are geared towards the attainment of developmental goals, although many of these also perform a further role of addressing urban-municipal issues (Woo 2017b, pp. 4–5). These all suggest a strong degree of coherence between the Smart Nation initiative and Singapore's developmental state approach. While I will discuss these developmental state aspects of the Smart Nation initiative in the following

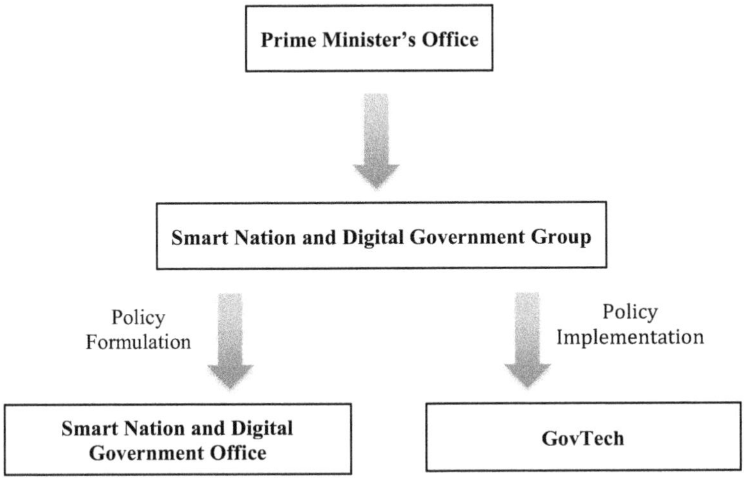

Figure 5.2 Organization structure of Smart Nation and Digital Government Group (SNDGG).

chapter, it is nonetheless necessary to address the politico-administrative context within which the initiative is embedded.

As the world's only 'fully-functioning city-state' (Long 2015), Singapore's approach to establishing itself as a smart city differs from those of other cities. In particular, the conflation of city and state in Singapore suggests the convergence of a national–local divide in smart city strategies (Angelidou 2014), and an elevation of urban and municipal issues to the national policy agenda, allowing for greater policy expediency when compared to countries with more layers of government (Balakrishnan 2016, Lim 2016). As Hoe has noted, what separates Singapore's Smart Nation from other smart cities is the availability of national-level resources and political legitimacy (Hoe 2016, p. 329).

More importantly, Singapore's status as a city-state has imbued it with both city-level and national-level resources and advantages. Indeed, Calder attributes the success of Singapore's smart city transformation to this dual identity as city and nation, arguing that:

> Singapore thus has two dimensions: as a *city* and as a *state*. Both are a source of strength on the international scene and allow Singapore to enjoy the best of both the national and municipal worlds. On the one hand, its diminutive city-state characteristic facilitates the pragmatic, flexible, nonideological domestic politics typical of cities that Barber describes. On the other hand, its national standing provides the legitimacy and resources required to play credibly on the international scene in areas of its clear competence.
>
> (Calder 2016, p. 3)

It is therefore instructive at this point to note that Singapore's digitization experience, by virtue of its position as a city-state, differs from that of other smart cities. This is reflected in its Smart Nation initiative, which emphasizes the nation-state, especially its strategic concerns, as its definitional basis. Based on the case of Singapore, Hoe (2016, p. 330) proposes the following working definition: 'A smart nation applies digital technology and data to address strategic issues through a whole-of-government approach and in collaboration with citizens'. As Hoe further notes:

> the distinguishing characteristics of a smart nation are strategic issues, digital technology and data, whole-of-government and collaboration with citizens. It is strategic because a smart nation tackles long-term survival issues which affect the nation. It applies digital technology and data because current technological trends are pointing to 'digitalization' as the 'next big thing' and using data to drive decision-making and engage the citizens. It uses a whole-of-government approach instead of just tackling problems at the urban, municipal, city or provincial level. Finally, it involves collaborating with citizens to co-design and co-create human-centric solutions which tap into the creativity of the population.
>
> (Hoe 2016, p. 330)

Furthermore, Singapore's unique position as city-state has also made its smart city initiatives more centralized and far more extensive than those implemented in other cities (Watts and Purnell 2016). This is evident in the Smart Nation initiative, which represents a comprehensive set of policy tools designed to facilitate Singapore's digitization efforts. Such a centralized approach is aided by the relatively high level of political and administrative centralization in Singapore,[1] which allows for swift decision-making and hence the ability to quickly implement large-scale policy changes (Low 2006, Tan 2012, Woo 2016b).

Hong Kong

Despite their many similarities, such as a highly developed economy, well-educated workforce, reputation for administrative efficiency and good governance that is underpinned by a British common law system, Hong Kong lags behind Singapore in its efforts to transform itself into a smart city (Woo 2017c, Yeung and Singh 2017). While Singapore had released its Smart Nation initiative in 2014, the Hong Kong government only plans to release its first Smart City Blueprint in the third quarter of 2018 (Yeung and Singh 2017).

This means that while Singapore is already in the process of implementing its Smart Nation initiatives, Hong Kong remains in the planning phase of its smart city strategy. This disparity between the two cities has been attributed to Singapore's more proactive approach to smart city planning and providing support for entrepreneurs and start-ups (Woodhouse 2016). This difference in pace and scale of the two cities' smart city strategies also reflects their different approaches to economic development and industrial policy.

Specifically, Hong Kong's historical predilection towards laissez-faire and free market principles may have resulted in delays to its smart city planning efforts, especially when compared to Singapore, which has proven itself more willing to rely on state interventions to stimulate economic growth and industry development. Nonetheless, the Hong Kong government's desire to catch up with other smart cities displays a willingness to introduce greater state intervention, particularly through the implementation of its forthcoming Smart City Development Blueprint (Koh 2017).

Given its late start in smart city development (when compared to Singapore at least), information on Hong Kong's smart city strategies is relatively sparse. Nonetheless, the Hong Kong government has given some indications of the policy and strategic directions that will underpin its smart city drive. I will discuss these in the remainder of this section.

Like Singapore, Hong Kong's current efforts to transform itself into a smart city are built upon an existing foundation of e-government policies. From 1998, the Hong Kong government has sought to expand the use of ICT in both the public and private sectors through a series of 'Digital 21' strategies (Government of Hong Kong Special Administrative Region 2017a). Figure 5.3 provides a timeline of Hong Kong's Digital 21 strategies.

While earlier Digital 21 Strategies were focused on building up ICT infrastructure, the latest iteration of the strategy emphasizes data sharing and collaboration, fostering an ICT industry, and delivering e-services to the public, and propelling economic development (IBM 2013, p. 5, Government of Hong Kong Special Administrative Region 2017a, p. 21). Entitled 'Smarter Hong Kong, Smarter Living', the latest iteration of the Digital 21 Strategy heralds a shift from instrumental goals, i.e. infrastructure building and public service delivery, to emphasizing greater public involvement and interactions, through fostering public–private collaboration.

During a launch of the 2014 Digital 21 Strategy, Secretary for Commerce & Economic Development Gregory So highlighted four strategic thrusts that underpin the Strategy (eGov Innovation 2013):

- Empowering people and businesses
- Igniting business innovation
- Supporting a thriving ICT industry
- Transforming and integrating public services

Aside from the Digital 21 Strategy, Hong Kong has also progressively expanded its e-government efforts, beginning with the creation of government websites in the early 2000s to more comprehensive efforts such as the

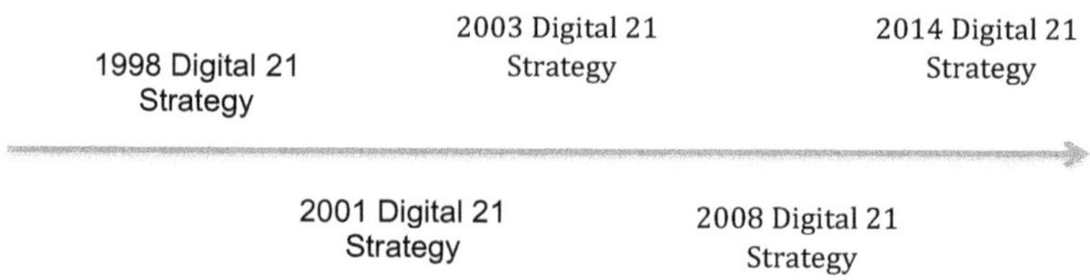

Figure 5.3 Hong Kong's Digital 21 Strategies.

establishment of GovHK, a public e-services portal, in 2007 as well as its subsequent evolution into the more citizen-centric MyGovHK Portal in 2010 and the formation of a Mobile MyGovHK in 2013 (IBM 2013, pp. 25–26). However, these prior initiatives tended to be centred on introducing greater public service efficiency, by incorporating ICT into government institutions and processes.

In other words, they remain very much within the realm of e-government. In contrast, Hong Kong's more recent smart city drive extends beyond public service delivery to include policy objectives such as public–private collaboration, entrepreneurship and innovation, urban policy issues, as well as improving the general well-being of citizens. This reflects a broader and more comprehensive approach that addresses a wider set of stakeholders.

Hong Kong's current smart city strategies are driven by a PWC study that was commissioned by the office of the Hong Kong Government Chief Information Officer (Basu 2017). Entitled 'Report of Consultancy Study on Smart City Blueprint for Hong Kong', the PWC study serves to provide the Hong Kong government with advice and recommendations for formulating its smart city development blueprint (PWC 2017, p. 4). Specifically, the report identifies five urban megatrends that can potentially be addressed by Hong Kong's smart city strategy (PWC 2017, p. 5):

- Ageing population
- Global and regional economic shifts
- Rapid urbanization
- Climate and resource scarcity
- Technological breakthroughs

This emphasis on five megatrends somewhat resembles the five key domains that were identified by Singapore's Smart Nation initiative, albeit with differences in some of the trends/domains that were identified. Hong Kong's Smart City Blueprint also emphasizes three main policy objectives (Office of the Government Chief Information Officer 2016b):

- Addressing urban challenges, enhancing the effectiveness of city management and improving people's quality of living as well as Hong Kong's

sustainability, efficiency and safety through the use of innovation and technology (I&T)
- Enhancing Hong Kong's attractiveness to global businesses and talents
- Inspiring continuous city innovation and sustainable economic development

Like the Smart Nation initiative, Hong Kong's Smart City Blueprint emphasizes economic (business development, talent management), social (quality of living, sustainability), and urban-municipal (addressing urban problems, enhancing city management) goals. These social and urban-municipal goals represent a shift from the developmental state's overarching focus on economic objectives as well as e-government's emphasis on public service delivery and administrative efficiency. As I will further explicate in Chapter 6, both Singapore and Hong Kong's smart city transformation involve a strategy adaptation of their respective developmental state models.

In order to achieve these objectives, the Blueprint lays out Hong Kong's smart city developmental plans for the next five years, with policy initiatives focused on six major areas (Office of the Government Chief Information Officer 2016b, PWC 2017):

- Smart mobility
- Smart living
- Smart environment
- Smart people
- Smart government
- Smart economy

Table 5.1 provides a summary of the various policy recommendations and initiatives that make up the Smart City Blueprint.

It is also important to note that Hong Kong's Smart City Blueprint is not entirely technology-oriented. For instance, initiatives such as improving waste management or reducing carbon emissions do not overtly emphasize the use of data or digital technologies. Rather, these initiatives are based on traditional policy instruments, such as a charging scheme for municipal solid waste or replacing coal-fired electricity generation with natural gas and non-fossil fuel sources (Office of the Government Chief Information Officer 2016b).

This suggests that Hong Kong has taken a broader and less techno-centric understanding of what it means to be a 'smart' city. More than simply incorporating advanced ICT and data analytics, Hong Kong's definition of a smart city also includes the efficient use of resources. As the Hong Kong Development Bureau states (Hong Kong Development Bureau 2017):

> There is not yet a universal definition of smart city. Some definitions put particular emphasis on leveraging Information and Communications

> Technology (ICT) to enhance the efficiency of a city's systems, operations and services. We think that the definition of smart city should be wider. Apart from ICT, a smart city should also leverage human and social capital to facilitate the sustainable growth of society and increase quality of living.

Aside from policy initiatives, the Smart City Blueprint also includes procedural recommendations such as encouraging more public–private collaboration in the implementation of the Blueprint as well as organizational reforms such as the proposed formation of a Smart City Office to coordinate smart city projects across government (Office of the Government Chief Information Officer 2016b). Like Singapore's SNDGG, this

Table 5.1 Components of Hong Kong's Smart City Blueprint

Key area	*Strategies and initiatives*
Smart mobility	Intelligent transport system and traffic management systems Real-time information for public transport interchanges, bus stops and car parks Environmentally friendly transportation technology Smart airport with facial biometric system and driverless vehicles
Smart living	Expand free public Wi-Fi Develop digital payment systems Introduce electronic identity (eID) Support elderly and disabled through technology Establish platform for big data analytics and electronic record sharing in healthcare
Smart environment	Reduce carbon emissions and promote energy efficiency Encourage green and intelligent buildings Improve waste management Pollution monitoring through remote sensing devices
Smart people	Nurture young talent in science, technology, engineering and mathematics (STEM) as well as information technology (IT) Promote innovation and entrepreneurial culture through financial and non-financial support, training and incubation
Smart government	Promote and expand open data initiatives Develop smart city infrastructure (fifth generation mobile networks, eID, big data analytics, public cloud services, cybersecurity, etc.) Promote adoption of technology in government departments to improve public service delivery
Smart economy	Using innovation and technology to enhance current strengths (FinTech, smart tourism) Promote sharing economy Develop new economic pillars and industries (R&D, advanced manufacturing, data technology industry, etc.)

last recommendation – forming a Smart City Office – suggests growing centralization of Hong Kong's smart city resources and capabilities.

More importantly for the purposes of this book, the proposed formation of a Smart City Office aligns Hong Kong's smart city strategy more closely to its developmental state model, i.e. the formation of a pilot agency. Indeed, this predilection towards centralization already exists within Hong Kong's smart city policy milieu. Similar to Singapore, Hong Kong's smart city strategies are currently led by a centralized agency. Specifically, the Innovation and Technology Bureau plays a key role in supporting the innovation and technology sector, of which the ICT industry is part, and encouraging R&D in both the private and public sectors (Innovation and Technology Bureau 2015).

However, it is the Office of the Government Chief Information Officer (OFCIO), which is situated within the Bureau, that is tasked with formulating Hong Kong's Smart City Blueprint (Office of the Government Chief Information Officer 2017). As discussed above, the OFCIO has already commissioned several studies to support this later role of formulating the Smart City Blueprint. However, this is where the similarities end. While Singapore's SNDGG consolidates ICT and digital expertise and resources from across the government, the OFCIO has instead sought to establish a 'core team' of digital experts that will in turn train other government departments to manage their own digitization efforts (Basu 2017).

Hence Hong Kong takes a more decentralized approach by building up digital expertise within individual government departments, rather than consolidating them within a singly centralized entity, as Singapore did when it merged the SNPO, Digital Government Directorate, and Government Technology Policy Department within the SNDGO. Nonetheless, there is an emerging tendency towards centralization, with the Innovation and Technology Bureau and the Development Bureau playing key roles in leading and steering Hong Kong's transformation into a smart city. The roles of pilot agencies in the two cities' smart city strategies will be discussed in the following chapter.

While the Smart City Blueprint lays out the proposed strategies and initiatives needed for Hong Kong to transform itself into a smart city, it is also important to note that the Hong Kong government has already implemented several smart city initiatives. For instance, the government has established an open data platform, DATA.GOV.SG that provides public access to government data sets for commercial and non-commercial reuse (Government of Hong Kong Special Administrative Region 2017b). Led by the Office of the Government Chief Information Officer, DATA.GOV.SG also involves other government departments and public/private organizations (Government of Hong Kong Special Administrative Region 2017c).

Aside from the open data platform, pilot trials have allowed the government to test new technological solutions, often in collaboration with non-state actors such as businesses and universities, within controlled environments. These include joint regulatory sandboxes by the Hong Kong Monetary Authority, Securities and Futures Commission and Insurance Authority, testing of autonomous vehicles within the Hong Kong International Airport, joint technological adoption initiatives by the Hong Kong Science Park and the Chinese University of Hong Kong, as well as the designation of Kowloon East as a test bed for smart city solutions (Office of the Government Chief Information Officer 2016b).

As a direct urban manifestation of Hong Kong's smart city ambitions, the Kowloon East district plays an important role in Hong Kong's smart city strategy. Like Singapore's Jurong Lake District, the Kowloon East district is envisioned to be a second core business district (CBD) for Hong Kong, with smart city technologies contributing to the competitiveness of the district by enhancing its urban infrastructure and livability (Hong Kong Development Bureau 2017). While the Development Office leads the development of the Kowloon East smart city test bed, the Energizing Kowloon East Office is tasked with its implementation, along with the implementation of other municipal-economic policies within the district (Govada et al. 2017).

This convergence of smart city initiatives and economic developmental goals, especially in terms of the government's aim to transform Kowloon East into a digitally augmented core business district, is also present in Singapore. As discussed above, Singapore's JLD initiative aims to achieve a similar goal of transforming the district into a second central business district, as well as a smart city test bed. Hence while test beds and pilot trials represent a key component of both cities' smart city strategies, they remain oriented towards developmental goals, specifically industrial policy and development.

Conclusion

In this chapter, I have sought to provide a broad overview of the ongoing transformation of Singapore and Hong Kong into smart cities. As this chapter has revealed, both cities have taken a highly state-centric approach. This is evident in the broad strategic policy frameworks that the two cities have enacted, such as Singapore's Smart Nation initiative and Hong Kong's Smart City Blueprint. Comprising a set of desired smart city policy objectives and the policy initiatives needed to achieve these objectives, the Smart Nation initiative and Smart City Blueprint serve to consolidate and guide the two cities' efforts in transforming themselves into leading smart cities.

Aside from these strategic policy frameworks, there are many similarities in the approaches that Singapore and Hong Kong have taken in their smart city transformation. First, both cities emphasize the three policy objectives of economic/industrial development, citizen engagement and urban livability. In both cases, 'smart' technologies such as sensors, data analytics, and advanced ICT provide policymakers and urban planners with a set of tools that can address complex urban issues, enhance economic productivity and innovation, facilitate public–private collaboration, as well as support the development of new digital industries.

Secondly, the Smart Nation initiative and Smart City Blueprint feature similar policy initiatives or tools. These include pilot trials and test beds such as the JLD or Kowloon East district, subsidies and investments in R&D, start-up incubators and accelerators, and regulatory sandboxes, among others. More importantly, most of these initiatives involve direct state interventions, whether in terms of government investments in R&D, state-owned start-up accelerators, or the steering role of central agencies such as the Innovation and Technology Bureau or the SNDGG.

This prevalent role of the state, particularly through key centralized agencies, alludes to the continued influence of the developmental state model. While the existing smart city narrative tends to place a strong emphasis on civic culture, citizen engagement and policy co-creation, the smart city ambitions of Singapore and Hong Kong do not necessarily obviate their pre-existing developmental state approaches to economic governance. Rather, the Smart Nation initiative and Smart City Blueprint retain many of the key elements of the developmental state model, albeit with modifications and adaptations.

Such retention of the developmental state model amid ongoing smart city transformations suggests a need to revisit the conceptual and theoretical foundations of the developmental state model, with the conceptual model of the developmental state model adapted to the emerging reality of such 'smart' developmental states. More than simply the application of advanced ICT and data technologies to economic policy processes and institutions, such smart developmental states reflect deeper ontological shifts in the institutions, processes and ideas that underpin the Asian developmental state.

Given the smart city ambitions of other East Asian developmental states such as China, South Korea and Japan, such shifts are likely to pervade much of the region, giving rise to a new class of smart developmental states. In the following chapter, I will discuss the theoretical and conceptual implications of these shifts, focusing in particular on the cases of Singapore and Hong Kong. This will allow for a preliminary explication of the conceptual foundations of the smart developmental state in Chapter 7.

Note

1 The ruling People's Action Party (PAP) has consistently won a comfortable majority in all general elections since independence.

References

Angelidou, M., 2014. Smart city policies: A spatial approach. *Cities*, 41, Supplement 1, S3–S11.

Ansell, C. and Gash, A., 2008. Collaborative Governance in Theory and Practice. *Journal of Public Administration Research and Theory*, 18 (4), 543–571.

Aoki, N., 2015. Institutionalization of New Public Management: The case of Singapore's education system. *Public Management Review*, 17 (2), 165–186.

Arun, M. and Yap, M.T., 2000. Singapore : The Development of an Intelligent Island and Social Dividends of Information Technology. *Urban Studies*, 37 (10), 1749–1756.

Azhar, S. and Zaharia, M., 2016. In race to be Asia's fintech hub, Singapore leads Hong Kong. *Reuters*, 3 Jul.

Bakıcı, T., Almirall, E., and Wareham, J., 2012. A Smart City Initiative: the Case of Barcelona. *Journal of the Knowledge Economy*, 4 (2), 135–148.

Balakrishnan, V., 2016. *Opening Speech by Dr Vivian Balakrishnan, Minister-In-Charge of the Smart Nation Initiative.*

Basu, M., 2017. Exclusive: Hong Kong's vision for Artificial Intelligence. *GovInsider.*

Batty, M., 2013. Big data, smart cities and city planning. *Dialogues in Human Geography*, 3 (3), 274–279.

Calder, K.E., 2016. *Singapore: Smart City, Smart State.* Washington, D.C: Brookings Institution Press.

Carroll, T. and Jarvis, D.S.L., 2014. Introduction: Financialisation and Development in Asia under Late Capitalism. *Asian Studies Review*, 38 (4), 533–543.

Chadwick, A., 2003. Bringing E-Democracy Back In: Why it Matters for Future Research on E-Governance. *Social Science Computer Review*, 21 (4), 443–455.

Chan, C.M.L., 2013. *From Open Data to Open Innovation Strategies: Creating e-Services Using Open Government Data.* Hawaii, USA, Hawaii International Conference on System Sciences No. 46.

Chow, J., 2017. Transforming Hong Kong into a smart city [online]. *South China Morning Post.* Available from: http://www.scmp.com/special-reports/property/topics/weekend-property/article/2106369/transforming-hong-kong-smart-city [Accessed 3 Dec 2017].

Cocchia, A., 2014. Smart and Digital City: A Systematic Literature Review. *In*: R.P. Dameri and C. Rosenthal-Sabroux, eds. *Smart City.* Springer, Cham, 13–43.

Colebatch, H.K., 2009. Governance as a conceptual development in the analysis of policy. *Critical Policy Studies*, 3 (1), 58–67.

Cyber Security Agency Singapore, 2017. Our Organisation [online]. *Cyber Security Agency.* Available from: http://www.csa.gov.sg/about-us/our-organisation [Accessed 26 December 2017].

Dameri, R.P., 2017. Urban Smart Dashboard. Measuring Smart City Performance. *In*: R.P. Dameri, ed. *Smart City Implementation.* Springer International Publishing, 67–84.

Dameri, R.P. and Ricciardi, F., 2017. Leveraging Smart City Projects for Benefitting Citizens: The Role of ICTs. *In*: S.Th. Rassia and P.M. Pardalos, eds. *Smart City Networks.* Springer, Cham, 111–128.

Dawes, S.S., 2008. The Evolution and Continuing Challenges of E-Governance. *Public Administration Review*, 68, S86–S102.

Duit, A. and Galaz, V., 2008. Governance and Complexity—Emerging Issues for Governance Theory. *Governance*, 21 (3), 311–335.

Duit, A., Galaz, V., Eckerberg, K., and Ebbesson, J., 2010. Governance, complexity, and resilience. *Global Environmental Change*, 20 (3), 363–368.

eGov Innovation, 2013. Hong Kong opens 2014 Digital 21 Strategy for public consultation [online]. *Enterprise Innovation | Asia's Premier Business and Technology Publication.* Available from: https://www.enterpriseinnovation.net/article/

hong-kong-opens-2014-digital-21-strategy-public-consultation-108719266 [Accessed 26 Dec 2017].

Ferguson, R.B., 2013. Smart Cities and Economic Development: What to Consider. *MIT Sloan Management Review.*

Filipponi, L., Vitaletti, A., Landi, G., Memeo, V., Laura, G., and Pucci, P., 2010. Smart City: An Event Driven Architecture for Monitoring Public Spaces with Heterogeneous Sensors. *In*: *2010 Fourth International Conference on Sensor Technologies and Applications (SENSORCOMM)*. Presented at the 2010 Fourth International Conference on Sensor Technologies and Applications (SENSORCOMM), 281–286.

Fukuyama, F., 2013. What Is Governance? *Governance*, 26 (3), 347–368.

Gil-Garcia, J.R., 2012. Towards a smart State? Inter-agency collaboration, information integration, and beyond. *Information Polity*, 17 (3, 4), 269–280.

Goldsmith, S. and Crawford, S., 2014. *The Responsive City: Engaging Communities Through Data-Smart Governance.* 1st ed. San Francisco, C.A.: Jossey-Bass.

Goodspeed, R., 2015. Smart cities: moving beyond urban cybernetics to tackle wicked problems. *Cambridge Journal of Regions, Economy and Society*, 8 (1), 79–92.

Govada, S.S., Spruijt, W., and Rodgers, T., 2017. Kowloon East: Hong Kong's New Smart CBD. *In*: V. Kumar, ed. *Smart Economy in Smart Cities.* Springer, Singapore, 229–243.

Government of Hong Kong Special Administrative Region, 2017a. Digital 21 Strategy [online]. *Government of the Hong Kong Special Administrative Region.* Available from: http://www.digital21.gov.hk/eng/# [Accessed 26 Dec 2017].

Government of Hong Kong Special Administrative Region, 2017b. DATA.GOV.HK [online]. Available from: https://data.gov.hk/en/ [Accessed 26 Dec 2017].

Government of Hong Kong Special Administrative Region, 2017c. FAQ | DATA.GOV.HK [online]. *DATA.GOV.HK.* Available from: https://data.gov.hk/en/faq [Accessed 26 Dec 2017].

GovTech Singapore, 2017. eGov Masterplans [online]. *eGov Masterplans.* Available from: http://www.tech.gov.sg/About-Us/Corporate-Publications/eGov-Masterplan [Accessed 6 May 2017].

Greco, I. and Bencardino, M., 2014. The Paradigm of the Modern City: SMART and SENSEable Cities for Smart, Inclusive and Sustainable Growth. *In*: B. Murgante, S. Misra, A.M.A.C. Rocha, C. Torre, J.G. Rocha, M.I. Falcão, D. Taniar, B.O. Apduhan, and O. Gervasi, eds. *Computational Science and Its Applications – ICCSA 2014.* Presented at the International Conference on Computational Science and Its Applications, Springer International Publishing, 579–597.

Gubbi, J., Buyya, R., Marusic, S., and Palaniswami, M., 2013. Internet of Things (IoT): A vision, architectural elements, and future directions. *Future Generation Computer Systems*, 29 (7), 1645–1660.

Haque, M.S., 2002. Structures of New Public Management in Malaysia and Singapore: Alternative Views. *The Journal of Comparative Asian Development*, 1 (1), 71–86.

Hashem, I.A.T., Chang, V., Anuar, N.B., Adewole, K., Yaqoob, I., Gani, A., Ahmed, E., and Chiroma, H., 2016. The role of big data in smart city. *International Journal of Information Management*, 36 (5), 748–758.

Hoe, S.L., 2016. Defining a smart nation: the case of Singapore. *Journal of Information, Communication and Ethics in Society*, 14 (4), 323–333.

Hollands, R.G., 2008. Will the real smart city please stand up? *City*, 12 (3), 303–320.

Hong Kong Development Bureau, 2017. Smart City – Kowloon East [online]. *Smart City Kowloon East*. Available from: http://www.smartke.hk/eng/smartke.php [Accessed 28 Dec 2017].

IBM, 2013. *Smarter Hong Kong, Smarter Living*. Hong Kong: IBM, Consultancy Services for the Digital 21 Strategy Review for the Office of the Government Chief Information Officer.

Innovation and Technology Bureau, 2015. Innovation and Technology Bureau: Our Role [online]. *Government of the Hong Kong Special Administrative Region*. Available from: http://www.itb.gov.hk/en/about_us/role/ [Accessed 19 Oct 2017].

Janssen, M., Charalabidis, Y., and Zuiderwijk, A., 2012. Benefits, Adoption Barriers and Myths of Open Data and Open Government. *Information Systems Management*, 29 (4), 258–268.

Janssen, M., Matheus, R., Longo, J., and Weerakkody, V., 2017. Transparency-by-design as a foundation for open government. *Transforming Government: People, Process and Policy*, 11 (1), 2–8.

Jessop, B., 2016. The Developmental State in an Era of Finance-Dominated Accumulation. *In*: Y. Chu, ed. *The Asian Developmental State*. Palgrave Macmillan US, 27–55.

Juniper Research, 2016a. *Worldwide Smart Cities: Energy, Transport & Lighting 2016–2021*. Basingstoke, UK: Juniper Research.

Juniper Research, 2016b. Singapore Named 'Global Smart City – 2016' [online]. Available from: https://www.juniperresearch.com/press/press-releases/singapore-named-global-smart-city-2016 [Accessed 17 Dec 2017].

Kitchin, R., 2014. The real-time city? Big data and smart urbanism. *GeoJournal*, 79 (1), 1–14.

Kitchin, R. and McArdle, G., 2016. *Urban data and city dashboards: Six key issues*. Maynooth: Maynooth University, Working Paper No. 21.

Koh, D., 2017. Chief Secretary Matthew Cheung outlines Hong Kong's Smart City development plans | OpenGovAsia [online]. *OPENGOV*. Available from: https://www.opengovasia.com/articles/7686-chief-secretary-matthew-cheung-outlines-hong-kongs-smart-city-development-plans [Accessed 25 Dec 2017].

Kraemer, K. and King, J.L., 2006. Information Technology and Administrative Reform: Will E-Government Be Different? *International Journal of Electronic Government Research (IJEGR)*, 2 (1), 1–20.

Larson, J.F. and Park, J., 2014. From developmental to network state: Government restructuring and ICT-led innovation in Korea. *Telecommunications Policy*, 38 (4), 344–359.

Layne, K. and Lee, J., 2001. Developing fully functional E-government: A four stage model. *Government Information Quarterly*, 18 (2), 122–136.

Lee, E.W.Y. and Haque, M.S., 2006. The New Public Management Reform and Governance in Asian NICs: A Comparison of Hong Kong and Singapore. *Governance*, 19 (4), 605–626.

Lee, H.L., 2014. *Smart Nation: Better living, more opportunities, stronger communities*.

Lee, J. and Lee, H., 2014. Developing and validating a citizen-centric typology for smart city services. *Government Information Quarterly*, 31 (Supplement 1), S93–S105.

Lim, Y.L., 2016. Trust between citizens, Government key for Smart Nation: PM Lee Hsien Loong. *The Straits Times*, 12 Jul.

Loke, K.F., 2017. Government to call for S$2.4b of ICT tenders this year for Smart Nation projects [online]. *Channel NewsAsia.* Available from: http://www.channelnewsasia.com/news/singapore/government-to-call-for-s-2-4b-of-ict-tenders-this-year-for-smart-8879506 [Accessed 25 May 2017].

Long, S., 2015. The Singapore exception. *The Economist.*

Low, L., 2006. *The Political Economy of a City-State Revised.* Singapore: Marshall Cavendish.

Ma, L., Chung, J., and Thorson, S., 2005. E-government in China: Bringing economic development through administrative reform. *Government Information Quarterly*, 22 (1), 20–37.

Marche, S. and McNiven, J.D., 2003. E-Government and E-Governance: The Future Isn't What It Used To Be. *Canadian Journal of Administrative Sciences / Revue Canadienne des Sciences de l'Administration*, 20 (1), 74–86.

Meijer, A. and Bolívar, M.P.R., 2016. Governing the smart city: a review of the literature on smart urban governance. *International Review of Administrative Sciences*, 82 (2), 392–408.

Menon, R., 2015. *A Smart Financial Centre.*

Misuraca, G., Mureddu, F., and Osimo, D., 2014. Policy-Making 2.0: Unleashing the Power of Big Data for Public Governance. *In*: M. Gasco-Hernandez, ed. *Open Government: Opportunities and Challenges for Public Governance.* New York, N.Y.: Springer, 171–181.

Monetary Authority of Singapore, 2016. MAS FinTech Regulatory Sandbox [online]. *MAS Website.* Available from: http://www.mas.gov.sg/Singapore-Financial-Centre/Smart-Financial-Centre/FinTech-Regulatory-Sandbox.aspx [Accessed 18 Jan 2017].

Nam, T. and Pardo, T.A., 2011. Smart City As Urban Innovation: Focusing on Management, Policy, and Context. *In*: *Proceedings of the 5th International Conference on Theory and Practice of Electronic Governance.* New York, N.Y., USA: ACM, 185–194.

Newman, J., Barnes, M., Sullivan, H., and Knops, A., 2004. Public Participation and Collaborative Governance. *Journal of Social Policy*, 33 (2), 203–223.

Ng, J.S., 2017. Parliament: Punggol North to become Singapore's first 'enterprise district', home to digital and cyber-security industries. *The Straits Times*, 7 Mar.

Norris, D.F. and Reddick, C.G., 2013. Local E-Government in the United States: Transformation or Incremental Change? *Public Administration Review*, 73 (1), 165–175.

Noveck, B.S., 2015. *Smart Citizens, Smarter State: The Technologies of Expertise and the Future of Governing.* Cambridge, M.A.: Harvard University Press.

Office of the Government Chief Information Officer, 2016a. Smart Hong Kong [online]. *Government of the Hong Kong Special Administrative Region.* Available from: https://www.smartcity.gov.hk/ [Accessed 3 Dec 2017].

Office of the Government Chief Information Officer, 2016b. *The Smart City Blueprint for Hong Kong.* Hong Kong: Government of the Hong Kong Special Administrative Region.

Office of the Government Chief Information Officer, 2017. OGCIO: About Us [online]. *Government of the Hong Kong Special Administrative Region.* Available from: https://www.ogcio.gov.hk/en/about_us/ [Accessed 26 Dec 2017].

Paskaleva, K., Cooper, I., and Concilo, G., 2018. Co-producing Smart City Services: Does One Size Fit All? *In*: *Smart Technologies for Smart Governments.* Springer, Cham, 123–158.

Paskaleva, K.A., 2011. The smart city: A nexus for open innovation? *Intelligent Buildings International*, 3 (3), 153–171.

Pereira, G.V., Cunha, M.A., Lampoltshammer, T.J., Parycek, P., and Testa, M.G., 2017. Increasing collaboration and participation in smart city governance: a cross-case analysis of smart city initiatives. *Information Technology for Development*, 23 (3), 526–553.

Perera, C., Zaslavsky, A., Christen, P., and Georgakopoulos, D., 2014. Sensing as a service model for smart cities supported by Internet of Things. *Transactions on Emerging Telecommunications Technologies*, 25 (1), 81–93.

PWC, 2017. *Report of Consultancy Study on Smart City Blueprint for Hong Kong*. Hong Kong: PricewaterhouseCoopers Advisory Services Limited.

Ratti, C. and Claudel, M., 2016. *The City of Tomorrow: Sensors, Networks, Hackers, and the Future of Urban Life*. New Haven; London: Yale University Press.

Resch, B., Britter, R., and Ratti, C., 2012. Live Urbanism – Towards SENSEable Cities and Beyond. *In*: S.T. Rassia and P.M. Pardalos, eds. *Sustainable Environmental Design in Architecture*. Springer New York, 175–184.

Rhodes, R.A.W., 1996. The New Governance: Governing without Government. *Political Studies*, 44 (4), 652–667.

Rhodes, R.A.W., 1997. *Understanding governance: policy networks, governance, reflexivity, and accountability*. London: Open University Press.

Schedler, K. and Scharf, M.C., 2001. Exploring the Interrelations Between Electronic Government and the new Public Management. *In*: B. Schmid, K. Stanoevska-Slabeva and V. Tschammer, eds. *Towards the E-Society*. Boston, M.A.: Springer, 775–788.

Seow, J., 2017. Boost for Smart Nation push with agencies under one roof, 25 Mar.

Shichiyakh, R.A., Klyuchnikov, D.A., Balashova, S.P., Novoselov, S.N., and Novosyolova, N.N., 2016. Smart City as the Basic Construct of the Socio-economic Development of Territories. *International Journal of Economics and Financial Issues*, 6 (1S), 157–162.

Singapore General Hospital, 2007. Press Release: Just transmit X-rays for fast results [online]. *Singapore General Hospital*. Available from: https://www.sgh.com.sg/about-us/newsroom/news-release/2007/Pages/Just-transmit-X-rays-for-fast-results-The-Straits-Times--20071203.aspx [Accessed 17 Dec 2017].

Smart Nation and Digital Government Office, 2017. Strategic National Projects to Build a Smart Nation [online]. *Smart Nation Singapore*. Available from: http://www.smartnation.sg/happenings/press-releases/strategic-national-projects-to-build-a-smart-nation [Accessed 24 Dec 2017].

Smart Nation Programme Office, 2016. About Smart Nation [online]. Available from: http://www.smartnation.sg/about-smart-nation [Accessed 22 Oct 2016].

Smart Nation Programme Office, 2017. Smart Nation Initiatives [online]. *Smart Nation Singapore*. Available from: http://www.smartnation.sg/initiatives/ [Accessed 15 Feb 2017].

Soh, C., Neo, B.S., and Markus, M.L., 1993. IT2000: A critical appraisal of Singapore's state-wide strategic planning process for information technology. *The Journal of Strategic Information Systems*, 2 (4), 351–372.

Spencer, J., 2015. How Smart Cities Are Boosting Economic Development Using GIS [online]. Available from: http://www.govtech.com/dc/articles/How-Street-Smart-Cities-Are-Boosting-Economic-Development-Using-GIS.html [Accessed 17 Dec 2017].

SPRING Singapore, 2016. Setting the standard worldwide: intelligent city, Smart Nation [online]. *SPRING Singapore*. Available from: https://www.spring.gov.sg/Inspiring-Success/Enterprise-Stories/Pages/Setting-the-standard-worldwide-intelligent-city-Smart-Nation.aspx [Accessed 20 Apr 2017].

Sriramesh, K. and Rivera-Sánchez, M., 2006. E-government in a corporatist, communitarian society: the case of Singapore. *New Media & Society*, 8 (5), 707–730.

Stéphane Roche, 2014. Geographic Information Science I: Why does a smart city need to be spatially enabled? *Progress in Human Geography*, 38 (5), 703–711.

Stimmel, C.L., 2015. *Building Smart Cities: Analytics, ICT, and Design Thinking.* Boca Raton: Auerbach Publications.

Tan, K.P., 2012. The Ideology of Pragmatism: Neo-liberal Globalisation and Political Authoritarianism in Singapore. *Journal of Contemporary Asia*, 42 (1), 67–92.

Tham, I., 2014. Jurong Lake District to be test bed for 'smart nation'. *Straits Times*, 18 Jun.

Torres, L., Pina, V., and Acerete, B., 2005. E-government developments on delivering public services among EU cities. *Government Information Quarterly*, 22 (2), 217–238.

Torres, L., Pina, V., and Royo, S., 2005. E-government and the transformation of public administrations in EU countries: Beyond NPM or just a second wave of reforms? *Online Information Review*, 29 (5), 531–553.

Townsend, A.M., 2014. *Smart Cities: Big Data, Civic Hackers, and the Quest for a New Utopia.* 1st ed. New York: W. W. Norton & Company.

Urban Redevelopment Authority, 2016. Punggol Creative Cluster and Learning Corridor [online]. Available from: https://www.ura.gov.sg/uol/master-plan/view-master-plan/master-plan-2014/Growth-Area/Punggol-Creative-Cluster/Punggol-Creative-Cluster [Accessed 8 Jun 2017].

Urban Redevelopment Authority, 2017a. A Smart and Sustainable District of the Future [online]. *Jurong Lake District.* Available from: https://www.jld.sg/Draft-Master-Plan/A-Smart-and-Sustainable-District-Of-The-Future [Accessed 29 Dec 2017].

Urban Redevelopment Authority, 2017b. Jurong Lake District [online]. Available from: https://www.jld.sg/ [Accessed 29 Dec 2017].

Urban Redevelopment Authority, 2017c. A Hub For The Future Economy [online]. *Jurong Lake District.* Available from: https://www.jld.sg/Draft-Master-Plan/A-Hub-for-the-Future-Economy [Accessed 29 Dec 2017].

Urban Redevelopment Authority, 2017d. Precincts [online]. *Jurong Lake District.* Available from: https://www.jld.sg/The-Second-CBD/Precincts [Accessed 29 Dec 2017].

Van der Meer, A. and Van Winden, W., 2003. E-governance in Cities: A Comparison of Urban Information and Communication Technology Policies. *Regional Studies*, 37 (4), 407–419.

Watts, J.M. and Purnell, N., 2016. Singapore Is Taking the 'Smart City' to a Whole New Level. *Wall Street Journal*, 25 Apr.

Weiss, T.G., 2000. Governance, good governance and global governance: Conceptual and actual challenges. *Third World Quarterly*, 21 (5), 795–814.

West, D.M., 2004. E-Government and the Transformation of Service Delivery and Citizen Attitudes. *Public Administration Review*, 64 (1), 15–27.

Wong, K., 2008. Reinventing Singapore's Electronic Public Services. *Ethos*, (4).

Woo, J.J., 2016a. *Business and Politics in Asia's Key Financial Centres – Hong Kong, Singapore and Shanghai.* 1st ed. Singapore: Springer.

Woo, J.J., 2016b. *Singapore as an International Financial Centre: History, Politics and Policy.* London: Palgrave Macmillan.

Woo, J.J., 2017a. *3-in-1: Governing a Global Financial Centre.* Singapore: World Scientific.

Woo, J.J., 2017b. *Singapore's Smart Nation Initiative – A Policy and Organisational Perspective.* Singapore: Lee Kuan Yew School of Public Policy, National University of Singapore.

Woo, J.J., 2017c. Arresting the painful decline of Hong Kong's financial centre status [online]. *Channel NewsAsia.* Available from: http://www.channelnewsasia.com/news/asiapacific/commentary-arresting-the-painful-decline-of-hong-kong-s-9030492 [Accessed 3 Dec 2017].

Woodhouse, A., 2016. Hong Kong faces challenge from Singapore in 'smart city' planning. *South China Morning Post*, 22 Jun.

World Bank Group, 2017. Smart Cities [online]. *World Bank.* Available from: http://www.worldbank.org/en/topic/ict/brief/smart-cities [Accessed 5 Dec 2017].

Yahya, Y., 2017. Insurance start-up PolicyPal graduates from MAS fintech regulatory sandbox. *Straits Times*, 29 Aug.

Yeung, R. and Singh, 2017. Why Singapore is a much smarter city than Hong Kong. *South China Morning Post*, 8 Nov.

Zanella, A., Bui, N., Castellani, A., Vangelista, L., and Zorzi, M., 2014. Internet of Things for Smart Cities. *IEEE Internet of Things Journal*, 1 (1), 22–32.

6 Conceptual and theoretical implications

The developmental state model has for various reasons faced significant challenges to its relevance and applicability as a conceptual and analytical framework. Indeed, the decline in popularity of the developmental state model first began with the exponential globalization of the early 1990s, with the 1997 Asian Financial Crisis being the proverbial final nail in the coffin. While a highly globalized economy negated states' efforts to groom and protect national champions from foreign competition, the Crisis revealed the 'crony capitalism' that often accompanied embedded autonomy in many developmental states.

The fate of the developmental state model was further sealed by many developmental states' inability to address the growing urban complexity that had accompanied their rapid urbanization, as well as increasing digitization of the global economy. This latter point is particularly salient, with global corporations increasingly hailing from the technology sector, and digital innovation causing disruption in traditional industries. As a consequence, developmental states that had hitherto relied on state-driven economic development found themselves at a disadvantage, with top-down efforts to stimulate innovation yielding limited success (Carroll and Jarvis 2017).

At the turn of the twenty-first century, prospects for the Asian developmental state appear bleak. As Calder (2016, pp. 14–15) has noted:

> In today's volatile globalizing world, the paradigms of the past are rapidly losing their normative and predictive value. No longer are nation-states the intrinsically dominant and autonomous actors that they have long been assumed to be. No longer are the technological frontiers and political-economic parameters clear enough for states to confidently and strategically plan in 'developmental' fashion.

Hence as global economic liberalization and urban complexity continue to grow apace, 'the "developmental state" concept is growing decidedly passé in the world of economic development' (Calder 2016, p. 15). However, such a view may be overly pessimistic and tends to underestimate the role of agency in developmental states' efforts to remain viable and relevant in the global economy. As I have discussed in previous chapters, developmental states such as Hong Kong and Singapore have sought to adapt in response to new challenges and demands, giving rise to the smart developmental state.

While new global challenges and rising expectations from an increasingly affluent and politicized populace had given rise to a need for both governments to reinvent their developmental states and build up state capacity (Cheung 2008), the emergence of a new digital economy and the availability of technologically augmented tools of governance have imbued such efforts with a technological slant. As this book has thus far shown, both Hong Kong and Singapore have taken concrete steps to adapt and reform their developmental states in response to such emerging challenges and needs by seeking to transform themselves into smart cities.

More importantly, both cities have taken a top-down and state-centric approach to their smart city transformations, through broad strategic policy frameworks such as the Smart Nation initiative and Smart City Blueprint. Hence the ongoing transformation of Singapore and Hong Kong into smart cities does not necessarily mean a shift away from the developmental state approach. Rather, the smart cities of Singapore and Hong Kong represent modifications and adaptations to their developmental state models, with 'smart' technologies seen as ways to enhance or augment the various components of the developmental state.

As Calder has noted, despite growing pressures from its highly liberalized and digitized economy, Singapore's developmental state approach to economic governance, albeit tempered with the inclusion of technology and a technocratic approach to governance, continues to thrive (Calder 2016, p. 15). Indeed, and as this book has shown, it is precisely the incorporation of technological solutions in its policy and governing milieu that has allowed for the continued proliferation of Singapore's developmental state. As I will discuss below, both Singapore's Smart Nation initiative and Hong Kong's Smart City Blueprint exhibit, and even reproduce, key elements of their respective developmental state models.

These observations also raise a deeper, and more pressing, point. Specifically, efforts by Hong Kong and Singapore to adapt and technologically augment their developmental states as a response to emerging challenges pose significant theoretical implications for future studies of the Asian developmental state model. In the remainder of this chapter, I will discuss these conceptual and developmental implications by focusing on the different components of the developmental state. As this chapter will show, shifts and adaptations have taken place within these components, as Hong Kong and Singapore continue to transform themselves into 'smart developmental states'.

Developmental elite

By virtue of their existing political systems and institutions, the developmental elite has retained its dominance over economic governance as well as smart city initiatives in both cities. While Singapore's ruling People's Action Party (PAP) has retained its political authority and legitimacy through a strong showing during the 2015 general election (Tan 2016, Morgenbesser 2017), proposed constitutional reforms aimed at introducing universal suffrage in Hong Kong have reached an impasse (Mushkat and Mushkat 2016, Poon 2018).

In both cases, political power remains concentrated within the incumbent governments. As a consequence, the smart city initiatives of both Singapore and Hong Kong continue to be driven by their respective governments and geared towards developmental goals. While the existing smart cities literature correlates smart city formation with greater citizen engagement and, to a certain extent, democratization of the policy process, Singapore and Hong Kong have instead exhibited greater centralization of their policy processes, with the Smart Nation initiative and Smart City Blueprint led by the respective governments.

Furthermore, and as I have discussed in Chapter 5, both initiatives have retained a strong developmental slant, with both governments emphasizing the economic potential of new 'smart' industries such as data analytics or the Internet of things. Given the continued dominance of Singapore and Hong Kong governments over their respective smart city initiatives and the strong developmental slant of these initiatives, it is clear that economic development and smart city transformation in both Singapore and Hong Kong remain driven by a closely knit developmental elite.

However, this is not to say that the developmental elite has remained static. Given the growing significance of emerging 'smart' industries, the developmental elite increasingly includes private sector elites from the technological sector. This is evident in the growing participation and influence of technology industry actors in the government's policy processes.

For instance, a Hong Kong government consultation exercise on its 2014 Digital 21 Strategy involved the participation of technology firms such as Microsoft and Hutchison, as well as technology industry associations such as the Hong Kong Information Technology Industry Council, Hong Kong Electronics and Technologies Association and Hong Kong Internet Service Providers Association, among others (Office of the Government Chief Information Officer 2014). Indeed, the very foundation Hong Kong's smart city development, its Smart City Blueprint, was developed by PriceWaterHouseCoopers, a private sector consultancy firm (PWC 2017).

Similarly, Singapore's Smart Nation initiative, as well as its overall efforts to develop its technology industry, involved the participation of technology firms and start-ups through its Future Economy Dialogues (Committee on the Future of Economy Secretariat 2015, Committee on the Future Economy 2017). Specifically, the Future Economy Dialogues involved technology firms such as Google, Oracle Corporation and Huawei Technologies, as well as key personnel involved in the digitization of traditional businesses, such as the Chief Innovation Officer of DBS Bank and UOB Bank's Head of

Group Channels and Digitization, among others (Committee on the Future Economy 2017, pp. 110–117).

As I have noted elsewhere, such policy consultation mechanisms play a crucial role in fostering policy co-creation in Singapore and Hong Kong, with private sector actors able to influence policy outcomes and processes through their feedback and inputs (Woo 2015a, 2015b, 2016, 2016). Hence while policy consultation mechanisms have long existed in the two cities (Economic Review Committee 2003, Menon 2013, Topping 2013, Tsang 2013, Woo 2016), the digitization of the two cities' economies has resulted in the growing role of technology firms and start-ups in policy consultation and facilitated their (formal and informal) membership in the developmental elite, often through deep and frequent interactions with other developmental elite members within policy consultation initiatives and exercises.

Nonetheless, state actors remain in the driving seat of both cities' smart city initiatives. This is especially evident in Singapore's Industry Transformation Maps (Committee on the Future Economy 2017, p. 49). While these Industry Transformation Maps (ITMs) incorporate to some extent the inputs of private sector stakeholders, the Singapore government remains very much in the driving seat, determining both the direction and content of these ITMs. This dominant role of the state is often borne out in the activities of its pilot agencies, which represent the lead agencies tasked with planning and leading sectorial development. I will now discuss the shifting roles of pilot agencies in Singapore and Hong Kong.

Pilot agencies

While developmental elite composition has remained constant, there has been a shift towards further decentralization of pilot agency roles. Specifically, new pilot agencies have been established to lead smart city transformation and government digitization. These agencies take the form of Singapore's Smart Nation and Digital Government Group (SNDGG) in Singapore and Hong Kong's Office of the Government Chief Information Office (OGCIO). While economic pilot agencies such as the Economic Development Board or the Development Bureau continue to lead overall economic development, the Smart Nation and Digital Government Group (SNDGG) and OGCIO act as lead agencies within the realm of smart city development.

This reflects a broader and ongoing trend of administrative decentralization in the two cities, beginning with the New Public Management (NPM) movement and culminating in more recent technologically enabled forms of administrative decentralization, such as e-government and e-governance. Having emerged in the late 1990s and early 2000s, NPM emphasizes the decentralization, privatization and outsourcing of public services, with the aim of enhancing public sector efficiency (Hood 1991, Osborne and Gaebler 1993, Hood 1995, Pollitt and Bouckaert 2011).

Both Singapore and Hong Kong have enacted administrative reforms aimed at incorporating NPM into their public administrative systems (Burns 1994, Cheung 1996, Haque 2002, Lee and Haque 2006, Sarker 2006, Shen et al. 2006, Aoki 2015). Yet despite the adoption of NPM reforms such as liberalization, deregulation and privatization, the Singapore and Hong Kong states remain firmly in control of their economic governance, with NPM reforms aimed at enhancing economic development and consolidating the developmental elite's authority over economic affairs (Lee and Haque 2006).

Similarly, and as I have discussed in Chapter 5, the two cities' efforts at introducing e-government and e-governance initiatives are similarly geared towards goals of economic development and administrative efficiency. More importantly, this drive towards administrative decentralization, whether through NPM reforms or e-government/e-governance initiatives, has given rise to the formation of decentralized pilot agencies tasked with leading the development of a specific industry or sector, with the rationale for the formation of these decentralized pilot agencies being a need for specialized technical knowledge in the governing of certain sectors.

These include the Monetary Authority of Singapore and Hong Kong Monetary Authority (financial sector), and Info-communications Media Development Authority of Singapore and Communications Authority of Hong Kong (telecommunications market), among others. The SNDGG and OGCIO function as pilot agencies for Singapore and Hong Kong's smart city transformations, as well as the development of new 'smart' sectors such as data analytics or the Internet of things. The proliferation of decentralized pilot agencies such as the SNDGG and OGCIO therefore represents a significant adaptation to the developmental state model.

While the developmental state model had emphasized the role and presence of a single pilot agency that oversees economic governance and development, the increasing complexity and diversity of the economy has necessitated the formation of decentralized pilot agencies that possess the necessary knowledge and expertise to manage, promote and regulate specific sectors or industries. Paradoxically, such decentralization of pilot agency roles also necessitates greater centralized control over these decentralized units. This is especially evident in the location of the SNDGG within the Prime Minister's Office, while the OGCIO is situated within the Innovation and Technology Bureau, which in turn operates under the purview of the Financial Secretary.

In both cases, decentralized pilot agencies were established to drive smart city transformation and the development of new 'smart' sectors, although these agencies report directly to the offices of key political leaders such as the Prime Minister or the Financial Secretary. Indeed, and as I have discussed in Chapter 5, the SNDGG and OGCIO were both established to centralize oversight and governance of smart city processes and sectors, even as they themselves represent a certain decentralization of pilot agency functions.

In other words, there are simultaneous movements of centralization and decentralization, with the decentralization of pilot agency functions giving rise to new pilot agencies that centralize policy functions within their specified sectors and are themselves subject to centralized control and oversight.

As such, the shift from developmental state to smart developmental state has given rise to new and sectorially defined pilot agencies. While these new pilot agencies reflect the decentralization that has occurred among smart cities and proponents of e-government/e-governance, their roles remain highly circumscribed and defined by the developmental elite. There is therefore a need to extend beyond current understandings of the developmental state model that emphasize a single pilot agency to a more nuanced understanding of the multiple and various pilot agencies that exist within the smart developmental state.

Embedded autonomy

Likewise, the shift from developmental state to smart developmental state has resulted in changes to the socio-political milieu within which developmental elites and pilot agencies are embedded, giving rise to new forms of public–private interactions and collaboration. Given the importance of such interactions and networks for stimulating growth and innovation in a knowledge-based and innovation-driven economy, embedded autonomy has become even more crucial for smart developmental states seeking to stimulate sectorial growth and economic development, with advanced ICT serving as a conduit through which embedded autonomy can be exercised and sustained.

However, the embedded autonomy that is practised by smart developmental states differs from that of traditional Asian developmental states. While traditional notions of embedded autonomy had emphasized the role of the state as *driver* of economic growth, the new knowledge-based economy requires instead the state to act as a *catalyst* of technological innovation and entrepreneurship. In other words, the emphasis has shifted from 'autonomy' to 'embedded', with the smart developmental state seeking to facilitate and support the activities of technology start-ups and entrepreneurs, rather than direct or influence them (although these occasionally occur as well).

Both Singapore and Hong Kong have sought to enhance their embedded autonomy by expanding opportunities for public–private collaboration and deepening networks between public agencies, technology start-ups and entrepreneurs, as well as citizens. For instance, both cities have established open data platforms that encourage policy co-creation with businesses and citizens, with the respective governments publishing public sector data on these platforms for public access. Hence while the state retains control over data access, the sharing of public sector data allows non-state entities such as firms, start-ups and citizens to participate in its smart city initiatives.

Furthermore, both cities have sought to support start-ups and entrepreneurs through incubators, accelerators, and investments in R&D. Such initiatives allow for the creation of 'collaborative public spaces' that allow public agencies to connect firms and start-ups with research institutions and laboratories, whether state- or privately owned, in the process facilitating the sharing of new technologies and ideas (Lester and Piore 2006, Block and Negoita 2016). Furthermore, applications such as Singapore's OneService app further embed public agencies within the public milieu, with policymakers gaining access to real-time policy feedback.

Hence while the traditional developmental state established its embedded autonomy by intentionally establishing close state–business relations, smart developmental states like Singapore and Hong Kong have taken a broader approach by establishing platforms that allow for public–private collaborations, not just with selected industry partners, but with the general public. Open data platforms and public engagement apps allow for the embedding of public agencies and policy processes within the broader socio-political context. This allows for the collection of public feedback and co-creation of policy solutions.

However, it is also important to note that these platforms and apps continue to be led by the state, with the SNDGG and OGCIO facilitating the establishment of these 'collaborative public spaces' through financial and non-financial means and, more importantly, defining the terms and conditions within which public engagement and collaboration occur in these arenas. Such collaboration can involve both business and societal actors. I will now turn my attention to these two sets of actors, and their roles in the smart developmental state model.

Management of non-state interests

Given that the smart city strategies of smart developmental states such as Hong Kong and Singapore continue to place a premium on driving economic growth and facilitating (smart) industry development, there has also been a continuation of the type of state–business relations that have characterized the traditional developmental state, i.e. the alignment of transnational and domestic business interests with the state's developmental agenda.

Even as it seeks to transition to a knowledge-based and innovation-driven economy, Singapore continues to rely on its strategy of attracting and establishing relationships with global MNCs to drive economic growth, with the state's Economic Development Board increasingly seeking to attract technology firms such as Apple, Google and Facebook to encourage innovation (Swan Gin 2017).

Such efforts include a recent revamp of EntrePass – a government scheme for attracting global start-ups – that involved removing a SG $50, 000 paid-up capital requirement and adding a 'business networks' criteria for assessing applicants (Yahya 2017). This omission of paid-up capital requirements and inclusion of a 'business networks' criterion suggest a growing emphasis on network and relational variables. Hence, firms' relations with the state and other firms are increasingly seen as a crucial driver of industry growth – more so than monetary investments.

Similarly, Hong Kong's stock exchange (HKEx) has recently overhauled its listing rules to attract technology firms to raise capital in the city, with technology firms already overtaking financial, energy, industrial and commercial firms in terms of both market values and economic influence (Yiu and Zhang 2017). Other initiatives to attract technology firms and start-ups include a campaign by InvestHK, a government department that aims to attract foreign direct investments, to attract established Financial Technology (FinTech) firms to expand their operations to Hong Kong, as well as a proposed HKEx Private Market that serves as a 'nursery' for early stage start-ups and companies (InvestHK 2012, Terekhova 2017).

Such efforts to attract technology firms by providing incentives and subsidies (both direct and implicit) are reminiscent of earlier efforts to attract banks and financial institutions through incentives such as reductions in withholding taxes (Ng 1998, Jarvis 2011, Woo 2016) and hence an enduring part of the two cities' developmental state approach to industrial policy and development. Seen from this perspective, little has changed in terms of the ways in which the Singapore and Hong Kong governments have sought to develop, manage and sustain their relations with non-state economic entities such as businesses or start-ups.

What has changed, however, is the *types* of firms that the two governments have sought to attract and hence develop a relationship with. While prior efforts have focused on large multinational corporations (MNCs), whether in manufacturing, finance, pharmaceuticals or retail, both Singapore and Hong Kong are aiming to attract a wide spectrum of technology firms and start-ups. Indeed, emergence of the new digital economy has also given rise to a wider diversity in the size and organizational form of technology firms, with a firm's size not necessarily a determinant of its innovative capacity.

This desire to attract both large and small firms is perhaps most evident in the recent reforms to Singapore's EntrePass scheme, with paid-up capital requirements entirely removed. However, this is not to downplay the significance of large firms, especially in light of the growing presence of firms such as Google, Facebook and Amazon in Singapore. Rather, both cities' efforts to attract a broader swathe of technology firms and start-ups suggest growing complexity in managing this wider range of non-state economic entities.

While the traditional developmental state model had assumed the presence of a single state organ or public agency that is tasked with managing the state's relations with a set of relatively uniform MNCs or global conglomerates, the smart developmental state relies on multiple public agencies to manage a complex web of relations with a broad range of small-, medium- and large-sized firms and start-ups. Hence economic development agencies (such as Singapore's Economic Development Board or Hong Kong's Development Bureau) and decentralized pilot agencies (such as the SNDGG, MAS, OGCIO and HKMA) are all involved in managing the smart developmental state's relations with non-state economic interests.

Similar to the discussion on pilot agencies above, there is a need to take a more nuanced view of how smart developmental states manage their relations with non-state economic interests. Whether in terms of public agencies or corporate entities, there is a greater diversity and a concomitant growth in number of organizations or actors involved. This proliferation of organizational types and forms, as well as a need for greater inter-agency cooperation, also suggests a need for greater policy capacity among public agencies and policymakers, a topic that I will return to in the next chapter. Similarly, while smart developmental states do not appear to differ from traditional developmental states in their relations with civil society, there have in reality been subtle shifts in state–societal relations.

Civil society

The ongoing digitization and smart city transformation of Singapore and Hong Kong has given rise to new modalities of socio-political engagement and interactions. In particular, social media has emerged to become a key platform for citizen interaction and political mobilization (Skoric et al. 2012, Sreekumar and Vadrevu 2013, Yung and Leung 2014, Audrey Yue and Helen Hok-Sze Leung 2017). At the same time, social media has also become a key means through which policymakers and political leaders engage citizens (Sriramesh and Rivera-Sánchez 2006, Skoric et al. 2012, 2012) or manage dissent (Rodan 2003, George 2007).

Interactions between the smart developmental state and civil society are therefore increasingly mediated by technology, with social media platforms and new media outlets playing multiple roles, including but not restricted to:

- Facilitating citizen engagement by governments
- Enabling political mobilization by interest groups
- Policy participation and co-creation by citizens and interest groups
- The formation of online interest-based communities

In both Singapore and Hong Kong, the Internet has facilitated the formation of online political and civic communities, with social media platforms allowing for the formation of closer ties among civil society organizations and facilitating collective action (Chu and Tang 2005, Soon and Kluver 2007, Soon 2016). However, this civil society activity towards cyberspace is necessarily uniform among civil society organizations. For instance, Soon and Cho (2011) have found that political bloggers and political parties in Singapore tend to dominate cyberspace, while issue-based advocacy groups and media agencies tend to occupy less important positions.

This dominance of political parties alludes to a growing tendency of smart developmental states to manage, or even dominate, civil society in the cyber sphere. For instance, Soon and Soh (2014) have found that Singapore's political elite is increasingly relying on media tools such as Facebook, Twitter, and personal blogs to engage citizens and articulate its political message. Aside from these social media and new media tools, the Singapore government has also established an online feedback platform, named 'REACH', that allows it to gather public sentiments and feedback and engage with citizens and grassroots organizations (MCI REACH 2017).

Similarly, the Hong Kong government is increasingly relying on the Internet to engage citizens and civil society organizations, whether through social media platforms such as Facebook or online policy consultations (Govada et al. 2017). However, and unlike Singapore, the Hong Kong government has yet to establish a centralized online public engagement platform, with existing efforts to engage citizens and civil society issue-based and often dominated by pro-government business interests (Cheung 2011). Hence while Singapore's smart city transformation has given rise to fundamental shifts in its government's interactions with civil society, the Hong Kong government's efforts at citizen 'e-engagement' remain relatively fragmented and business-oriented.

Beyond public engagement through the new media and social media, smart cities have also come to be associated with new modalities of socio-political engagements, impacting the state's relationships with citizens and civil society. As Ho (2016, p. 3103) has noted, 'the smart city is fundamentally about redefining and reconfiguring *relations* within and between people, their community, government and the urban environment'. Hence, not only is the smart city inherently a *relational* subject or endeavour, but it also represents a more fundamental reconfiguration of governing logics and relations in the city.

Drawing on the case of Singapore, Ho has also noted that the smart city's control or dominance over its population approximates Foucauldian 'governmentality', with smart city initiatives often serving to perpetuate neoliberal logics of the state, 'thereby facilitating authoritarian consolidation in Singapore' (Ho 2016). Examples include 'attempts to re-shape values and priorities of household resource consumption through the lens of the market subject' through the implementation of 'smart homes' with advanced energy and water management systems or the reduction of elderly caregiving to a reductionist technological rationality through smart monitoring systems (Ho 2016, pp. 3107–3110).

In other words, the application of social media and advanced ICT tools to managing state–societal relations extends beyond simple public engagement to encompass more subtle efforts to (re)shape the public agenda and re-shape societal norms and values. For instance, the Smart Nation initiative has been seen as a means of reconfiguring the boundaries and modes of citizen participation towards that of 'smart urbanism', with its emphasis on computational skills and thinking obviating more contentious forms of political participation (Ho 2016, pp. 3110–3112).

However, it should also be noted that this technical (and technological) rationalization of civil society is neither new nor unique to Singapore. Indeed, such predilections for technical rationality and technologically mediated forms of civic participation are characteristic of many, if not all, smart cities. This is evident in the hackathons, open data platforms and co-creation of 'smart' solutions and applications that have emerged in smart cities across the world. However, the technical rationalization of civil society is particularly marked in Singapore, due to its relatively technocratic approach to policy and governance (Barr 2006, Tan 2012).

Hence in place of contentious politics or a vibrant civil society, such technologically mediated forms of urban participation serve to reiterate, and even reify, Singapore's technocratic form of elite governance (Barr 2006, 2014). This suggests a growing rationalization of the civil society sphere, with technological solutions replacing political mobilization, both as means of fostering state–societal relations and avenue for providing policy feedback or co-creating policy solutions. As Ho summarizes, 'participation in the Smart Nation is restricted to computational tinkering and tweaks that seek to improve efficiencies according to economic and technical rationality' (Ho 2016, p. 3112).

The emergence of the smart developmental state has therefore given rise to profound changes in the ways in which governments manage and interact with civil society organizations. While social media, new media and other advanced ICT tools provide governments with useful new tools for engaging with civil society, the growing technical rationalization of the civic sphere has also given rise to more subtle forms of social control. This latter point signifies a fundamental shift in the governance of civil society, with technology providing not only the means for engaging with and managing civil society organizations, but the discursive and epistemological foundations upon which civil society activities are based as well.

Furthermore, this growing focus on technical rationality melds neatly with the developmental state model's key driving ideology of performance legitimacy, which emphasizes economic performance and technical efficiency as bases of political legitimacy. I will now turn my attention to performance legitimacy, and its relevance to the smart developmental state.

Performance legitimacy

Given its continued emphasis on economic growth and development, performance legitimacy continues to form a crucial component of the smart developmental state. As I have discussed in Chapter 5, the smart city strategies of both Singapore and Hong Kong emphasize the economic potential of 'smart' industries such as data analytics and the Internet of things. More importantly, smart developmental states like Singapore and Hong Kong continue to draw political legitimacy from their ability to ensure strong economic growth and deliver material improvements to citizens' lives.

For instance, Singapore's Smart Nation initiative emphasizes the two goals of 'improving people's lives' and 'creating new economic opportunities' (Lee 2014, Smart Nation Programme Office 2016, Woo 2017a). Similarly, Hong Kong's Smart City Blueprint also emphasizes economic policy objectives such as enhancing Hong Kong's attractiveness to businesses and stimulating economic growth and innovation, along with improving citizens' quality of life, especially through more effective urban policy interventions (Office of the Government Chief Information Officer 2016, PWC 2017).

Hence in both Singapore and Hong Kong, smart city strategies remain development-oriented, with the goals and objectives of these strategies geared towards stimulating economic growth. At the same time, both cities emphasize goals of improving citizens' lives or 'quality of living' through technological means. This emphasis on economic development and material improvements to citizens' lives also alludes to the continued relevance, and importance, of performance legitimacy in ensuring public support for the two governments' smart city initiatives.

However, Singapore and Hong Kong vary in their level of performance legitimacy. While Singapore continues to enjoy high levels of performance legitimacy, with the ruling People's Action Party securing a significant gain in vote-share during the 2015 general election, which took place soon after the launch of the Smart Nation initiative (Tan 2016, Tan et al. 2016), Hong Kong has been experiencing a decline in its performance legitimacy, with declining confidence in the government giving way to mass social protests (Lam 2015, Chan and Chan 2017, Lam and Cooper 2017, Wong and Chan 2017).

Indeed, Cheung (2004, p. 20) has argued that the Hong Kong government's legitimacy deficit was increasingly exposed, as its capacity to deliver policy outcomes or manage citizen expectations declined. While this decline in Hong Kong's performance legitimacy has been attributed to deficiencies in its political system (Lam 2015), the introduction of a smart city strategy has not, as yet at least, bolstered Hong Kong's performance legitimacy. As of this writing, neither Hong Kong's social protests nor its decline in performance legitimacy are showing any signs of abatement (Griffiths 2017, ABC News 2018).

The diverging fortunes of Singapore and Hong Kong, in terms of their performance legitimacy, is related to the levels of political and policy capacity possessed by their respective governments. Specifically, Singapore's high levels of political and policy capacity – whether arising from its electoral system or the effectiveness of its policies – has bolstered its performance legitimacy considerably, while prominent policy failures coupled with stalled political reforms has resulted in a decline, or even decay, in Hong Kong's performance legitimacy (Lam 2015, Woo 2017b, 2017c, 2017d, 2017d). I will discuss this capacity aspect of the smart developmental state in the next chapter.

Conclusion

While critics of the Asian developmental state model have been quick to suggest its demise (Fine 1999, Kim 1999, Minns 2001, Hayashi 2010), the reality is much more nuanced. Faced with a highly globalized and increasingly digitized economy, developmental states such as Singapore and Hong Kong have adapted their approach to economic development and industrial policy by transforming themselves into 'smart developmental states'. This involves supporting the development of 'smart' industries such as data analytics and the Internet of things as well as incorporating advanced ICT and data analytics into policy and political processes.

As I have discussed in this chapter, the transformations of Singapore and Hong Kong into smart developmental states have given rise to major shifts in both cities' economic governance models. While both cities have retained the fundamental structure of the developmental state model, there have been modifications and adaptations to the individual components that make up this structure, i.e. developmental elite, pilot agency, embedded autonomy, management of non-state interests, civil society and performance legitimacy. These adaptations are listed in Table 6.1 below.

As Table 6.1 shows, the transformation from a traditional Asian developmental state to a 'smart developmental state' is not simply about the application of technological tools to development and governance; nor is it simply a matter of building up the necessary 'hardware', such as ICT infrastructure. Rather, there has been a deeper shift in governance styles and models. In particular, smart developmental states such as Singapore and Hong Kong have incorporated a significant extent of citizen and industry

Table 6.1 Adaptations to the developmental state model

Components	*Modifications*
Developmental elite	Growing role of technology firms and start-ups, although state remains dominant.
Pilot agency	Specialized and decentralized pilot agencies
Embedded autonomy	State as catalyst of technological innovation and entrepreneurship; Platforms for policy co-creation
Management of non-state interests	Growing focus on attracting both large and small firms and start-ups
Civil society	Engaging civil society through social media and new media; managing and control of civil society organizations through technical rationalization
Performance legitimacy	Use of smart city initiatives to enhance economic growth and improve material well-being of citizens

engagement and policy co-creation with these stakeholders. Furthermore, the state increasingly plays a supporting role in *facilitating* innovation and entrepreneurship, rather than generating new businesses and innovations through public agencies or state-owned entities (although efforts to do so have not been lacking).

However, it is also important to note that such shifts do not necessarily result in a complete overhaul of the traditional developmental state model. As I have shown in Chapter 5, Singapore and Hong Kong continue to take a state-centric approach to their smart city strategies, albeit with varying degrees of state control or intervention. Rather, the abovementioned shifts in governance style can be seen as a *layering on* of new modes of governance and civic engagement onto an existing developmental state framework. Hence while elements of the developmental state, such as the developmental elite or pilot agency, remain intact, they have been modified for greater policy responsiveness and efficiency, whether through co-opting technology firms into the developmental elite or creating specialized and decentralized pilot agencies.

In other words, the smart developmental state represents a revised and refreshed version of the developmental state model, taking into account new technologies and shifting socio-political landscapes, rather than an entirely new model of economic governance. More importantly, this suggests a significant extent of agency and adaptability among developmental states. Faced with potentially disruptive economic, socio-political and technological changes, smart developmental states such as Singapore and Hong Kong have exhibited a strong ability to adapt and adjust their style of governance, organizational form, and even ideological bases in response to such shifting realities.

This poses significant theoretical and conceptual implications for the Asian developmental state model. While existing studies on the Asian developmental state tend to take a static and descriptive approach, there is a need to understand the dynamism and adaptability that is characteristic of many developmental states. While I have sought to address these theoretical implications within this chapter, there is much scope and need for further research on the evolution of the Asian developmental state in a rapidly shifting environment.

References

ABC News, 2018. China warned not to meddle further by Hong Kong protesters [online]. *ABC News*. Available from: http://www.abc.net.au/news/2018-01-02/hong-kong-democracy-protesters-sound-warning-to-china/9297720 [Accessed 9 Jan 2018].

Aoki, N., 2015. Institutionalization of New Public Management: The case of Singapore's education system. *Public Management Review*, 17 (2), 165–186.

Audrey Yue and Helen Hok-Sze Leung, 2017. Notes towards the queer Asian city: Singapore and Hong Kong. *Urban Studies*, 54 (3), 747–764.

Barr, M.D., 2006. Beyond technocracy: The culture of elite governance in Lee Hsien Loong's Singapore. *Asian Studies Review*, 30 (1), 1–18.

Barr, M.D., 2014. *The ruling elite of Singapore: networks of power and influence.* London: I.B. Tauris.

Block, F. and Negoita, M., 2016. Beyond Embedded Autonomy: Conceptualizing the Work of Developmental States. *In*: Y. Chu, ed. *The Asian Developmental State: Reexaminations and New Departures.* New York, N.Y.: Palgrave Macmillan, 57–72.

Burns, J.P., 1994. Administrative reform in a changing political environment: The case of Hong Kong. *Public Administration and Development*, 14 (3), 241–252.

Calder, K.E., 2016. *Singapore: Smart City, Smart State.* Washington, D.C.: Brookings Institution Press.

Carroll, T. and Jarvis, D.S.L., 2017. *Asia after the Developmental State: Disembedding Autonomy.* Cambridge, UK: Cambridge University Press.

Chan, E. and Chan, J., 2017. Hong Kong 2007–2017: a backlash in civil society. *Asia Pacific Journal of Public Administration*, 39 (2), 135–152.

Cheung, A.B.L., 1996. Efficiency As the Rhetoric: Public-Sector Reform in Hong Kong Explained. *International Review of Administrative Sciences*, 62 (1), 31–47.

Cheung, A.B.L., 2004. Strong executive, weak policy capacity: The changing environment of policy-making in Hong Kong. *Asian Journal of Political Science*, 12 (1), 1–30.

Cheung, A.B.L., 2008. The story of two administrative states: state capacity in Hong Kong and Singapore. *The Pacific Review*, 21 (2), 121–145.

Cheung, P.T.Y., 2011. Civic engagement in the policy process in Hong Kong: Change and continuity. *Public Administration and Development*, 31 (2), 113–121.

Chu, Y.-W. and Tang, J.T.H., 2005. The Internet and Civil Society: Environmental and Labour Organizations in Hong Kong. *International Journal of Urban and Regional Research*, 29 (4), 849–866.

Committee on the Future Economy, 2017. *Report of the Committee on the Future Economy.* Singapore: Government of Singapore.

Committee on the Future of Economy Secretariat, 2015. Committee On The Future Economy To Review Singapore's Economic Strategies and Position Us For The Future. Singapore: Ministry of Finance, Press Release.

Economic Review Committee, 2003. *New Challenges, Fresh Goals: Towards a Dynamic Global City.* Singapore: Ministry of Trade and Industry.

Fine, B., 1999. The Developmental State Is Dead—Long Live Social Capital? *Development and Change*, 30 (1), 1–19.

George, C., 2007. Consolidating authoritarian rule: calibrated coercion in Singapore. *The Pacific Review*, 20 (2), 127–145.

Govada, S.S., Wong, F., Rodgers, T., Chow, H.Y.C., and Busa, K., 2017. E-Engagement in Hong Kong. *In*: B. Dahiya, ed. *E-Democracy for Smart Cities.* Springer, Singapore, 143–180.

Griffiths, J., 2017. Three years after Umbrella Movement, Hong Kongers back on the streets [online]. *CNN.* Available from: http://www.cnn.com/2017/10/01/asia/hong-kong-protest-umbrella/index.html [Accessed 9 Jan 2018].

Haque, M.S., 2002. Structures of New Public Management in Malaysia and Singapore: Alternative Views. *The Journal of Comparative Asian Development*, 1 (1), 71–86.

Hayashi, S., 2010. The developmental state in the era of globalization: beyond the Northeast Asian model of political economy. *The Pacific Review*, 23 (1), 45–69.

Ho, E., 2016. Smart subjects for a Smart Nation? Governing (smart)mentalities in Singapore. *Urban Studies*, 0042098016664305.

Hood, C., 1991. A Public Management for All Seasons? *Public Administration*, 69 (1), 3–19.

Hood, C., 1995. The 'new public management' in the 1980s: Variations on a theme. *Accounting, Organizations and Society*, 20 (2–3), 93–109.

InvestHK, 2012. Information and Communications Technology | English [online]. *Government of the Hong Kong Special Administrative Region*. Available from: http://www.investhk.gov.hk/business-opportunities/information-communications-technology.html [Accessed 5 Jan 2018].

Jarvis, D.S.L., 2011. Race for the money: international financial centres in Asia. *Journal of International Relations and Development*, 14 (1), 60–95.

Kim, Y.T., 1999. Neoliberalism and the decline of the developmental state. *Journal of Contemporary Asia*, 29 (4), 441–461.

Lam, J.T.M., 2015. Political Decay in Hong Kong After the Occupy Central Movement. *Asian Affairs: An American Review*, 42 (2), 99–121.

Lam, W. and Cooper, L., 2017. *Citizenship, Identity and Social Movements in the New Hong Kong: Localism after the Umbrella Movement*. London: Routledge.

Lee, E.W.Y. and Haque, M.S., 2006. The New Public Management Reform and Governance in Asian NICs: A Comparison of Hong Kong and Singapore. *Governance*, 19 (4), 605–626.

Lee, H.L., 2014. Smart Nation: Better living, more opportunities, stronger communities.

Lester, R.K. and Piore, M.J., 2006. *Innovation—The Missing Dimension*. Cambridge, M.A.: Harvard University Press.

MCI REACH, 2017. About REACH [online]. *Government of Singapore*. Available from: https://www.reach.gov.sg/about-us/about-reach [Accessed 8 Jan 2018].

Menon, R., 2013. Interview.

Minns, J., 2001. Of miracles and models: The rise and decline of the developmental state in South Korea. *Third World Quarterly*, 22 (6), 1025–1043.

Morgenbesser, L., 2017. The autocratic mandate: elections, legitimacy and regime stability in Singapore. *The Pacific Review*, 30 (2), 205–231.

Mushkat, M. and Mushkat, R., 2016. The Political Economy of Constitutional Incrementalism in Hong Kong. *Northwestern Interdisciplinary Law Review*, 9, 1–46.

Ng, B.K., 1998. *Hong Kong and Singapore as International Financial Centres: A Comparative Functional Perspective*. Singapore: Nanyang Technological University, SABRE Working Paper No. 6–98.

Office of the Government Chief Information Officer, 2014. Digital 21 Strategy – Public Consultation and Submissions [online]. *Government of the Hong Kong Special Administrative Region*. Available from: http://www.digital21.gov.hk/eng/relatedDoc/submissions2013.htm [Accessed 12 Jan 2018].

Office of the Government Chief Information Officer, 2016. *The Smart City Blueprint for Hong Kong*. Hong Kong: Government of the Hong Kong Special Administrative Region.

Osborne, D. and Gaebler, T., 1993. *Reinventing government: how the entrepreneurial spirit is transforming the public sector*. New York, N.Y.: Plume.

Pollitt, C. and Bouckaert, G., 2011. *Public Management Reform: A Comparative Analysis – New Public Management, Governance, and the Neo-Weberian State*. 3rd ed. Oxford; New York: Oxford University Press.

Poon, K., 2018. The Impasse Over Constitutional Reform: Negotiating Democracy in Hong Kong. *In*: B.C.H. Fong and T.-L. Lui, eds. *Hong Kong 20 Years after the Handover*. Palgrave Macmillan, Cham, 3–19.

PWC, 2017. *Report of Consultancy Study on Smart City Blueprint for Hong Kong*. Hong Kong: PricewaterhouseCoopers Advisory Services Limited.

Rodan, G., 2003. Embracing electronic media but suppressing civil society: Authoritarian consolidation in Singapore. *The Pacific Review*, 16 (4), 503–524.

Sarker, A.E., 2006. New public management in developing countries: An analysis of success and failure with particular reference to Singapore and Bangladesh. *International Journal of Public Sector Management*, 19 (2), 180–203.

Shen, L.-Y., Platten, A., and Deng, X.P., 2006. Role of public private partnerships to manage risks in public sector projects in Hong Kong. *International Journal of Project Management*, 24 (7), 587–594.

Skoric, M.M., Pan, J., and Poor, N.D., 2012. *Social Media and Citizen Engagement in a City-State: A Study of Singapore*. Dublin, Ireland: AAAI, Proceedings of the Sixth International AAAI Conference on Weblogs and Social Media.

Smart Nation Programme Office, 2016. About Smart Nation [online]. Available from: http://www.smartnation.sg/about-smart-nation [Accessed 22 Oct 2016].

Soon, C., 2016. Civil society and technology: whither the change? *In*: C. Soon and G. Koh, eds. *Civil Society and the State in Singapore*. Singapore: World Scientific, 87–109.

Soon, C. and Cho, H., 2011. Flows of Relations and Communication among Singapore Political Bloggers and Organizations: The Networked Public Sphere Approach. *Journal of Information Technology & Politics*, 8 (1), 93–109.

Soon, C. and Kluver, R., 2007. The Internet and Online Political Communities in Singapore. *Asian Journal of Communication*, 17 (3), 246–265.

Soon, C. and Soh, Y.D., 2014. Engagement@web 2.0 between the government and citizens in Singapore: dialogic communication on Facebook? *Asian Journal of Communication*, 24 (1), 42–59.

Sreekumar, T.T. and Vadrevu, S., 2013. Subpolitics and Democracy: The Role of New Media in the 2011 General Elections in Singapore. *Science Technology & Society*, 18 (2), 231–249.

Sriramesh, K. and Rivera-Sánchez, M., 2006. E-government in a corporatist, communitarian society: the case of Singapore. *New Media & Society*, 8 (5), 707–730.

Swan Gin, B., 2017. Singapore's long game in innovation. *The Straits Times*, 23 Aug.

Tan, K.P., 2012. The Ideology of Pragmatism: Neo-liberal Globalisation and Political Authoritarianism in Singapore. *Journal of Contemporary Asia*, 42 (1), 67–92.

Tan, K.P., 2016. Singapore in 2015. *Asian Survey*, 56 (1), 108–114.

Tan, T.H., Tng, Y.H., and Yeo, A., 2016. Normalization versus Equalization Effects of the Internet for Political Parties: Singapore's General Election 2015 as a Case Study. *In*: *2016 Conference for E-Democracy and Open Government (CeDEM)*. Presented at the 2016 Conference for E-Democracy and Open Government (CeDEM), 84–95.

Terekhova, M., 2017. Here's why Chinese tech giants are choosing to list in Hong Kong [online]. *Business Insider*. Available from: http://www.businessinsider.com/heres-why-chinese-tech-giants-are-choosing-to-list-in-hong-kong-2017-12 [Accessed 5 Jan 2018].

Topping, S., 2013. Interview.

Tsang, D., 2013. Interview.

Wong, Y.C. and Chan, J.K.H., 2017. Civil disobedience movements in Hong Kong: a civil society perspective. *Asian Education and Development Studies*, 6 (4), 312–332.

Woo, J.J., 2015a. Policy Relations and Policy Subsystems: Financial policy in Hong Kong and Singapore. *International Journal of Public Administration*, 38 (8), 553–561.

Woo, J.J., 2015b. Beyond the Neoliberal orthodoxy: Alternative financial policy regimes in Asia's financial centres. *Critical Policy Studies*, 9 (3), 297–316.

Woo, J.J., 2016. *Business and Politics in Asia's Key Financial Centres – Hong Kong, Singapore and Shanghai.* 1st ed. Singapore: Springer.

Woo, J.J., 2017a. *Singapore's Smart Nation Initiative – A Policy and Organisational Perspective.* Singapore: Lee Kuan Yew School of Public Policy, National University of Singapore.

Woo, J.J., 2017b. *3-in-1: Governing a Global Financial Centre.* Singapore: World Scientific.

Woo, J.J., 2017c. Arresting the painful decline of Hong Kong's financial centre status [online]. *Channel NewsAsia.* Available from: http://www.channelnewsasia.com/news/asiapacific/commentary-arresting-the-painful-decline-of-hong-kong-s-9030492 [Accessed 3 Dec 2017].

Woo, J.J., 2017d. Commentary: Hong Kong, a cautionary tale for Singapore, a lesson for the future [online]. *Channel NewsAsia.* Available from: https://www.channelnewsasia.com/news/singapore/commentary-hong-kong-a-cautionary-tale-for-singapore-a-lesson-9093180 [Accessed 9 Jan 2018].

Yahya, Y., 2017. EntrePass scheme enhanced to attract global start-ups to Singapore. *The Straits Times*, 2 Aug.

Yiu, E. and Zhang, S., 2017. New economy stocks hog the limelight in the age of technology. *South China Morning Post*, 30 Dec.

Yung, B. and Leung, L.Y.-M., 2014. Diverse roles of alternative media in Hong Kong civil society: from public discourse initiation to social activism. *Journal of Asian Public Policy*, 7 (1), 83–101.

7 The smart developmental state

As Asia enters the new digital economy (Bain & Company 2017, Sheng 2017), its nations and cities are undergoing extensive digitization, giving rise to a proliferation of smart cities that seek to leverage the latest digital and data technologies to address emerging policy issues and drive economic development.

Yet while smart cities in Western developed economies have emphasized greater civic engagement and policy co-creation or co-production between the state and its citizens (Bakıcı 2012, Crivello 2014, Goldsmith and Crawford 2014, Kitchin 2014, Neirotti et al. 2014), Asian smart cities have retained a strong focus on spurring economic development through the application of smart technologies or the development of new industries associated with this digitization of the economy, with the state continuing to play an outsized role in smart city formation.

This is especially evident in the two cases that I have examined in this book: Singapore and Hong Kong. It is by no means a matter of coincidence that Singapore and Hong Kong have taken similar trajectories and governing approaches to developing their smart cities. As I have discussed in Chapters 3 and 4, Singapore and Hong Kong are archetypal Asian developmental states, with both cities possessing the six key components of a typical developmental state (Leftwich 1995):

- Developmental elite
- Pilot agency
- Embedded autonomy
- Management of non-state economic interests
- Civil society
- Performance legitimacy

Indeed, both cities have leveraged their mastery of (and over) these six key developmental state components to achieve strong and consistent economic growth. Despite the occasional emergence of political resistance to certain elements of the their developmental state models such as control over civil society or an over-emphasis of economic over socio-political development

(Chong 2012, Tan 2012, Chan and Chan 2017, Lam and Cooper 2017), both Singapore and Hong Kong continue to rely on a developmental state approach to economic development and governance (Lim 2015, Cheng 2016, Woo 2016, Yeung 2017).

This persistence of the developmental state model in Singapore and Hong Kong also flows into their respective smart city initiatives, with both cities' digitization and transformation into smart cities very much predicated upon economic motivations and driven by development-oriented policy initiatives. As I have discussed in Chapters 5 and 6, the ongoing transformation of Singapore and Hong Kong into leading smart cities has involved the retention of key developmental state components, with the result being the emergence of a 'smart developmental state' that incorporates and leverages advanced ICT and 'smart' technologies to further its developmental agenda. Table 7.1 provides a broad overview of the components of this emerging smart developmental state.

As Table 7.1 shows, the smart developmental state comprises a set of modified developmental state components, with varying degrees of modification or adaptation. For instance, the smart developmental state continues to be driven by a developmental elite, although there have been growing efforts to include or co-opt technology firms and start-ups into the fold of the developmental elite.

Hence while the governments of Singapore and Hong Kong had previously sought to include private sector actors from sectors such as manufacturing, services and finance into their developmental elite, the growing

Table 7.1 Components of the smart developmental state

Developmental state					
Developmental elite	Pilot agency	Embedded autonomy	Management of non-state economic interests	Civil society	Performan legitima
Smart developmental state					
Developmental elite remains intact, with inclusion/co-optation of technology firms/ start-ups	Smart city-specific pilot agencies, e.g. Smart Nation and Digital Government Group; Innovation and Technology Bureau	More 'embedded than 'autonomy', but state remains in charge.	Greater diversity in firms; asymmetric relationship	Technologically mediated civic participation	Economic and technica rational

significance and prominence of 'smart industries' as future drivers of growth has prompted policymakers and political leaders to include representatives from these emerging sectors in key policy decision-making mechanisms such as policy consultations and advisory committees.

However, it is also important to note that this growing role of technology firms and start-ups in the developmental elite does not necessarily conform to traditional developmental state politics. Specifically, the advanced ICT tools and platforms that have emerged in tandem with the smart city, such as social media and big data, have given rise to new modes of public–private interactions and communications. As I have discussed in Chapters 5 and 6, this has resulted in changes to the ways in which developmental states interact with civil society and non-state economic interests.

In terms of non-state economic interests, new 'smart' tools such as open data platforms have facilitated closer interactions between the state and business interests. More importantly, such technologically augmented interactions have given rise to the co-creation of policy solutions and initiatives (Woo 2017a). Aside from open data platforms, policymakers have also sought to co-develop 'smart' technologies through research collaborations, pilot trials, state-sponsored start-up incubators and state investments in R&D. In all instances, technological tools and platforms have become the nexus around which the developmental state is able to interact and collaborate with its industry partners.

To some extent, the same can be said about the smart developmental state's relations with civil society. While data analytics and sensor technologies have enhanced public service delivery through the efficient collection and interpretation of data, feedback platforms such as Singapore's One-Service app have allowed policymakers to engage directly with citizens, who are now able to provide feedback on emerging policy issues. However, and as scholars have noted, the smart city has also been employed as a means of control and dominance over citizens and civil society through a heightened emphasis on technical rationality (Ho 2016).

Hence while smart technologies have provided new platforms for policymakers and political leaders to engage citizens and other stakeholders, these have also allowed for greater control over civil society, often through more subtle means. In short, the smart developmental state's approach to managing civil society is not very different from that of the traditional developmental state, with the only difference being the technologically augmented means through which control over civil society is exercised.

This ability to engage citizens more deeply, yet at the same time retain state control over civil society and the overall public consciousness, also points towards the continued relevance of embedded autonomy as a key ideological foundation of the developmental state model. Through the various technological tools and platforms that were discussed in earlier chapters, smart developmental states are able to embed themselves more deeply within the socio-political milieu. Yet at the same time, and through top-down ownership and oversight of these various tools and platforms, such public–private interactions often take place within the terms and conditions of the state.

As the case of Singapore has shown, platforms such as the OneService app, FinTech regulatory sandbox and open data platforms are all owned and operated by public agencies, with these platforms organized under the rubrics of the Smart Nation initiative. Furthermore, the formulation and implementation of smart city initiatives such as the Smart Nation initiative or Smart City Blueprint remain solely within the purview of the respective governments, with private sector involvement typically restricted to that of consultancy. As such, the policy autonomy of both the Singapore and Hong Kong governments remain strong, with policy initiatives driven by public agencies and these agencies relatively insulated from socio-political pressures.

At the pinnacle of such politically insulated public agencies sits the pilot agency. Here, there has been a significant departure from the traditional developmental state model. While the traditional developmental state has relied on a single pilot agency to drive its economic development policies, smart developmental states such as Singapore and Hong Kong have established decentralized pilot agencies such as the Smart Nation and Digital Government Group (SNDGG) and Office of the Government Chief Information Officer (OGCIO) to lead sectorial development. Such decentralized pilot agencies are not new, with agencies such as the Monetary Authority of Singapore and Hong Kong Monetary Authority, among others, playing the role of sectorial pilot agencies (in this case, financial sector development).

However, there is a key difference between smart city pilot agencies such as the SNDGG or OGCIO and other decentralized pilot agencies. Specifically, digitization and smart city initiatives tend to take a 'whole-of-government' approach, with almost all, if not all, government departments subject to some extent of digitization. Given their role in driving the overall smart city transformation, smart city pilot agencies therefore operate across sectorial boundaries and policy domains. For instance, Singapore's Smart Nation initiative encompasses policy domains such as public transport, healthcare, financial regulation, public housing and education, among others.

This requires the SNDGG to coordinate Smart Nation initiatives across the various government departments and public agencies. This suggests a greater extent of centralization than other decentralized pilot agencies. More importantly, the smart city pilot agency works in tandem with the overall pilot agency, such as Singapore's Economic Development Board or Hong Kong's Development Bureau, to coordinate the digitization and developmental activities of sectorial pilot agencies, such as the Monetary Authority of Singapore and Hong Kong Monetary Authority in financial sector development. This is illustrated in Table 7.2.

As the last column of Table 7.1 shows, the inter-linkages and synergies among the various pilot agencies allow for the establishment and

Table 7.2 Inter-linkages between pilot agencies

	Sectorial pilot agency	*Sectorial pilot agency*	*Sectorial pilot agency*	Linkages between smart city and economy
Overall pilot agency	Economic development + sectorial development	Economic development + sectorial development	Economic development + sectorial development	
Smart city pilot agency	Digitization + economic/sectorial development	Digitization + economic/ sectorial development	Digitization + economic/ sectorial development	

development of the various linkages between smart city development and economic growth. As I have discussed in Chapter 5, the smart city initiatives of both Singapore and Hong Kong are geared towards stimulating economic growth and development, whether by fostering technologically enabled productivity and innovation or developing new 'smart' sectors such as data analytics or the Internet of things. This increasingly complex and interlocking system of pilot agencies represents a significant modification to the developmental state model, requiring further research and conceptualization.

As I have shown in this book and summarized in this chapter thus far, the transformation of developmental states such as Singapore and Hong Kong into smart cities has given rise to modifications and adaptations to the developmental state model, with the end result being the emergence of the smart developmental state. While it retains the major components of the developmental state model, the smart developmental state encapsulates significant modifications and adaptations within these major components. These have been discussed above.

Taking a policy-centric understanding of the developmental state

Fundamentally driven by policy initiatives such as the Smart Nation initiative and Smart City Blueprint, the shift from developmental state to smart developmental state also suggests a need to take a policy-oriented approach to understanding the developmental state. While the developmental state model has thus far been rooted in political economy and political science (Douglass 1994, Johnson 1995, Leftwich 1995, Woo-Cumings 1999, Evans 2010), there is also a need to situate the developmental state within its broader policy context.

This will allow for a more dynamic understanding of the developmental state that takes into account the impacts of policy shifts and changes. As this book has shown, broad policy shifts such as public sector digitization and smart city transformations can result in significant changes in a country or city's developmental state. In particular, the developmental state model may benefit from incorporating insights from two emerging streams of public policy literature: policy capacity and policy design.

In the remainder of this chapter, I will provide a brief discussion of these two emerging public policy theoretical concepts that can contribute to a policy-centric understanding of the developmental state.

Policy capacity

Given its focus on economic performance, there is a strong emphasis on the state's competence and ability to deliver strong and consistent economic growth. Such state competence has been variously described as state strength (Ikenberry 1986, Sørensen 1993, Volgy and Bailin 2003, Shen and Williamson 2005) or state capacity (Rondinelli and Cheema 2003, Besley and Persson 2010, Hendrix 2010, Savoia and Sen 2012, Mietzner 2017). These notions of state strength have been applied to research on Singapore and Hong Kong (Cheung 2008, Lee 2009).

However, it has been argued that state-centric approaches such as state capacity or state strength tend to underestimate the role of private sector and societal actors in resolving policy issues (Doner 1992). Others have gone even so far as to argue that state capacity is no longer relevant, with private authority overtaking the state as key policy actor (Strange 1996, Cutler et al. 1999, Haufler 2001). However, such an overemphasis on the policy role of private actors is also limited by the fact that states continue to exercise authority over policy formulation processes (Howlett and Lejano 2013, Capano et al. 2015).

There is therefore a need for a balanced understanding of a state's capacity or ability to attain its policy goals that takes into account the roles of both public and private sector actors. To this end, more recent literature on 'policy capacity' may prove instructive (Bakvis 2000, Painter and Pierre 2005, Gleeson et al. 2011). Specifically, Wu et al. (2015, p. 166, 2018, p. 3) define policy capacity as the 'set of skills and resources – or competencies and capabilities – necessary to perform policy functions'.

According to Wu *et al.*, policy capacity can further be broken down into analytical, operational and political capacities at the individual, organizational and systemic levels (Wu et al. 2018, p. 4). Aside from providing conceptual depth, these various permutations of policy capacities can also be easily applied to the developmental state. For instance, systemic political capacities such as 'legitimation capacity' are closely related to performance legitimacy, with a state's ability to generate public trust and support for its policies dependent on its levels of legitimation capacity, which may in turn draw from the state's ability to ensure strong economic performance (Pal and Clark 2015, Woo et al. 2015).

At the organizational level, organizational policy capacities determine the ability of pilot agencies and other public agencies to lead economic development, whether in terms of their analytical and operational ability to handle complex policy issues (Gleeson et al. 2011, Peters 2015) or their ability to navigate the socio-political milieu in discharging their duties, i.e. embedded autonomy (Anne 2015, Dunlop 2015). In short, policy capacity provides a potentially useful tool for understanding development states and reframing the developmental state model in terms of policy capacity. This may in turn allow for more systematic appraisals of developmental state performance and capabilities.

As it stands, there are growing efforts to understand the developmental states of Singapore and Hong Kong in terms of policy capacity (Cheung 2004, 2008, Woo et al. 2016), although these studies could do with greater conceptual specification. Aside from scholarly work, policy capacity is also slowly entering the lexicon of policymakers and practitioners. For instance, training and reskilling initiatives such as the SkillsFuture scheme have been seen as part of the Singapore government's efforts at 'capacity building', i.e. developing more ICT talent and specialists (Hoe 2016, p. 328).

Another example can be found in the 'industry transformation maps' (ITMs) that were published by the Singapore Government's Committee for the Future Economy and which aim to guide the development of specific industries in order to ensure productivity and competitiveness in these industries (Committee on the Future Economy 2017, pp. 48–52). In particular, the Committee emphasizes that ITMs are not about 'picking winners' but aim to 'build capacities at the industry level' (Committee on the Future Economy 2017, p. 49).

Hence whether at the individual, organizational or industry level, smart city initiatives tend to emphasize capacity building. Certainly, the discussions in Chapter 5 have also alluded to the potential for smart technologies to enhance the various policy capacities that were identified by Wu *et al.* For instance, data analytics and sensor technologies can be seen as means of enhancing the analytical capacity of governments and their public agencies, while citizen engagement platforms such as open data platforms or Singapore's OneService app can contribute towards political capacity by fostering closer public–private relations and trust.

Certainly, there is much scope for future research on policy capacity in smart developmental states. Aside from policy capacity, there are also merits to taking a policy design approach to understanding the developmental state model. I will now discuss these potential linkages between policy design and the developmental state.

Policy design

Policy design has been defined as the 'deliberate and conscious attempt to define policy goals and connect them to instruments or tools expected to realize these objectives' (Howlett et al. 2015, p. 291). While this tool-based understanding has formed the foundations of policy design (Hood

1986, Woodside 1986, Elmore 1987, Bressers and Klok 1988, Howlett 1991, Bemelmans-Videc et al. 1998, Vedung 1998), more recent research in policy design has sought to address the procedural aspects of formulating and implementing policy instruments (Howlett 2000) as well as the socio-political context within which policy design takes place (Howlett 2009, Schneider and Sidney 2009, Howlett 2011, Madrian 2014).

More importantly, the policy design literature is increasingly taking a broader and more systematic view that addresses the efforts of policy designers to formulate and implement packages of tools, or 'policy mixes' that seek to achieve a set of desired policy objectives as well as the myriad ways in which tools within a given policy mix interact with each other (Grabosky 1995, Gunningham *et al.* 1998, Howlett 2004, Howlett et al. 2009). These efforts have given rise to what are known as 'new governance arrangements' that involve the 'layering' or 'patching' on of new policy instruments to an existing policy mix (Béland 2007, Howlett and Rayner 2007, Rayner and Howlett 2009, Howlett and Rayner 2013, 2014).

This latter stream of research on 'new governance arrangements' has proven particularly relevant to smart city strategies such as Singapore's Smart Nation initiative and Hong Kong's Smart City Blueprint. In both instances, a broad policy framework comprising a well-defined set of policy goals and policy tools or initiatives was established (Office of the Government Chief Information Officer 2016, Smart Nation Programme Office 2017). For instance, Singapore's Smart Nation initiative includes three broad policy goals – enhancing economic opportunities, addressing urban issues, and fostering community development – and provides a list of policy tools, in the form of policy 'enablers' (Lee 2014, Smart Nation Programme Office 2017, Woo 2017b).

As I have noted elsewhere, Singapore's Smart Nation initiative is highly design-oriented, with specific policy tools matched with desired policy goals (Woo 2017b). Beyond smart city strategies, policy design also provides a potentially powerful analytical framework for understanding the internal workings of developmental states. Indeed, much of the existing developmental state literature tends to take a highly descriptive approach that focuses on the components of the developmental state or its historical development. Aside from discussions of industrial policy, much of this literature does not sufficiently address the policy initiatives that form the developmental state's policy activities as well as sustain its continued existence.

Indeed, industrial policy can be seen as a form of policy design, with specific policy initiatives such as incentives, subsidies, and infrastructural support making up the policy tools that are typically implemented to achieve the developmental state's policy goals of economic and sectorial development. Such a design-centric understanding of the developmental state can also go beyond such traditional 'substantive' policy tools to include the procedural and political aspects of policy design (Howlett 2000). This allows for the retention of the developmental state's political economy focus, while at the same time introduce a much-needed policy focus.

For instance, the embedded autonomy within which developmental states exercise their authority as well as manage their relations with non-state economic interests or civil society can be reframed in terms of procedural policy instruments, such as the financial regulatory infrastructure, anti-trust laws, rules governing civil society activity and even the sort of policy consultative mechanisms that I have discussed in prior chapters. As I have discussed elsewhere, such procedural policy tools have become increasingly important in Singapore and Hong Kong, with policy consultations and policy co-creation contributing to the two cities' economic development (Woo 2015a, 2015b, 2016).

As it was the case with policy capacity, there is much scope for further research and conceptualization on the design aspects of the developmental state. Taking such a design-centric approach will allow for a delineation of the policy tools and policy goals that represent the developmental state's day-to-day policy activities. Perhaps most importantly, policy capacity and policy design address both the technical aspects (substantive policy tools, operational policy capacities) and political bases (political or legitimation capacity, procedural policy tools) of policymaking. Incorporating these two policy approaches to the study of the developmental state allows for a deeper focus on policy, without neglecting the fundamental political-economic basis of the developmental state model.

Moving forward

Despite expectations of its demise, the developmental state has proven its longevity, with Asian developmental states such as Singapore and Hong Kong continuing to pursue their developmental agendas. Furthermore, developmental states do not remain static. Rather, they have displayed a strong ability to adapt and adjust themselves in response to shifting political and economic circumstances. The emergence of a knowledge-based and innovation-driven digital economy has prompted efforts by Singapore and Hong Kong to transform themselves into smart cities, with the goal of exploring new economic opportunities, addressing urban issues and fostering community development.

As I have discussed in Chapters 5 and 6, such efforts have resulted in adaptations to key components of the developmental state model, giving rise to what I have termed the 'smart developmental state'. More than 'old wine in new bottles' but not entirely a reinvention of the developmental state, the smart developmental state leverages new 'smart' technologies such as data analytics and sensors to enhance policy capacities, develop new industries and stimulate innovation, create new platforms for public–private engagements while at the same time create new tools for managing civil society, as well as generate material improvements to citizens' lives.

To answer the research questions that I have posed at the beginning of this book, the developmental state is not only relevant, but very much alive and well in today's globalized knowledge economy. Indeed, smart developmental states such as Singapore and Hong Kong have successfully integrated themselves into the new digital and knowledge-based economy through adroit adaptations to their developmental state models, whether through the incorporation of technology or introduction of administrative reforms. In both Singapore and Hong Kong, smart city strategies are beginning to yield fruit, with emerging sectors such as the Internet of things or the sharing economy contributing to their developmental goals.

These modifications to the developmental states of Singapore and Hong Kong also suggest a need for corresponding conceptual adaptations and modifications to the developmental state model, in order to ensure the continued relevance of the model as a framework of analysis. I have discussed some of these theoretical adaptations in Chapter 6. However, and as I have discussed above, more work needs to be done, in order that the developmental state model remains useful as a conceptual framework capable of addressing the ongoing transformation of developmental states into smart cities and smart developmental states.

Hopefully, this book has provided some useful starting points for future research and theorization on the smart developmental state.

References

Anne, T., 2015. The dilemmas of organisational capacity. *Policy and Society*, 34 (3–4), 209–217.

Bain & Company, 2017. *Digital economy takes off in Southeast Asia as the number of connected consumers surges 50 percent in the last year to 200 million*. Boston, M.A.: Bain & Company, Press Release.

Bakıcı, T., Almirall, E., and Wareham, J., 2012. A Smart City Initiative: the Case of Barcelona. *Journal of the Knowledge Economy*, 4 (2), 135–148.

Bakvis, H., 2000. Rebuilding Policy Capacity in the Era of the Fiscal Dividend: A Report from Canada. *Governance*, 13 (1), 71–103.

Béland, D., 2007. Ideas and Institutional Change in Social Security: Conversion, Layering, and Policy Drift*. *Social Science Quarterly*, 88 (1), 20–38.

Bemelmans-Videc, M.-L., Rist, R.C., and Vedung, E., eds., 1998. *Carrots, Sticks, and Sermons: Policy Instruments and Their Evaluation*. New Jersey: Transaction Publishers.

Besley, T. and Persson, T., 2010. State Capacity, Conflict, and Development. *Econometrica*, 78 (1), 1–34.

Bressers, H. and Klok, P.-J., 1988. Fundamentals for a Theory of Policy Instruments. *International Journal of Social Economics*, 15 (3/4), 22–41.

Capano, G., Howlett, M., and Ramesh, M., 2015. Bringing Governments Back in: Governance and Governing in Comparative Policy Analysis. *Journal of Comparative Policy Analysis: Research and Practice*, 17 (4), 311–321.

Chan, E. and Chan, J., 2017. Hong Kong 2007–2017: a backlash in civil society. *Asia Pacific Journal of Public Administration*, 39 (2), 135–152.

Cheng, J., 2016. Business-government nexus: the special case of Hong Kong. *Asian Education and Development Studies*, 5 (4), 454–467.

Cheung, A.B.L., 2004. Strong executive, weak policy capacity: The changing environment of policy-making in Hong Kong. *Asian Journal of Political Science*, 12 (1), 1–30.
Cheung, A.B.L., 2008. The story of two administrative states: state capacity in Hong Kong and Singapore. *The Pacific Review*, 21 (2), 121–145.
Chong, T., 2012. A Return to Normal Politics: Singapore General Elections 2011. *Southeast Asian Affairs*, 2012 (1), 283–298.
Committee on the Future Economy, 2017. *Report of the Committee on the Future Economy*. Singapore: Government of Singapore.
Crivello, S., 2014. Urban Policy Mobilities: The Case of Turin as a Smart City. *European Planning Studies*, 1–13.
Cutler, A.C., Haufler, V., and Porter, T., 1999. *Private authority and international affairs*. Albany: State University of New York Press.
Doner, R.F., 1992. Limits of State Strength: Toward an Institutionalist View of Economic Development. *World Politics*, 44 (3), 398–431.
Douglass, M., 1994. The 'Developmental State' and the Newly Industrialised Economies of Asia. *Environment and Planning A*, 26 (4), 543–566.
Dunlop, C.A., 2015. Organizational political capacity as learning. *Policy and Society*, 34 (3–4), 259–270.
Elmore, R.F., 1987. Instruments and Strategy in Public Policy. *Review of Policy Research*, 7 (1), 174–186.
Evans, P.B., 2010. Constructing the 21st Century Developmental State: Potentialities and Pitfalls. *In*: O. Edigheji, ed. *Constructing a Democratic Developmental State in South Africa: Potentials and Challenges*. Cape Town, South Africa: HSRC Press, 37–58.
Gleeson, D., Legge, D., O'Neill, D., and Pfeffer, M., 2011. Negotiating Tensions in Developing Organizational Policy Capacity: Comparative Lessons to be Drawn. *Journal of Comparative Policy Analysis: Research and Practice*, 13 (3), 237–263.
Goldsmith, S. and Crawford, S., 2014. *The Responsive City: Engaging Communities Through Data-Smart Governance*. 1st ed. San Francisco, C.A.: Jossey-Bass.
Grabosky, P.N., 1995. Regulation by Reward: On the Use of Incentives as Regulatory Instruments. *Law & Policy*, 17 (3), 257–282.
Gunningham, N., Grabosky, P., and Sinclair, D., 1998. *Smart Regulation: Designing Environmental Policy*. New York: Oxford University Press.
Haufler, V., 2001. *A public role for the private sector: industry self-regulation in a global economy*. Washington: Carnegie Endowment for International Peace.
Hendrix, C.S., 2010. Measuring state capacity: Theoretical and empirical implications for the study of civil conflict. *Journal of Peace Research*, 47 (3), 273–285.
Ho, E., 2016. Smart subjects for a Smart Nation? Governing (smart)mentalities in Singapore. *Urban Studies*, 0042098016664305.
Hoe, S.L., 2016. Defining a smart nation: the case of Singapore. *Journal of Information, Communication and Ethics in Society*, 14 (4), 323–333.
Hood, C., 1986. *The Tools of Government*. London: Chatham House Publishers.
Howlett, M., 1991. Policy Instruments, Policy Styles, and Policy Implementation. *Policy Studies Journal*, 19 (2), 1–21.
Howlett, M., 2000. Managing the 'hollow state': procedural policy instruments and modern governance. *Canadian Public Administration*, 43 (4), 412–431.
Howlett, M., 2004. Beyond Good and Evil in Policy Implementation: Instrument Mixes, Implementation Styles, and Second Generation Theories of Policy Instrument Choice. *Policy and Society*, 23 (2), 1–17.

Howlett, M., 2009. Governance modes, policy regimes and operational plans: A multi-level nested model of policy instrument choice and policy design. *Policy Sciences*, 42 (1), 73–89.

Howlett, M., 2011. *Designing Public Policies: Principles and Instruments*. 1st ed. London: Routledge.

Howlett, M. and Lejano, R.P., 2013. Tales From the Crypt The Rise and Fall (and Rebirth?) of Policy Design. *Administration & Society*, 45 (3), 357–381.

Howlett, M., Mukherjee, I., and Woo, J.J., 2015. From Tools to Toolkits in Policy Design Studies: The New Design Orientation and Policy Formulation Research. *Policy and Politics*, 43 (2), 291–311.

Howlett, M., Ramesh, M., and Perl, A., 2009. *Studying Public Policy: Policy Cycles and Policy Subsystems*. 3rd ed. Oxford: Oxford University Press.

Howlett, M. and Rayner, J., 2007. Design Principles for Policy Mixes: Cohesion and Coherence in 'New Governance Arrangements'. *Policy and Society*, 26 (4), 1–18.

Howlett, M. and Rayner, J., 2013. Patching vs Packaging in Policy Formulation: Assessing Policy Portfolio Design. *Politics and Governance*, 1 (2), 170–182.

Howlett, M. and Rayner, J., 2014. Patching Vs Packaging in Policy Formulation: Complementary Effects, Goodness of Fit, Degrees of Freedom and Feasibility in Policy Portfolio Design. *Politics and Governance*, 1 (2).

Ikenberry, G.J., 1986. The irony of state strength: comparative responses to the oil shocks in the 1970s. *International Organization*, 40 (1), 105–137.

Johnson, C., 1995. *Japan: Who Governs?: The Rise of the Developmental State*. New York: W. W. Norton & Company.

Kitchin, R., 2014. The real-time city? Big data and smart urbanism. *GeoJournal*, 79 (1), 1–14.

Lam, W. and Cooper, L., 2017. *Citizenship, Identity and Social Movements in the New Hong Kong: Localism after the Umbrella Movement*. London: Routledge.

Lee, H.L., 2014. *Smart Nation: Better living, more opportunities, stronger communities*.

Lee, J., 2009. Developmentalism, social welfare and state capacity in East Asia: integrating housing and social security in Singapore. *Journal of Asian Public Policy*, 2 (2), 157–170.

Leftwich, A., 1995. Bringing politics back in: Towards a model of the developmental state. *Journal of Development Studies*, 31 (3), 400–427.

Lim, L.Y.C., 2015. *Singapore's Economic Development: Retrospection and Reflections*. Singapore: World Scientific.

Madrian, B.C., 2014. Applying Insights from Behavioral Economics to Policy Design. *Annual Review of Economics*, 6 (1), 663–688.

Mietzner, M., 2017. Authoritarian elections, state capacity, and performance legitimacy: Phases of regime consolidation and decline in Suharto's Indonesia. *International Political Science Review*, 0192512116687139.

Neirotti, P., De Marco, A., Cagliano, A.C., Mangano, G., and Scorrano, F., 2014. Current trends in Smart City initiatives: Some stylised facts. *Cities*, 38, 25–36.

Office of the Government Chief Information Officer, 2016. *The Smart City Blueprint for Hong Kong*. Hong Kong: Government of the Hong Kong Special Administrative Region.

Painter, M. and Pierre, J., 2005. Unpacking policy capacity: issues and themes. *In*: M. Painter and J. Pierre, eds. *Challenges to State Policy Capacity: Global Trends and Comparative Perspectives*. Basingstoke: Palgrave Macmillan, 1–18.

Pal, L.A. and Clark, I.D., 2015. Making reform stick: Political acumen as an element of political capacity for policy change and innovation. *Policy and Society*, 34 (3–4), 247–257.

Peters, B.G., 2015. Policy capacity in public administration. *Policy and Society*, 34 (3–4), 219–228.

Rayner, J. and Howlett, M., 2009. Introduction: Understanding integrated policy strategies and their evolution. *Policy and Society*, 28 (2), 99–109.

Rondinelli, D.A. and Cheema, G.S., 2003. *Reinventing Government for the Twenty-first Century: State Capacity in a Globalizing Society*. Bloomfield, C.T.: Kumarian Press.

Savoia, A. and Sen, K., 2012. *Measurement and Evolution of State Capacity: Exploring a Lesser Known Aspect of Governance*. Manchester, UK: Effective States and Inclusive Development Research Centre (ESID), Effective States and Inclusive Development Research Centre Working Paper No. 10.

Schneider, A. and Sidney, M., 2009. What Is Next for Policy Design and Social Construction Theory? *Policy Studies Journal*, 37 (1), 103–119.

Shen, C. and Williamson, J.B., 2005. Corruption, Democracy, Economic Freedom, and State Strength: A Cross-national Analysis. *International Journal of Comparative Sociology*, 46 (4), 327–345.

Sheng, A., 2017. Asean will march into digital economy to beat of own drum. *The Straits Times*, 26 Aug.

Smart Nation Programme Office, 2017. Smart Nation Initiatives [online]. *Smart Nation Singapore*. Available from: http://www.smartnation.sg/initiatives/ [Accessed 15 Feb 2017].

Sørensen, G., 1993. Democracy, authoritarianism and state strength. *The European Journal of Development Research*, 5 (1), 6–34.

Strange, S., 1996. *The Retreat of the State: The Diffusion of Power in the World Economy*. Cambridge: Cambridge University Press.

Tan, K.P., 2012. Singapore in 2011: A 'New Normal' in Politics? *Asian Survey*, 52 (1), 220–226.

Vedung, E., 1998. Policy Instruments: Typologies and Theories. *In*: M.-L. Bemelmans-Videc, R.C. Rist, and E. Vedung, eds. *Carrots, Sticks & Sermons: Policy Instruments & Their Evaluation*. New Jersey: Transaction Publishers, 21–58.

Volgy, T.J. and Bailin, A., 2003. *International Politics & State Strength*. London: Lynne Rienner Publishers.

Woo, J.J., 2015a. Policy Relations and Policy Subsystems: Financial policy in Hong Kong and Singapore. *International Journal of Public Administration*, 38 (8), 553–561.

Woo, J.J., 2015b. Beyond the Neoliberal orthodoxy: Alternative financial policy regimes in Asia's financial centres. *Critical Policy Studies*, 9 (3), 297–316.

Woo, J.J., 2016. *Business and Politics in Asia's Key Financial Centres – Hong Kong, Singapore and Shanghai*. 1st ed. Singapore: Springer.

Woo, J.J., 2017a. *3-in-1: Governing a Global Financial Centre*. Singapore: World Scientific.

Woo, J.J., 2017b. *Singapore's Smart Nation Initiative – A Policy and Organisational Perspective*. Singapore: Lee Kuan Yew School of Public Policy, National University of Singapore.

Woo, J.J., Ramesh, M., and Howlett, M., 2015. Legitimation Capacity: System-Level Resources and Political Skills in Public Policy. *Policy & Society*, 34 (3–4), 271–283.

Woo, J.J., Ramesh, M., Howlett, M., and Coban, M.K., 2016. Dynamics of global financial governance: Constraints, opportunities, and capacities in Asia. *Policy and Society*, 35 (3), 269–282.

Woo-Cumings, M., 1999. *The Developmental State*. Ithaca, N.Y.: Cornell University Press.

Woodside, K., 1986. Policy Instruments and the Study of Public Policy. *Canadian Journal of Political Science*, 19 (04), 775–794.

Wu, X., Ramesh, M., and Howlett, M., 2015. Blending Skill and Resources Across Multiple Levels of Activity: Competences, Capabilities and the Policy Capacities of Government. *Policy & Society*, 34 (3–4), 165–171.

Wu, X., Ramesh, M., and Howlett, M., 2018. Policy Capacity: Conceptual Framework and Essential Components. *In*: X. Wu, M. Howlett and M. Ramesh, eds. *Policy Capacity and Governance*. Palgrave Macmillan, Cham, 1–25.

Yeung, H.W., 2017. State-led development reconsidered: the political economy of state transformation in East Asia since the 1990s. *Cambridge Journal of Regions, Economy and Society*, 10 (1), 83–98.

Index

For Product Safety Concerns and Information please contact our EU representative GPSR@taylorandfrancis.com
Taylor & Francis Verlag GmbH, Kaufingerstraße 24, 80331 München, Germany

www.ingramcontent.com/pod-product-compliance
Ingram Content Group UK Ltd.
Pitfield, Milton Keynes, MK11 3LW, UK
UKHW011017180926
475701UK00004B/791